MW00785274

HOW TO
START A
BUSINESS IN
TEXAS

with forms

HOW TO
START A
BUSINESS IN
TEXAS

with forms

William R. Brown
Mark Warda
Attorneys at Law

Sphinx Publishing
A Division of Sourcebooks, Inc.
Naperville, IL • Clearwater, FL

Copyright © 1983, 1990, 1992, 1995, 1999 by William R. Brown and Mark Warda
Cover design © 1999 by Sourcebooks, Inc.

All rights reserved. No part of this book may be reproduced in any form or by any electronic or mechanical means including information storage and retrieval systems—except in the case of brief quotations embodied in critical articles or reviews—without permission in writing from its publisher, Sourcebooks, Inc. Purchasers of the book are granted a license to use the forms contained herein for their own personal use. No claim of copyright is made in any official government forms reproduced herein.

Second edition, 1999

Published by: **Sphinx® Publishing, a division of Sourcebooks, Inc.®**

Naperville Office	Clearwater Office
P.O. Box 372	P.O. Box 25
Naperville, Illinois 60566	Clearwater, Florida 33757
630-961-3900	727- 587-0999
Fax: 630-961-2168	Fax: 727-586-5088

Interior Design and Production: Amy S. Hall, Sourcebooks, Inc.

This publication is designed to provide accurate and authoritative information in regard to the subject matter covered. It is sold with the understanding that the publisher is not engaged in rendering legal, accounting, or other professional service. If legal advice or other expert assistance is required, the services of a competent professional person should be sought.

From a Declaration of Principles Jointly Adopted by a Committee of the
American Bar Association and a Committee of Publishers and Associations

Library of Congress Cataloging-in-Publication Data

Brown, William R. (William Robert)
    How to start a business in Texas : with forms / William R. Brown
and Mark Warda. -- 2nd ed.
       p.   cm.
    Includes bibliographical references and index.
    ISBN 1-57071-365-0 (pbk.)
    1. Business enterprises--Law and legislation--Texas--Popular
works. 2. Business law--Texas. I. Warda, Mark. II. Title.
KFT1405.Z9B76 1999
346.764'065--dc21   99-13348
                                                                     CIP

Printed and bound in the United States of America.

Paperback — 10 9 8 7 6 5 4 3 2 1

CONTENTS

Using Self-Help Law Books

Whenever you shop for a product or service, you are faced with various levels of quality and price. In deciding what product or service to buy, you make a cost/value analysis on the basis of your willingness to pay and the quality you desire.

When buying a car, you decide whether you want transportation, comfort, status, or sex appeal. Accordingly, you decide among such choices as a Neon, a Lincoln, a Rolls Royce, or a Porsche. Before making a decision, you usually weigh the merits of each option against the cost.

When you get a headache, you can take a pain reliever (such as aspirin) or visit a medical specialist for a neurological examination. Given this choice, most people, of course, take a pain reliever, since it costs only pennies; whereas a medical examination costs hundreds of dollars and takes a lot of time. This is usually a logical choice because rarely is anything more than a pain reliever needed for a headache. But in some cases, a headache may indicate a brain tumor, and failing to see a specialist right away can result in complications. Should everyone with a headache go to a specialist? Of course not, but people treating their own illnesses must realize that they are betting on the basis of their cost/value analysis of the situation, they are taking the most logical option.

The same cost/value analysis must be made in deciding to do one's own legal work. Many legal situations are very straight forward, requiring a simple form and no complicated analysis. Anyone with a little intelligence and a book of instructions can handle the matter without outside help.

But there is always the chance that complications are involved that only an attorney would notice. To simplify the law into a book like this, several legal cases often must be condensed into a single sentence or paragraph. Otherwise, the book would be several hundred pages long and too complicated for most people. However, this simplification necessarily leaves out many details and nuances that would apply to special or unusual situations. Also, there are many ways to interpret most legal questions. Your case may come before a judge who disagrees with the analysis of our authors.

Therefore, in deciding to use a self-help law book and to do your own legal work, you must realize that you are making a cost/value analysis and deciding that the chance your case will not turn out to your satisfaction is outweighed by the money you will save in doing it yourself. Most people handling their own simple legal matters never have a problem, but occasionally people find that it ended up costing them more to have an attorney straighten out the situation than it would have if they had hired an attorney in the beginning. Keep this in mind while handling your case, and be sure to consult an attorney if you feel you might need further guidance.

INTRODUCTION

Each year about a hundred thousand new corporations are registered in Texas and thousands more partnerships and proprietorships open for business. Texas is booming! Nearly 1,000 people move to the state each day and the demand for new products and services keeps growing. Some have said Texas is now what California was to the '60s, a thriving, trend-setting center of activity where little shops can bloom into expansive enterprises.

The best way to take part in this boom is to run your own business. Be your own boss and be as successful as you dare to be.

But if you don't follow the laws of the state, your progress can be slowed or stopped by government fines, civil judgments or even criminal penalties.

This book is intended to give you the framework for legally opening a business in Texas. It also includes information on where to find special rules for each type of business. If you have problems which are not covered by this book, you should seek out an attorney who can be available for your ongoing needs.

In order to cover all of the aspects of any business you are thinking of starting, you should read through this entire book, rather than skipping to the parts which look most interesting. There are many laws which may not sound like they apply to you, but which do have provisions which will affect your business.

In recent years the government bureaucracies have been amending and lengthening their forms regularly. The forms included in this book were the most recent available at the time of publication. It is possible that some may be revised at the time you read this book, but in most cases previous versions of the forms will still be accepted.

DECIDING TO START A BUSINESS 1

If you are reading this book, then you have probably made a serious decision to take the plunge and start your own business. Hundreds of thousands of people make the same decision each year and many of them become very successful. Some merely eke out a living, others become billionaires, but a lot of them also fail. Knowledge can only help your chances of success. You need to know why some succeed while others fail. Some of what follows may seem obvious, but to someone wrapped up in a new business idea, some of this information is occasionally overlooked.

KNOW YOUR STRENGTHS

The last thing a budding entrepreneur wants to hear is that he is not cut out for running his own business. Those "do you have what it takes" quizzes are ignored with the fear that the answer might be one the entrepreneur doesn't want to hear. But even if you lack some skills you can be successful if you know where to get them.

You should consider all of the skills and knowledge that running a successful business means and decide whether you have what it takes. If you don't, it doesn't necessarily mean you are doomed to be an employee all your life. Perhaps you just need a partner who has the skills you lack, or perhaps you can hire the skills you need, or can structure your business to avoid areas where you are weak. If those don't work, maybe you can learn the skills.

For example, if you are not good at dealing with employees (either you are too passive and get taken advantage of, or too tough and scare them off) you can:

☞ handle product development yourself and have a partner or manager deal with employees

☞ take seminars in employee management

☞ structure your business so that you don't need employees. Either use independent contractors or set yourself up as an independent contractor

Here are some of the factors to consider when planning your business:

☞ If it takes months or years before your business turns a profit do you have the resources to hold out? Businesses have gone under or been sold just before they were about to take off and staying power is an important ingredient to success.

☞ Are you willing to put in a lot of overtime to make your business a success? Owners of businesses do not set their own hours, the business sets them for the owner. Many business owners work long hours seven days a week, but they enjoy running their business more than family picnics or fishing.

☞ Are you willing to do the dirtiest or most unpleasant work of the business? Emergencies come up and employees are not always dependable. You might need to mop up a flooded room, spend a weekend stuffing 10,000 envelopes or work Christmas if someone calls in sick.

☞ Do you know enough about the product or service? Are you aware of the trends in the industry and what changes new technology might bring? Think of the people who started typesetting or printing businesses just before type was replaced by laser printers.

☛ Do you know enough about accounting and inventory to manage the business? Do you have a good "head for business?" Some people naturally know how to save money and do things profitably. Others are in the habit of buying the best and the most expensive of everything. The latter can be fatal to a struggling new business.

☛ Are you good at managing employees?

☛ Do you know how to sell your product or service? You can have the best product on the market but people don't beat a path to your door. If you are a wholesaler, shelf space in major stores is hard to get, especially for a new company without a record, a large line of products, or a large advertising budget.

☛ Do you know enough about getting publicity? The media receive thousands of press releases and announcements each day. Most are thrown away. Don't count on free publicity to put your name in front of the public.

KNOW YOUR BUSINESS

You don't only need to know the concept of a business, you need the experience of working in a business. Maybe you always dreamed of running a bed and breakfast or having your own pizza place and now that you are laid off, you think it's time to use your savings to fulfill your dream. Have you ever worked in such a business? If not, you may have no idea of the day-to-day headaches and problems of the business. For example, do you really know how much to allow for theft, spoilage, and unhappy customers.

You might feel silly taking an entry level job at a pizza place when you'd rather start your own, but it might be the most valuable preparation you could have. A few weeks of seeing how a business operates could mean the difference between success and failure.

Working in a business as an employee is one of the best ways to be a success at running such a business. New people with new ideas who work in old stodgy industries have been known to revolutionize them with obvious improvements that no one before dared to try.

DO THE MATH

Conventional wisdom says you need a business plan before committing yourself to a new venture, but lots of businesses are started successfully without the owner even knowing what a business plan is. They have a great concept, put it on the market and it takes off. But you at least need to do some basic calculations to see if the business can make a profit. Here are some examples:

☛ If you want to start a retail shop, figure out how many people are close enough to become customers and how many other stores will be competing for those customers. Visit some of those other shops and see how busy they are. Without giving away your plans to compete, ask some general questions like "how's business?" and maybe they'll share their frustrations or successes.

☛ Whether you sell a good or a service, do the math to find out how much profit is in it. For example: if you plan to start a house painting company, find out what you will have to pay to hire painters; what it will cost you for all of the insurance; bonding and licensing you will need; and what the advertising will cost you. Figure out how many jobs you can do per month and what other painters are charging. In some industries in some areas of the country, there may be a large margin of profit or there may be almost no profit.

☛ Find out if there is a demand for your product or service. Suppose you have designed a beautiful new kind of candle and your friends all say you should open a shop because "everyone will want them." Before making a hundred of them and renting a store, bring a few to craft shows or flea markets and see what happens.

☛ Figure out what the income and expenses would be for a typical month of your new business. List monthly expenses such as rent, salaries, utilities, insurance, taxes, supplies, advertising, services, and other overhead. Then figure out how much profit you will average from each sale. Next, calculate how many sales you will need to cover your overhead and divide by the number of business days in the month. Can you reasonably expect that many sales? How will you get those sales?

Most types of businesses have trade associations, which often have figures on how profitable its members are. Some even have start-up kits for people wanting to start businesses. One good source of information on such organizations is the *Encyclopedia of Associations* published by Gale Research Inc. and available in many library reference sections. Producers of products to the trade often give assistance to small companies getting started to win their loyalty. Contact the largest suppliers of the products your business will be using and see if they can be of help.

SOURCES OF FURTHER GUIDANCE

The following offices offer free or low cost guidance for small businesses.

Service Corps of Retired Executives. This is a nonprofit group of retired people who offer free guidance to small businesses.

Abilene SCORE
2106 Federal Post Office & Court
Abilene, TX 79601
Phone: (915) 677-1857

Austin SCORE
2501 S. Congress
Austin, TX 78701
Phone: (512) 442-7235
Fax: (512) 442-7528

Golden Triangle SCORE
P.O. Box 3150
Beaumont, TX 77704
Phone: (409) 838-6581
Fax: (409) 833-6718

Brazos Valley SCORE
Norwest Bank Building
3000 Briarcrest, Suite 302
Bryan, TX 77802
Phone: (409) 776-8876

Corpus Christi SCORE
651 Upper North Broadway, Suite 654
Corpus Christi, TX 78477
Phone: (512) 888-4322
Fax: (512) 888-3418

Dallas SCORE
Comerica Bank-Second Floor
6260 E. Mockingbird
Dallas, TX 75214-2619
Phone: (214) 828-2471
Fax: (214) 828-2803

El Paso SCORE
10737 Gateway West, 320
El Paso, TX 79935
Phone: (915) 540-5155
Fax: (915) 540-5636

Fort Worth SCORE
100 East 15th Street #24
Ft. Worth TX 76102
Phone: (817) 871-6002
Fax: (817) 871-6031

L Rio Grande Vly SCORE
222 E. Van Buren, Suite 500
Harlingen TX 78550
Phone: (956) 427-8533
Fax: (956) 427-8537

Houston SCORE
9301 Southwest Freeway, Suite 550
Houston, TX 77074
Phone: (713) 773-6565
Fax: (713) 773-6550

Lubbock SCORE
1205 Texas Avenue, Room 411D
Lubbock, TX 79401
Phone: (806) 472-7462
Fax: (806) 472-7487

San Antonio SCORE
c/o SBA, Federal Building
727 E. Durango, Room #A527
San Antonio, TX 78206
Phone: (210) 472-5931
Fax: (210) 472-5935

Texarkana SCORE
P.O. Box 1468
Texarkana, TX 75504
Phone: (903) 792-7191
Fax: (903) 793-4304

East Texas SCORE
RTDC
1530 SSW Loop 323, Ste. 100
Tyler, TX 75701
Phone: (903) 510-2975

Waco SCORE
401 Franklin Avenue
Waco, TX 76701
Phone: (254) 754-8898
Fax: (254) 756-0776

Wichita Falls SCORE
Hamilton Building
PO Box 1860
Wichita Falls, TX 76307
Phone: (817) 723-2741

SMALL BUSINESS
DEVELOPMENT
CENTERS

Educational programs for small businesses are offered through the Small Business Development Centers at many Texas colleges and universities. You should check their programs for courses in any areas in which you are weak.

Abilene Christian University
Caruth Small Business
Development Center
College of Business Administration
648 East Highway 80
Abilene, TX 79601
Phone: (915) 670-0300
Fax: (915) 670-0311

Sul Ross State University
Small Business Development Center
P.O. Box C-47, Room 319
Alpine, TX 79832
Phone: (915) 837-8694
Fax: (915) 837-8104

West Texas A&M University
Small Business Development Center
T. Boone Pickens School of Business:
1800 South Washington, Suite 209
Amarillo, TX 79102
Phone: (806) 372-5151
Fax: (806) 372-5261

Trinity Valley Community College
Small Business Development Center
500 South Prairieville
Athens, TX 75751
Phone: (903) 675-7403; (800) 335-7232
Fax: (903) 675-5199

Lower Colorado River Authority
Small Business Development Center
3700 Lake Austin Boulevard
Jack Miller Bldg Mail Stop M104
Austin, TX 78767
Phone: (512) 473-3510
Fax: (512) 473-3285

Lee College Small Business
Development Center
200 Lee Drive
Rundell Hall
Baytown, TX 77522-0818
Mailing Address:
P.O. Box 818
Baytown, TX 77522-0818
Phone: (281) 425-6309
Fax: (281) 425-6307

Lamar University
Small Business Development Center
855 E. Florida Avenue, Suite 101
Beaumont, TX 77705
Phone: (409) 880-2367
Fax: (409) 880-2201

Bonham Satellite Small
Business Development Center
Sam Rayburn Library
1201 E. 9th St., Bldg. 2
Bonham, TX 75418
Phone: (903) 583-7565
Fax: (903) 583-6706

Blinn College
Small Business Development Center
902 College Avenue
Brenham, TX 77833
Phone: (409) 830-4137
Fax: (409) 830-4135

Brazos Valley Small Business
Development Center
4001 East 29th Street, Suite 175
Bryan, TX 77805
Mailing Address:
P.O. Box 3695
Bryan, TX 77805-3695
Phone: (409) 260-5222
Fax: (409) 260-5229
Website: http://www.bvsbdc.org

Greater Corpus Christi Business Alliance
Small Business Development Center
1201 North Shoreline
Corpus Christi, TX 78403
Phone: (512) 881-1847
Fax: (512) 882-4256

Navarro Small Business
Development Center
120 North 12th Street
Corsicana, TX 75110
Phone: (903) 874-0658; (800) 320-7232
Fax: (903) 874-4187

International Assistance Center
Small Business Development Center
World Trade Center, Suite #150
2050 Stemmons Freeway
P.O. Box 58299
Dallas, TX 75258
Phone: (214) 747-1300; (800) 337-7232
Fax: (214) 748-5774

North Texas Small Business
Development Center
Dallas County Community College
1402 Corinth Street
Dallas, TX 75215
Phone: (214) 860-5835; (800) 350-7232
Fax: (214) 860-5813

Center for Government
Contracting/Technology
Assistance Center
Small Business Development Center
1402 Corinth Street
Dallas, TX 75215
Phone: (214) 860-5841; (800) 348-7232
Fax: (214) 860-5881

Dallas County Community College
Small Business Development Center
1402 Corinth Street
Dallas, TX 75215
Phone: (214) 860-5850
Fax: (214) 860-5881

Grayson County College
Small Business Development Center
6101 Grayson Drive
Denison, TX 75020
Phone: (903) 463-8787; (800) 316-7232
Fax: (903) 463-5437

Denton Satellite Small
Business Development Center
P.O. Drawer P
Denton, TX 76201
Phone: (254) 380-1849
Fax: (254) 382-0040

Best Southwest Small Business
Development Center
214 South Main, Suite 102A
Duncanville, TX 75116
Phone: (972) 709-5878; (800) 317-7232
Fax: (972) 709-6089

University of Texas-Pan American
Small Business Development Center
1201 West University
Edinburg, TX 78539-2999
Phone: (956) 316-2610
Fax: (956) 316-2612

El Paso Community College
Small Business Development Center
103 Montana Avenue, Suite 202
El Paso, TX 79902-3929
Phone: (915) 534-3410
Fax: (915) 534-4625

Tarrant County Junior College
Small Business Development Center
7917 Highway 80 West
Ft. Worth, TX 76102
Mailing Address:
1500 Houston Street, Room 163
Ft. Worth, TX 76102
Phone: (817) 871-6028
Fax: (817) 871-0031

Small Business Development
Center for Enterprise Excellence
7300 Jack Newell Boulevard, South
Fort Worth, TX 76118
Phone: (817) 272-5930
Fax: (817) 272-5952

North Central Texas College
Small Business Development Center
1525 West California
Gainesville, TX 76240
Phone: (254) 668-4220; (800) 351-7232
Fax: (254) 668-6049

Galveston College
Small Business Development Center
5001 Avenue U
Galveston, TX 77550
Mailing Address:
4015 Avenue Q
Galveston, TX 77550
Phone: (409) 740-7380
Fax: (409) 740-7381

Texas Gulf Coast Small
Business Development Center
University of Houston
1100 Louisiana, Suite 500
Houston, TX 77002
Phone: (713) 752-8425
Fax: (713) 756-1500
e-mail: fyoung@uh.edu

Houston Community College System
Small Business Development Center
10405 Stancliff, Suite 100
Houston, TX 77099
Phone: (281) 933-7932
Fax: (281) 568-3690

UH International Trade Center
Small Business Development Center
University of Houston
1100 Louisiana, Suite 500
Houston, TX 77002
Phone: (713) 752-8404
Fax: (713) 756-1515

North Harris Montgomery County
College District
Small Business Development Center
250 North Sam Houston Parkway East
Houston, TX 77060
Phone: (281) 260-3174
Fax: (281) 260-3162

UH Texas Information
Procurement Service
University of Houston
Small Business Development Center
1100 Louisiana, Suite 500
Houston, TX 77002
Phone: (713) 752-8477; (800) 252-7232
Fax: (713) 756-1515

Texas Mfg. Assistance Center
- Gulf Coast
1100 Louisiana, Suite 500
Houston, TX 77002
Phone: (713) 752-8440
Fax: (713) 756-1500

Sam Houston State University
Small Business Development Center
843 South Sam Houston Avenue
Huntsville, TX 77341-3738
Mailing Address:
P.O. Box 2058
Huntsville, TX 77341-2058
Phone: (409) 294-3737
Fax: (409) 294-3612
Website: http://www.shsu.edu/~sbd_tab

Kingsville Chamber of Commerce
Small Business Development Center
635 East King
Kingsville, TX 78363
Phone: (512) 595-5088
Fax: (512) 592-0866

Brazosport College
Small Business Development Center
500 College Drive
Lake Jackson, TX 77566
Phone: (409) 266-3380
Fax: (409) 266-3482

Laredo Development Foundation
Small Business Development Center
616 Leal Street
Laredo, TX 78041
Phone: (210) 722-0563
Fax: (210) 722-6247

Kilgore College Small Business
Development Center
Triple Creek Shopping Plaza
110 Triple Creek Drive, Suite #70
Longview, TX 75601
Phone: (903) 757-5857; (800) 338-7232
Fax: (903) 753-7920

Northwestern Texas
Small Business Development Center
Texas Tech University
Spectrum Plaza
2579 South Loop 289, Suite 114
Lubbock, TX 79423
Phone: (806) 745-3973
Fax: (806) 745-6207
e-mail: odbea@ttacs.ttu.edu

Angelina Community College
Small Business Development Center
P.O. Box 1768
Lufkin, TX 75902-1768
Phone: (409) 639-1887
Fax: (409) 639-3863

Northeast/Texarkana
Small Business Development Center
Mr. Bob Wall, Director
P.O. Box 1307
Mt. Pleasant, TX 75455
Phone: (903) 572-1911; (800) 357-7232
Fax: (903) 572-0598
Website: http://www.bizcoach.org

University of Texas/Permian Basin
Small Business Development Center
4901 East University
Odessa, TX 79762
Phone: (915) 552-2455
Fax: (915) 552-2433

Paris Junior College
Small Business Development Center
2400 Clarksville Street
Paris, TX 75460
Phone: (903) 784-1802
Fax: (903) 784-1801

Courtyard Center for Professional
and Economic Development
Small Business Development Center
4800 Preston Park Boulevard
Suite A126/Box 15
Plano, TX 75093
Phone: (972) 985-3770
Fax: (972) 985-3775

Angelo State University
Small Business Development Center
2610 West Avenue N
Campus Box 10910
San Angelo, TX 76909
Phone: (915) 942-2098
Fax: (915) 942-2096

South Texas Border
Small Business Development Center
University of Texas
at San Antonio Downtown
USTA Downtown
1222 North Main, Suite 450
San Antonio, TX 78212
Phone: (210) 458-2450
Fax: (210) 458-2464
e-mail: rmckinley@utsa.edu

International Trade Center
University of Texas at San Antonio
Small Business Development Center
1222 North Main, Suite 450
San Antonio, TX 78212
Phone: (210) 458-2470
Fax: (210) 458-2464

Technology Center
Small Business Development Center
University of Texas at San Antonio
1222 North Main, Suite 450
San Antonio, TX 78212
Phone: (210) 458-2458
Fax: (210) 458-2464

University of Texas
at San Antonio Downtown
Small Business Development Center
1222 North Main, Suite 450
San Antonio, TX 78212
Phone: (210) 458-2460
Fax: (210) 458-2464

Tarleton State University
Small Business Development Center
College of Business Administration
Box T-0650
Stephenville, TX 76402
Phone: (817) 689-4373
Fax: (817) 689-4374

College of the Mainland
Small Business Development Center
1200 Amburn Road
Texas City, TX 77591
Phone: (281) 280-3991 ext. 494;
(409)-938-1211 ext. 494
Fax: (409) 938-7578

Tyler Junior College
Small Business Development Center
1530 South SW Loop 323, Suite 100
Tyler, TX 75701
Phone: (903) 510-2975
Fax: (903) 510-2978

Middle Rio Grande
Development Council
Small Business Development Center
209 North Getty Street
Uvalde, TX 78801
Phone: (210) 278-2527
Fax: (210) 278-2929

University of Houston-Victoria
Small Business Development Center
700 Main Center, Suite 102
Victoria, TX 79901
Phone: (512) 575-8944
Fax: (512) 575-8852
e-mail: parks@jade.vic.uh.edu

McLennan Community College
Small Business Development Center
401 Franklin
Waco, TX 76701
Phone: (254) 714-0077; (800) 349-7232
Fax: (254) 714-1668

Lower Colorado River Authority
Coastal Plains
Small Business Development Center
301 West Milam
Wharton, TX 77488

Mailing Address:
P.O. Box 148
Wharton, TX 77488-0148
Phone: (409) 532-1007
Fax: (409) 532-0056

Wharton County Junior College
Small Business Development Center
Administration Building, Room 102
911 Boling Highway
Wharton, TX 77488-0080
Phone: (409) 532-0604
Fax: (409) 532-2410

Midwestern State University
Small Business Development Center
3410 Taft Boulevard
Wichita Falls, TX 76308
Phone: (817) 689-4373
Fax: (817) 689-4374

GOVERNMENT ASSISTANCE

Believe it or not, there are a few government programs that actually help a small and new business.

BUSINESS PERMIT OFFICE

The Texas Department of Commerce has an office which will assist and advise new businesses concerning permits needed to operate the business. Contact their offices at 1-800-888-0511.

DISADVANTAGED BUSINESSES

Federal and State law provide rules for certifying businesses owned and operated by minorities and women and for disadvantaged businesses. This certification makes them eligible for some preferential treatment in contracting with the government, such as city and county construction. Also. many large companies will use a certain number of certified disadvantaged businesses. If your business is owned at least 51% by a minority or woman, you should look into getting certified. The Texas General Services Commission administers a program for certification for state contracts. Call (512) 463-3419. In some large metropolitan areas, regional certification agencies have been established whose

www.tded.state.tx.us

certifications are accepted by most local governments. Consult with the city or county contracting office in your area to find out how to get certified. The Small Business Administration administers the program for contractors with the federal government. Contact their local office.

CHOOSING THE FORM OF YOUR BUSINESS 2

BASIC FORMS OF DOING BUSINESS

The four most common forms for a business in Texas are proprietorship, partnership, corporation and limited partnership. Laws have been passed in recent years which allowed creation of two new types of enterprises: *limited liability companies*, and *limited liability partnerships*. These offer new benefits for certain kinds of businesses. The characteristics, advantages and disadvantages of each are as follows:

PROPRIETORSHIP

Characteristics. A proprietorship is one person doing business in his or her own name or under a fictitious name.

Advantages. Simplicity is just one advantage. There is also no organizational expense, and no extra tax forms or reports.

Disadvantages. The proprietor is personally liable for all debts and obligations. Also, there is no continuation of the business after death. All profits directly taxable, certainly a disadvantage for the proprietor, and business affairs are easily mixed with personal affairs.

GENERAL PARTNERSHIP

Characteristics. A general partnership involves two or more people carrying on a business together and sharing the profits and losses.

Advantages. Partners can combine expertise and assets. A general partnership is formed by an agreement, and it allows liability to be spread among more persons. The business can be continued after the death of a partner if bought out by surviving partner.

Disadvantages. Each partner is liable for acts of other partners within the scope of the business. This means that if your partner harms a customer or signs a million-dollar credit line in the partnership name, you can be personally liable. Even if left in the business, all profits are taxable. Two more disadvantages: control is shared by all parties and the death of a partner may result in liquidation. In a general partnership, it is often hard to get rid of a bad partner.

CORPORATION ***Characteristics.*** A corporation is an artificial, legal "person" which carries on business through its officers for its shareholders. (In Texas one person may form a corporation and be the sole shareholder and officer.) Laws covering corporations are contained in the Texas Business Corporation Act. This legal person carries on business in its own name and shareholders are not necessarily liable for its acts.

An *S corporation* is a corporation which has filed IRS Form 2553 choosing to have all profits taxed to the shareholders, rather than to the corporation. An S corporation files a tax return but pays no federal or state tax. The profit shown on the S corporation tax return is reported on the owners' tax returns.

A C *corporation* is any corporation which has not elected to be taxed as an S corporation. A C corporation pays income tax on its profits. The effect of this is that when dividends are paid to shareholders they are taxed twice, once by the corporation, and once when they are paid to the shareholders. In Texas, both S and C corporation must pay corporate franchise tax.

A *professional corporation* is a corporation formed by a professional such as a lawyer or accountant. Texas has special rules for professional service corporations which differ slightly from those of other corporations. These rules are included in Article 1528e, Texas Revised Civil Statutes. There are also special tax rules for professional service corporations.

A *nonprofit corporation* is usually used for organizations such as churches and condominium associations. Texas' special rules for nonprofit corporations are included in Article 1396-101 et. seq., Texas Revised Civil Statutes.

Advantages. If properly organized, shareholders have no liability for corporate debts and lawsuits; officers usually have no personal liability for their corporate acts. The existence of a corporation may be perpetual. There are tax advantages allowed only to corporations. There is prestige in owning a corporation. Two excellent advantages: capital may be raised by issuing stock, and it is easy to transfer ownership upon death. A small corporation can be set up as an S corporation to avoid double taxation of corporate profits but still retain corporate advantages. The number of shareholders in an S corporation is limited. Some types of businesses can be set up as nonprofit corporations which provide significant tax savings.

Disadvantages. The start-up costs for forming a corporation are certainly a disadvantage; plus there are certain formalities such as annual meetings, separate bank accounts and tax forms. Unless a corporation registers as an S corporation, it must pay federal income tax separate from the tax paid by the owners along with Texas franchise tax.

LIMITED
PARTNERSHIP

Characteristics. A limited partnership has characteristics similar to both a corporation and a partnership. There are *general partners* who have the control and personal liability and there are *limited partners* who only put up money and whose liability is limited to what they paid for their share of the partnership (like corporate stock).

Advantages. Capital can be contributed by limited partners who have no control of the business or liability for its debts.

Disadvantages. A great disadvantage is high start-up costs. Also, an extensive partnership agreement is required because general partners are personally liable for partnership debts and for the each other's actions. (One solution to this problem is to use a corporation as the general partner.)

LIMITED
LIABILITY
COMPANY

Characteristics. Texas was one of the last states in the United States to allow a limited liability company. This new invention is like a limited partnership without general partners. It has characteristics of both a corporation and a partnership: none of the partners have liability and all can have some control. LLCs in Texas are subject to the corporate franchise tax.

Advantages. The limited liability company offers the tax benefits of a partnership with the protection from liability of a corporation. It offers more tax benefits than an S corporation because it may pass through more depreciation and deductions, have different classes of ownership, have an unlimited number of members, and have aliens as members. It is similar to a Latin-American "Limitada" or a German "GmbH & Co. K.G." and is expected to attract foreign investment to Texas.

Disadvantages. Start up and annual fees are higher than for a corporation. LLCs pay social security tax on all profits (up to a limit); whereas S corporation profits are exempt from social security tax. Because a limited liability company is a relatively new invention, there are not a lot of answers to legal questions which may arise. (However, the courts will probably rely on corporation and limited partnership law.) Limited liability companies are covered under Article 1528n, Texas Revised Civil Statutes (Texas Limited Liability Company Act).

LIMITED
LIABILITY
PARTNERSHIP

Characteristics. The limited liability partnership is like a general partnership but with limited personal liability. It was devised to allow partnerships of lawyers and other professionals to limit their personal liability without losing their partnership structure. It insulates one partner from liability for the error of another partner, but does not shelter the partner from liability for his own professional error. Both general and limited partnerships can register as LLPs.

Advantages. The limited liability partnership offers the flexibility and tax benefits of a partnership with the protection from liability of a corporation. LLPs are not subject to Texas franchise taxes.

Disadvantages. Start-up and annual fees are higher for LLPs than for a corporation. Also, the law requires the partnership to maintain certain minimum insurance.

START-UP PROCEDURES

PROPRIETORSHIP

In a proprietorship, all accounts and licenses are taken in the name of the owner. See chapter 3 for using a fictitious or assumed name.

PARTNERSHIP

To form a partnership, a written agreement should be prepared to spell out rights and obligations of the parties. It may be registered with the Secretary of State but this is not required. Sphinx Publishing publishes the book, *How to Form Your Own Partnership*, by Edward A. Haman, which includes all the necessary information and forms for starting a partnership. It can be obtained at your local bookstore, or by calling 1-800-432-7444. See chapter 3 for using a fictitious name. Most accounts, property, and licenses can be in either the partnership name or that of the partners.

CORPORATION

To form a corporation, *articles of incorporation* must be filed with the Secretary of State in Austin along with $300 in filing fees. An organizational meeting is then held. At the meeting, officers are elected, stock issued, by-laws are adopted and formalities are complied with in order to avoid the corporate entity being set aside later. Licenses and accounts are titled in the name of the corporation. Sphinx Publishing publishes *How to Form Your Own Corporation*, which includes the forms and instructions necessary for forming a corporation. One person or more may form a for profit corporation, but at least three persons are needed to form nonprofit corporation.

LIMITED PARTNERSHIP

A written limited partnership agreement must be drawn up and registered with the Secretary of State in Austin, and a lengthy disclosure document given to all prospective limited partners. Because of the complexity of securities laws and the criminal penalties for violation, it is advantageous to have an attorney organize a limited partnership.

LIMITED
LIABILITY
COMPANY

One or more persons may form a limited liability company by filing articles of organization with the Secretary of State in Austin. Licenses and accounts are in the name of the company. Sphinx will release an LLC book in 1999.

LIMITED
LIABILITY
PARTNERSHIP

Two or more persons may form a limited liability partnership by filing an application for registration as a Texas Registered Limited Liability Partnership with the Secretary of State in Austin. Licenses and accounts are in the name of the company.

	Sole Proprietorship	General Partnership	Limited Partnership	Limited Liability Co.	Corporation C or S	Nonprofit Corporation
Liability Protection	No	No	For limited partners	For all members	For all shareholders	For all members
Taxes	Pass through	Pass through	Pass through	Pass through	S corps. pass through C corps. pay tax	None on income Employees pay on wages
Minimum # of members	1	2	2	1	1	None
Startup fee	None	None	$750	$200	$300	$25
Annual fee	None	None	None	None	None	None
Diff. classes of ownership	No	Yes	Yes	Yes	S corps. No C corps. Yes	No ownership Diff. classes of membership
Survives after Death	No	No	Yes	Yes	Yes	Yes
Best for	1 person low-risk business or no assets	low-risk business	low-risk business with silent partners	All types of businesses	All types of businesses	Educational

BUSINESS START-UP CHECKLIST

- ❏ Make your plan
  - ❏ Obtain and read all relevant publications on your type of business
  - ❏ Obtain and read all laws and regulations affecting your business
  - ❏ Calculate whether your plan will produce a profit
  - ❏ Plan your sources of capital
  - ❏ Plan your sources of goods or services
  - ❏ Plan your marketing efforts
- ❏ Choose your business name
  - ❏ Check other business names and trademarks
  - ❏ Register your name, trademark, etc.
- ❏ Choose the business form
  - ❏ Prepare and file organizational papers
  - ❏ Prepare and file fictitious name if necessary
- ❏ Choose the location
  - ❏ Check competitors
  - ❏ Check zoning
- ❏ Obtain necessary licenses
  - ❏ City?   ❏ State?
  - ❏ County?   ❏ Federal?
- ❏ Choose a bank
  - ❏ Checking
  - ❏ Credit card processing
  - ❏ Loans
- ❏ Obtain necessary insurance
  - ❏ Worker's Comp   ❏ Automobile
  - ❏ Liability   ❏ Health
  - ❏ Hazard   ❏ Life/disability
- ❏ File necessary federal tax registrations
- ❏ File necessary state tax registrations
- ❏ Set up a bookkeeping system
- ❏ Plan your hiring
  - ❏ Obtain required posters
  - ❏ Obtain or prepare employment application
  - ❏ Obtain new hire tax forms
  - ❏ Prepare employment policies
  - ❏ Determine compliance with health and safety laws
- ❏ Plan your opening
  - ❏ Obtain all necessary equipment and supplies
  - ❏ Obtain all necessary inventory
  - ❏ Do all necessary marketing and publicity
  - ❏ Obtain all necessary forms and agreements
  - ❏ Prepare you company policies on refunds, exchanges, returns

YOUR BUSINESS NAME 3

PRELIMINARY CONSIDERATIONS

Before deciding upon a name for your business, you should be sure that it is not already being used by someone else. Many business owners have spent thousands of dollars on publicity and printing only to throw it all away because another company owned the name. A company that owns a name can take you to court and force you to stop using that name. It can also sue you for damages if it thinks your use of the name cost it a financial loss.

If you will be running a small local shop with no plans for expansion, you should at least check out whether the name has been trademarked. If someone else is using the same name anywhere in the country and has registered it as a federal trademark, they can sue you. If you plan to expand or to deal nationally, you should do a thorough search of the name.

The first places to look are the local phone books and official records of your county. Next, you should check with the Secretary of State's office in Austin to see if someone has registered a fictitious name or corporate name the same as or confusingly similar to the one you have chosen. This can be done either by calling them at 512-463-555 or by emailing them at corpinfo@sos.state.tx.us. They have a web site for searching names but there are fees to use it and you must have funds on deposit. the site is http://www.sos.state.tx.us/function/forms/direct.html.

To do a national search, you should check trade directories and phone books of major cities. These can be found at many libraries and are usually reference books which cannot be checked out. The *Trade Names Directory* is a two volume set of names compiled from many sources published by Gale Research Co.

If you have a computer with internet access, you can use it to search all of the yellow page listings in the U.S. at no charge at a number of sites. One website, http://www.infoseek.com, offers free searches of yellow pages for all states at once.

To be sure that your use of the name does not violate someone else's trademark rights, you should have a trademark search done of the mark in the United States Patent and Trademark Office. In the past, this required a visit to their offices or the hiring of a search for over a hundred dollars. But in 1999, the USPTO put its trademark records online and you can now search them at: http://www.uspto.gov/tmdb/index.html.

If you do not have access to the internet, you might be able to do it at a public library or have one of their employees, for a small fee, order an online search for you. If this is not available to you, you can have a search done through a firm. One such firm is Government Liaison Services, Inc., P. O. Box 10648, Arlington, VA 22210. Tel. (703) 524-8200. They also offer searches of 100 trade directories and 4800 phone books.

No matter how thorough your search is, there is no guarantee that there is not a local user somewhere with rights to the mark. For example, say you register a name for a new chain of restaurants and later find out that someone in Tucumcari, New Mexico has been using the name longer than you. That person will still have the right to use the name, but just in his local area. If you do not want his restaurant to cause confusion with your chain, you can try to buy him out. Similarly, if you are operating a small business under a unique name and a law firm in New York writes and offers to buy the right to your name, you can assume that some large corporation wants to start a major expansion under that name.

The best way to make sure a name you are using is not already owned by someone else is to make up a name. Names such as Xerox, Kodak and Exxon were made up and didn't have any meaning prior to their use. Remember that there are millions of businesses and even something you make up may already be in use. Do a search anyway.

ASSUMED NAMES

In Texas, as in most states, unless you do business in your own legal name, you must register the name you are using, called an "assumed name." A sole proprietor or general partnership must register with the County Clerk of the county where the business is located and in any other county where business is being conducted.

If a corporation, limited partnership, or limited liability company does business under a name other than its registered name, the assumed name must be registered with the Secretary of State and the county clerk's office in the county of its principal place of business. It should also be registered in any other county in which it does significant business. To register an assumed name, you must fill out and sign a Certificate of Assumed Name form and file it with each office. The fee for filing with the Secretary of State is $25 and the county filing fee varies with each county. Registrations are effective for ten years.

It is a misdemeanor to fail to register a fictitious name and you may not sue anyone unless you are registered. If someone sues you and you are not registered, they may be entitled to attorney's fees and court costs.

If your name is *John Doe* and you are operating a masonry business, you may operate your business as *John Doe, Mason* without registering it. But any other use of a name should be registered, such as:

Doe Masonry	Doe Masonry Company
Doe Company	Texas Sunshine Masonry

You cannot use the words, "corporation," "incorporated," "corp.," or "Inc." unless you are a corporation. However, corporations do not have to register the name they are using unless it is different from their registered corporate name.

When you use a fictitious name you are "doing business as" (d/b/a) whatever name you are using. Legally you would use the name "John Doe d/b/a Doe Masonry."

To register a fictitious name, you must file an Assumed Name Certificate with the Secretary of State. (See the appendix for blank form.) Unlike corporate names and trademarks which are carefully screened by the Secretary of State to avoid duplication, fictitious name registrations are accepted without regard to who else is using the name. If you apply for registration of a trademark or corporate name, the Secretary of State will check all other registrations and refuse registration if the name or a similar name is already registered. But the registration of a fictitious name does not bestow any rights to the name upon the registrant; it is merely notice to the world of which persons are behind the business. So the Secretary of State will allow anyone to register any name, even if 100 others have already registered that name. (At $50 per registration, this should be very profitable for the state.)

As discussed previously, you should do some research to see if the name you intend to use is already being used by anyone else. Even persons who have not registered a name can acquire some legal rights to the name through mere use.

Some businesses have special requirements for registration of their fictitious names. See chapter 6 for a list of state regulated professions with references to the laws which apply to them.

On pages 34-39 are the fictitious name instructions and a sample filled-in form. A blank form is included in the appendix.

CORPORATE NAMES

A corporation does not have to register a fictitious name because it already has a legal name. The name of a corporation must contain one of the following words:

Incorporated	Inc.
Company	Co.
Corporation	Corp.

It is not advisable to use only the word "Company" or "Co." because unincorporated businesses also use these words; therefore, a person dealing with you might not realize you are incorporated. If this happens, you might end up with personal liability for corporate debts. You can use a combination of two of the words, such as ABC Co., Inc.

If the name of the corporation does not contain one of the above words it will be rejected by the Secretary of State. It will also be rejected if the name used by it is already taken or is similar to the name of another corporation, or if it uses a forbidden word such as "Bank" or "Trust." To check on a name, you may call the corporate name information number in Austin: (512) 463-5555. Keep trying, they are often busy. You can also check their website listed on page 26.

If a name you pick is taken by another company, you may be able to change it slightly and have it accepted. For example, if there is already a Tri-City Upholstery, Inc., and it is in a different county, you may be allowed to use Tri-City Upholstery of Liberty County, Inc. *But*, even if this is approved by the Secretary of State, you might get sued by the other company if your business is close to theirs or there is a likelihood of confusion.

Also, don't have anything printed until your corporate papers are returned to you. Sometimes a name is approved over the phone and rejected when submitted. Once you have chosen a corporate name and know it is available, you should immediately register your corporation.

If a corporation wants to do business under a name other than its corporate name, it can register a fictitious name such as "Doe Corporation d/b/a Doe Industries." But if the name used leads people to believe that the business is not a corporation, the right to limited liability may be lost. If such a name is used, it should always be accompanied by the corporate name.

PROFESSIONAL CORPORATIONS

Professionals such as attorneys, doctors, dentists, and architects can form professional corporations, professional associations, limited liability partnerships or limited liability companies in which to practice. These are better than general partnerships because they protect the professional from the malpractice of his or her co-workers. Professionals can form limited liability companies and limit their personal liability while receiving tax treatment as a partnership (see page 20).

Professional partnerships can register as limited liability partnerships to limit the partner's liability to his or her own professional malpractice (see pages 20-21).

Under Texas law, a professional corporation cannot use the usual corporate designations, Inc., Corp., or Co., but must use the words *Professional Corporation*, or the abbreviation, *P.C.*. Other states use abbreviations such as *P.A.* (professional association) or *P.S.C.* (professional service corporation) but neither of these are legal in Texas for a professional corporation. Professional corporations are covered by Article 1528e, Texas Revised Statutes (Professional Corporation Act).

Physicians are expressly excluded from organizing as a professional corporation. Physicians can form professional associations. Professional Associations are covered by Article 1528f Texas Revised Civil Statutes (Professional Association Act). Professional associations do not limit the personal liability of its members.

THE WORD "LIMITED"

The words *Limited* or *Ltd.* should not be used unless the entity is a limited partnership, limited liability company, or a limited liability partnership. If a corporation wishes to use the word limited in its name, it must still use one of the corporate words or abbreviations such as *incorporated* or *corp.*

DOMAIN NAMES

Because the internet is so new and changing rapidly, all of the rules for internet names have not yet been configured. Originally, the first person to reserve a name owned it, and enterprising souls bought up the names of most of the Fortune 500 corporations and held them for ransom. Then a few of the corporations went to court and the rule was developed that if a company had a trademark for a name, that company could stop someone else from using it if the other person didn't have a trademark.

You cannot yet get a trademark merely for using a domain name. Trademarks are granted for the use of a name in commerce. Once you have a valid trademark you will be safe in using it for your domain name.

In the next few years there will probably be several changes to the domain name system to make it more flexible and useful throughout the world. One proposed change is the addition of more generic top level domains (gTLDs) which are the last parts of the names, like *com* and *gov.* Some of the suggested additions are *firm, store, web, arts, rec, nom,* and *info.* This should free up a lot of names since corporations like McDonald's are not in the arts business and would probably not be able to keep the names from legitimate users.

If you wish to protect your domain name, the best thing to do at this point is to get a trademark for it. To do this, you would have to use it on your goods or services. The following section gives some basic information about trademarks. To find out if a domain name is available, go to http://rs.internic.net.

TRADEMARKS

As your business builds goodwill, its name will become more valuable and you will want to protect it from others who may wish to copy it. To protect a name used to describe your goods or services, you can register it as a trademark (for goods) or a service mark (for services) with either the Secretary of State of the state of Texas or with the United States Patent and Trademark Office.

You cannot obtain a trademark for the name of your business, but you can trademark the name you use on your goods and services. In most cases, you use your company name on your goods as your trademark. In effect, it protects your company name. Another way to protect your company name is to incorporate. A particular corporate name can only be registered by one company in Texas.

STATE REGISTRATION

State registration would be useful if you only expect to use your trademark within the state of Texas. Federal registration would protect your mark anywhere in the country. The registration of a mark gives you exclusive use of the mark for the types of goods for which you register it. The only exception is persons who have already been using the mark. You cannot stop people who have been using the mark prior to your registration.

The procedure for state registration is simple and the cost is $50. First, you should write to the Secretary of State, Statutory Filing Division, Corporations Section, P.O. Box 13697, Austin, TX 78711. Or call (512) 463-5576 to ask them to search your name and tell you if it is available. For questions about filing the application, call the same number.

Before a mark can be registered, it must be used in Texas. For goods, this means it must be used on the goods themselves, or on containers, tags, labels, or displays of the goods. For services, it must be used in the sale or advertising of the services. The use must be in an actual transaction with a customer. A sample mailed to a friend is not an acceptable use.

The $50 fee will register the mark in only one "class of goods." If the mark is used on more than one class of goods, a separate registration must be filed. The registration is good for ten years. Six months prior to its expiration, it must be renewed. The renewal fee is $25 for each class of goods.

On pages 40-46 are instructions and a sample filled-in form for a Texas trademark. A blank form is in the appendix of this book.

FEDERAL REGISTRATION

For federal registration, the procedure is a little more complicated. There are two types of applications depending upon whether you have already made actual use of the mark or whether you merely have an intention to use the mark in the future. For a trademark which has been in use, you must file an application form along with specimens showing actual use and a drawing of the mark which complies with all of the rules of the United States Patent and Trademark Office. For an "intent to use" application you must file two separate forms, one when you make the initial application and the other after you have made actual use of the mark as well as the specimens and drawing. Before a mark can be entitled to federal registration, the use of the mark must be in "interstate commerce" or in commerce with another country. The fee for registration is $245, but if you file an "intent to use" application there is a second fee of $100 for the filing after actual use.

An explanation of the entire trademark registration procedure and the application forms are included in the book *How to Register Your Own Trademark* by Mark Warda, published by Sphinx Publishing. It is available through most bookstores, or directly from the publisher by calling 1-800-432-7444.

Office of the Secretary of State

Corporations Office
P.O. Box 13697
Austin, Texas 78711-3597

APPLICATION FOR
RESERVATION OF ENTITY NAME

The undersigned applicant hereby applies for reservation of the following entity name for a period of one hundred twenty (120) days:

Crazy Comp. Software

The name is being reserved for the following type of entity pursuant to the applicable statutory provision. The appropriate fee is enclosed with this application for the type of entity specified below:

✔ *Corporation* (including business, non-profit, professional and foreign corporations and professional associations) pursuant to Article 2.06 of the Texas Business Corporation Act <u>OR</u> Article 2.04A of the Texas Non-Profit Corporation Act (*$40.00*).

____ *Limited Liability Company* (including foreign limited liability companies pursuant to Article 2.04 of the Texas Limited Liability Company Act (*$25.00*).

____ *Limited Partnership* (including foreign limited partnerships) pursuant to Section 1.04 of the Texas revised Limited Partnership Act (*$50.00*).

<u>Name reservations filed under one statute cannot be used for, or transferred to, filing made under any other statute.</u> In addition, once the application is filed, the name reservation will be recorded exclusively in the name of the applicant. Transfer of the reservation to another person may be made by filing a notice of such transfer executed by the applicant for whom the name was reserved and paying the appropriate fee.

Name and Address of Applicant:

XYZ Products. Inc.

2431 South Dallas Street

Fort Worth, Texas 73000

Dated: March 3, 2001

Signature:

Xavier Y. Zork

34

APPLICATION FOR RESERVATION OF ENTITY NAME

The name of a corporation, limited liability company or limited partnership may be reserved for a period of 120 days. There is no provision for renewal of a name reservation. Consequently, a subsequent application for reservation of the same corporate, limited partnership, or limited liability company name will not be accepted for filing until the original reservation has expired. A registrant may terminate the reservation of a name prior to the expiration of the reservation period by filing an application to cancel the name reservation. The filing fee for cancellation of a corporate name reservation is $15, cancellation of a limited partnership name reservation is $25, and cancellation of a limited liability company reservation is $10.

Only persons intending to organize a Texas business or non-profit corporation, limited liability company or limited partnership, persons intending to qualify a foreign (out-of-state) corporation, foreign limited liability company or foreign limited partnership to transact business in Texas, or any such entity which intends to change its name may reserve a name using this reservation procedure. This form may be used to reserve the name of any of these types of entities.

The name reservation application should set forth the entity name to be reserved, specify the person for whom the reservation is made, and be signed by the applicant or the attorney or agent thereof. Prior to signing, please read the statements on this form carefully. A person commits an offense under the Texas Business Corporation Act, the Texas Limited Liability Company Act or the Texas Non-Profit Corporation Act if the person signs a document the person knows is false in any material respect with the intent that the document be delivered to the secretary of state for filing. The offense is a Class A misdemeanor.

Mail the completed form along with the correct filing fee to the address shown in the heading of this form. The delivery address is James Earl Rudder Office Building, 1019 Brazos, Austin, Texas 78701. Upon filing the reservation we will issue a certificate of name reservation and return it to the remitter. The telephone number is (512) 463-5555, TDD: (800) 735-2989, FAX: (512) 463-5709.

The applicable statutes and the secretary of state's name availability rules provide that a proposed name cannot be the same as, deceptively similar to, or similar to (without a letter of consent) that of any existing domestic or foreign corporation, limited partnership, limited liability company or any name reservation or registration filed with the secretary of state. Therefore, upon submission of the application, the name will be checked for availability in accordance with the name availability rules administered by the secretary of state. Name availability may be checked prior to submission by calling (512) 463-5555. This is only a preliminary clearance and should not be relied upon as final approval of the name. The final decision regarding name availability will be made when the document is submitted for filing.

Form No. 501
Revised 7/98

The office of the Secretary of State does not discriminate on the basis of race, color, national origin, sex, religion, age or disability in employment or the provision of services.

ASSUMED NAME RECORDS
CERTIFICATE OF OWNERSHIP FOR UNINCORPORATED BUSINESS OR PROFESSION

NOTICE: "CERTIFICATES OF OWNERSHIP" ARE VALID ONLY FOR A PERIOD NOT TO EXCEED 10 YEARS FROM THE DATE FILED IN THE COUNTY CLERK'S OFFICE (Chapter 36, Section 1, title 4 - Business and Commerce Code)

NAME IN WHICH BUSINESS IS OR WILL BE CONDUCTED
_____Chili Unlimited_____
BUSINESS ADDRESS: __1818 Stockyard Plaza_____
CITY: Abilene_____ STATE: Texas_____ ZIP CODE: __73000_____
PERIOD (Not to Exceed 10 years) DURING WHICH ASSUMED NAME WILL BE USED:
_____ten (10) years_____
BUSINESS IS TO BE CONDUCTED AS (Check one):
____ Proprietorship __X_ Sole Practioner ____ Joint Venture
____ General Partnership ____ Limited Partnership
____ Joint Stock Company ____ Real Estate Investment Trust
____ Other: _____

CERTIFICATE OF OWNERSHIP

I/We, the undersigned am/are the owner(s) of the above business and my/our name(s) and address(es) given is/are true and correct, and there is/are no ownership(s) in said business other than those listed herein below.

NAME OF OWNERS

NAME: Hank Dillon_____ SIGNATURE: ___*Hank Dillon*_____
ADDRESS: 1818 Stockyard Plaza, Abilene, TX 730000_____
NAME:_____ SIGNATURE: _____
ADDRESS: _____
NAME:_____ SIGNATURE: _____
ADDRESS: _____
NAME:_____ SIGNATURE: _____
ADDRESS: _____
NAME:_____ SIGNATURE: _____
ADDRESS: _____

STATE OF TEXAS   §
COUNTY OF __Taylor_____   §

BEFORE ME, THE UNDERSIGNED AUTHORITY, on this day personally appeared
_____
_____

known to me to be the person__ whose name__ is/are subscribed to the foregoing instrument and acknowledged to me that __he__ is/are the owner__ of the above-named business and that __he__ signed the same for the purpose and consideration therein expressed.
GIVEN UNDER MY HAND AND SEAL OF OFFICE on _____, _____.

_____
Notary Public in and for the State of Texas

My Commission Expires:

_____

36

ASSUMED NAME CERTIFICATE

1. The name of the corporation, limited liability company, limited partnership, or registered limited liability partnership as stated in its articles of incorporation, articles of organization, certificate of limited partnership, application for certificate of authority or comparable document is___XYZ Products, Inc._____

2. The assumed name under which the business or professional service is or is to be conducted or rendered is ___Crazy Comp. Software_____
_____

3. The state, country, or other jurisdiction under the laws of which it was incorporated, organized, or associated is _____Texas_____ , and the address of its registered or similar office in that jurisdiction is _2431 South_____

Dallas St., Fort Worth, Texas_____

4. The period, not to exceed 10 years, during which the assumed name will be used is___
___ten (10) years_____

5. The entity is a (circle one):

> (Business Corporation)
> Non-Profit Corporation
> Professional Corporation
> Professional Association
> Limited Liability Company
> Limited Partnership
> Registered Limited Liability Partnership

If the entity is some other type of incorporated business, professional or other association, please specify below:
_____N/A_____

6. If the entity is required to maintain a registered office in Texas, the address of the registered office is_2431 South Dallas St., Fort Worth, Texas_____
_____ and the name of its registered agent at such address is ____Xavier Y. Zork_____
The address of the principal office (if not the same as the registered office) is_____
_____same as registered office_____

7.   If the entity is not required to or does not maintain a registered office in Texas, the office address in Texas is _____N/A_____
and if the entity is not incorporated, organized or associated under the laws of Texas, the address of its place of business in Texas is ___N/A_____
and the office address elsewhere is _____N/A_____

8.   The county or counties where business or professional services are being or are to be conducted or rendered under such assumed name are (if applicable, use the designation "ALL" or "ALL EXCEPT"): _____ALL_____

Xavier Y. Zork
Signature of officer, general partner, manager, representative or attorney-in-fact of the entity

State of Texas   §
County of ___Tarrant_____   §

This instrument was acknowledged before me on ____March 3, 2000_____ by

_____Xavier Y. Zork_____
(name of person acknowledging)

(Notary Seal)

_____
Signature of Notary
Notary Public, State of Texas

Form No. 503
Revised 8/98

The Office of the Secretary or State does not discriminate on the basis of race, color, national origin, sex, religion, age or disability in employment or the provision of services.

INSTRUCTIONS FOR FILING ASSUMED NAME CERTIFICATE

1. A corporation, limited liability company, limited partnership or registered limited liability partnership which regularly conducts business or renders a professional service in this state under a name other than its true name, must file an assumed name certificate with the secretary of state. In addition, an assumed name certificate must be filed with the county clerk in the county which the principal office is located if these are not in the same county.

2. Send one originally executed certificate accompanied by the filing fee of $25 to the Secretary of State, Statutory Filings Division, Corporations Section, P.O. Box 13697, Austin, Texas 78711-3697. The delivery address is 1019 Brazos, Austin, Texas 78701. The telephone number is (512) 463-5555, TDD: (800) 735-2989, FAX: (512) 5463-5709.

3. All assumed name certificates to be filed with the county clerk must be sent directly to the appropriate county clerk and not to the secretary of state.

4. The information provided in paragraph 6 regarding the registered agent and registered office address in Texas must match the information on file in this office. To verify the information on file, you may contact our Public Information Team at (512) 463-5555 or e-mail at corpinfo@sos.state.tx.us.

5. A certificate executed and acknowledged by an attorney-in-fact shall include a statement that the attorney-in-fact had been duly authorized in writing by his principal to execute and acknowledge the same.

6. Whenever an event occurs that causes the information in the assumed name certificate to become materially misleading (*e.g.* change of registered agent/office or a change of name), a new certificate must be filed within 60 days after the occurrence of the event which necessitates the filing.

7. A registrant that ceases to transact business or render professional services under an assumed name for which a certificate has been filed may file an abandonment of use pursuant to the Texas Business and Commerce Code, §36.14. See secretary of state form number 504.

Form No. 503
Revised 8/98

The Office of the Secretary of State does not discriminate on the basis of race, color, national origin, sex, religion, age or disability in employment or the provision of services.

Office of the
Secretary of State

Corporations Office
P.O. Box 13697
Austin, Texas 78711-3597

APPLICATION FOR REGISTRATION
OF TRADEMARK OR SERVICE MARK

The undersigned applicant has adopted and used, and is now using, a certain trademark or service mark in Texas and hereby makes application for registration of such mark, in accordance with Chapter 16 of the Texas Business & Commerce Code.

1. Applicant: _____ Hank Dillon d/b/a Chili Unlimited _____

2. Address: _____ 1818 Stockyards Plaza _____
    City: __ Abilene __ State: __ Texas __ Zip: __ 73000 __

3. Applicant is incorporated or organized as a _____ sole proprietorship _____
    and is incorporated or organized under the laws of _____

4. Describe the mark (words and/or design) SHOWN ON THE ATTACHED DRAWING SHEET:

    _____ "Fire Breather Chili Kit" _____

    _____

5. Description of goods or services in connection with which the mark is being used: (BE SPECIFIC)

    _____ Packaged spice and recipe kit for consumer chili preparation _____

    _____

6. The manner in which the mark is being used (labels, tags on the goods, etc.; OR brochures, newspapers advertising the services, etc.): (A SAMPLE IS ATTACHED)

    _____ label on the package, in newspaper advertisements _____

    _____

7. Number and title of the class of goods or services: _____ Class 29, Meats & _____
    Processed Foods

8. Date mark first used by applicant (BOTH SPACES MUST BE COMPLETED):
    (a) Anywhere: February 30, 2000 (b) In Texas: __ February 30, 2000 __

40

9. Applicant hereby appoints the secretary of state of Texas as its agent for service of process only in suits relating to the registration which may be issued if the applicant is or becomes a nonresident individual, partnership or association or foreign corporation, limited partnership, or limited liability company without a certificate of authority to do business in this state or cannot be found in this state.

10. Applicant is the owner of the mark and, to the best of the applicant's knowledge, no other person is entitled to use the mark in this state in the identical form used by applicant, or in a form that is likely, when used in connection with the goods or services, to cause confusion or mistake, or to deceive, because of its resemblance to the mark used by the applicant.

Executed on this __31st__ day of __September__, __2000__.

Hank Dillon, d/b/a Chili Unlimited
(Name of Applicant)

Hank Dillon
(Signature of Applicant) (if applicable, title of officer, partner, or other authorized person)

INSTRUCTIONS

Submit an **ORIGINAL** and one copy of the application. <u>Prior to signing, please review carefully the statements set forth in the application. A person commits an offense under Section 16.31, Business & Commerce Code, if the person signs a document that is forged or that the person knows is false in any material respect with the intent that the document be delivered to the secretary of state for filing. The offense is a Class A misdemeanor. In addition, an application or registration procured by fraud is subject to cancellation pursuant to Sections 16.16 and 16.28, Business & Commerce Code.</u>

The application must by <u>typewritten</u> or <u>clearly printed in black ink.</u> Enclose two (2) copies of a <u>drawing</u> of the mark and two (2) <u>specimens</u> of use (examples of use listed in item 6).

The application processing fee of $50.00 also must be enclosed. Checks should be made payable to the secretary of state. <u>The processing fee is not refundable regardless of whether the application is subsequently registered, denied or abandoned.</u>

Documents should be mailed to the address shown in the heading of this form. The delivery address is James Earl Rudder Office Building, 1019 Brazos, Austin, Texas 78701. We will place one document on record and return a file stamped copy. The telephone number is (512) 463-5576, TDD: (800) 735-2989, FAX: (512) 463-5709.

TRADEMARK DRAWING SHEET

Applicant:

Hank Dillon d/b/a
Chili Unlimited

Address:

1818 Stockyards Plaza
Abilene, Texas 73000

Goods/Services:

Packaged chili spices
and recipe kit

TRADEMARKS

GENERAL INFORMATION

TRADEMARKS and SERVICE MARKS are commonly referred to as brand names, logos or slogans. Trademarks are used to identify tangible goods; service marks are used to identify services. The term "mark" is used to refer to both trademarks and service marks. A mark generally does not include "trade names," which are terms used only to identify a business organization, rather than to distinguish the goods or services provided by the business. A company name may be viewed to be merely a trade name, instead of a trademark or service mark, if it is advertised in such a way that it attracts little attention, if it is used in close proximity to an address or phone number, or if it is dominated by the presence of another, indisputable trademark. A trade name, however, may be registered as a trademark if it is shown to function as a trademark.

The registration of the trademark or service mark with the Office of the Secretary of State - creates a statewide priority of rights in the mark against any other person who subsequently adopts the same or a confusingly similar mark. Registration also provides "constructive notice" to all persons in the state of Texas of the priority of the registered mark and provides the owner with certain procedural advantages when the owner seeks judicial relief for infringement. For these reasons, it is beneficial for an owner of a mark who does business in Texas to register a trademark or service mark with the secretary of state.

Since identical or confusingly similar marks may not be registered by more than one person, a person planning to use or register a mark should take steps to determine whether others have priority of rights to that mark. One important step is checking the active trademark and service mark registration on file with the Secretary of State prior to submitting the trademark application.

APPLICATION FOR REGISTRATION

Registration of trademarks and service marks in Texas is based on <u>actual use</u> of the mark in Texas. For example, before an application can be submitted to the Office of the Secretary of State, the trademark must be used on a product, or the service mark must be used in association with the services rendered (during advertising or sale), and the goods must be sold or distributed in Texas or the services must be rendered in this state. A proposed mark may not be "reserved" prior to its actual use in Texas commerce or before the submission of a properly complete and filed application. If an application is submitted prior to actual use, the secretary of state will consider it void, registration will be refused, and the processing fee submitted with the application will not be refunded.

An application for trademark registration undergoes an examination process similar to the federal trademark registration process. A "Trademark Examiner" (either a Trademark Attorney or trademark Legal Assistant) reviews the application to ascertain whether the mark

proposed for registration is registrable under Chapter 16, Business & Commerce Code [Section 16.08] including whether the mark performs the identifying functions of a trademark or service mark. In addition, the Examiner compares the proposed mark with similar marks previously registered in Texas to determine whether the applicant's mark will cause a likelihood of confusion for consumers with ant state registered mark. Texas law, federal statutory law (upon which the Texas trademark statute is based), federal case law, and examining procedures similar to those used by the United States Patent Trademark Office are used by the secretary of state to conduct the examinations of trademark applications.

If the examiner determines that the application does not meet the standards for registration, a written office action specifying the reasons for denial of registration will be sent to the applicant or the applicant's agent. The applicant is given sixty (60) days within which to amend the application, to provide the information requested, or to respond to the denial. Failure to respond within the time specified will terminate the examination process and will result in abandonment of the application. Upon receipt pf the applicant's response. the examiner will re-examine the application. The examination procedures described may be repeated until the application is registered, finally denied, or abandoned by the applicant.

The Trademark Examiners cannot provide legal advice to potential or actual applicants with regard to trademark law applicable to a particular circumstance. Because trademark law is quite complex, the secretary of state recommends that persons seeking to register a mark consult with a private attorney.

INSTRUCTIONS FOR APPLICATIONS

Numbers 1 & 2 of the application form: The applicant should be the person who owns the trademark or service mark and controls the use of the mark. The complete name and address of the applicant is to be entered. A sole proprietor doing business under an assumed name should state the individual's name, followed by "d/b/a [assumed name]."

Number 3: If applicant is a corporation limited partnership, limited liability company or other business entity, please identify the type of business organization and the state of incorporation or organization. Out of state corporations or other out-of-state business entities seeking a trademark or service mark registration should also submit invoices or other material demonstrating the sale of goods or the rendition of services in Texas commerce.

Number 4: Registration of only one mark may be sought in one application. For example, if the mark includes words and a design element (a "composite mark"), and applicant also uses the same words apart from the design, applicant may have two separate marks, A single application may not be used to register words "with or without" an accompanying design, or with more than one design. In addition, the applicant should describe the mark exactly as it appears in the specimen accompanying the application.

The applicant also must submit with the application a "drawing sheet" that shows the mark exactly as it appears in the specimen accompanying the application and exactly as it is described in paragraph 4 of the application. If the mark includes a design, a drawing of the entire proposed mark (in clean, uniform black lines) must be attached to the application. If the mark described in the application consists only of a word, letter or numeral, or any combination thereof, and if the mark is not depicted in a special form, the mark may be typed in capital letters on the drawing sheet. Where color is a feature mark, the color or colors shall be designated by the linings accepted by the United States Patent and Trademark Office, which are shown on the drawing sheet. In addition, state in the description of the mark that "the mark is lined for the color 'X'."

Number 5: Describe <u>clearly and concisely</u> the goods or the services currently sold or provided by the applicant. Limited the description of goods or services to those goods or services that are classified under the same class heading. [See instructions for number 7.]

Number 6: The applicant should state the ways in which the mark is used, and/or the medium by which it is communicated to the consuming public. For example: tags or labels attached to the goods; or newspapers, brochures or signs advertising the services. Specimens consistent with the methods noted in the application must be submitted with the application.

Specimens: for trademark applications, include specimens such as actual labels or tags affixed to, or containers used with, the goods. A photograph of an actual display that appears in immediate proximity to the goods ("point-of-sale" display) is also an acceptable specimen. For service mark applications, submit actual materials used in selling or advertising the services, such as menus, newspaper advertisements, coupons and the like. Advertising samples submitted (including letterhead or business cards) <u>must</u> contain some understandable reference to the services described in the application.

Number 7: State the class in which the applicant believes the goods or services belong. The classification system is set forth below:

Goods

Class 1: Chemicals
Class 2: Paints
Class 3: Cosmetics & Cleaning Preparations
Class 4: Lubricants & Fuels
Class 5: Pharmaceuticals
Class 6: Metal Goods
Class 7: Machinery
Class 8: Hand Tools
Class 9: Electrical & Scientific Apparatus
Class 10: Medical Apparatus
Class 11: Environmental Control Apparatus
Class 12: Vehicles
Class 13: Firearms
Class 14: Jewelry
Class 15: Musical Instruments
Class 16: Paper Goods & Printed Matter
Class 17: Rubber Goods
Class 18: Leather Goods
Class 19: Non-metallic Building Materials
Class 20: Furniture
Class 21: Housewares & Glass
Class 22: Cordage & Fibers
Class 23: Yarns & Threads
Class 24: Fabrics
Class 25: Clothing
Class 26: Fancy Goods (*eg*., buttons, ribbons)
Class 27: Floor Coverings
Class 28: Toys & Sporting Goods
Class 29: Meats & Processed Foods
Class 30: Staple Foods (*e.g.*, coffee, sugar)
Class 31: Natural Agricultural Products
Class 32: Light Beverages
Class 33: Wine & Spirits
Class 34: Smokers' Articles

Services

Class 35: Advertising & Business
Class 36: Insurance and Financial
Class 37: Building Construction & repair
Class 38: Telecommunications
Class 39: Transportation & Storage
Class 40: Treatment of Materials
Class 41: Education & Entertainment
Class 42: Miscellaneous Services
(including providing of food & drink, legal services, temporary accommodation, medical, hygienic & beauty care, veterinary & agricultural services, computer programming, scientific & industrial research, and other services that do not fit into the other classes)

Number 8: The applicant should note accurately the date on which the mark was first publicly used to identify the goods or services being marketed. BOTH dates of first use "Anywhere" and in "Texas" MUST be indicated on the application. (If the date of first use was in Texas, both dates will be the same.) The month, day and year should be noted for each of first use, *e.g.*, "November 10, 1983."

Signature: The applicant must sign and date the application. The applicant's attorney of record may sign the application only with express authorization pursuant to a power of attorney. In addition, the application should not ne executed <u>before</u> the first date of use of the mark.

Form No. 901
Revised 9/97

The Office of the Secretary of State does not discriminate on the basis of race, color, national origin, sex, religion, age or disability in employment or the provision of services.

FINANCING YOUR BUSINESS 4

The way to finance your business is determined by how fast you want your business to grow and how much risk of failure you are able to handle. Letting the business grow with its own income is the slowest but safest way to grow. Taking out a personal loan against your house to expand quickly is the fastest but riskiest way to grow.

GROWING WITH PROFITS

Many successful businesses have started out with little money and used the profits to grow bigger and bigger. If you have another source of income to live on (such as a job or a spouse), you can plow all the income of your fledgling business into growth.

Some businesses start as hobbies or part time ventures on the weekend while the entrepreneur holds down a full time job. Many types of goods or services businesses can start this way. Even some multimillion dollar corporations, Apple Computer for example, started out this way.

This allows you to test your idea with little risk. If you find you're not good at running that type of business, or the time or location wasn't right for your idea, all you are out is the time you spent and your start-up capital.

However, a business can only grow so big from its own income. In many cases, as a business grows, it gets to a point where the orders are so big that money must be borrowed to produce the product to fill them. There is the risk, with this kind of order, that if the customer can't pay or goes bankrupt, the business will also fold. At such a point, a business owner should investigate the credit worthiness of the customer and weigh the risks. Some businesses have grown rapidly, some have gone under, and others have decided not to take the risk and stayed small. You can worry about that down the road.

USING YOUR SAVINGS

If you have savings you can tap to get your business started, that is the best source. You won't have to pay high interest rates and you won't have to worry about paying someone back relatives.

HOME EQUITY   If you have owned your home for several years, it is possible that the equity has grown substantially and you can get a second mortgage to finance your business. Some lenders will make second mortgages that exceed the equity if you have been in the home for many years and have a good record of paying your bills. Just remember, if your business fails, you may lose your house.

RETIREMENT ACCOUNTS   Be careful about borrowing from your retirement savings. There are tax penalties for borrowing from or against certain types of retirement accounts. Also, your future financial security may be lost if your business doesn't succeed.

HAVING TOO MUCH MONEY   It probably doesn't seem possible to have too much money with which to start a business, but many businesses have failed for that reason. With plenty of start-up capital available, a business owner doesn't need to watch expenses and can become wasteful. Employees get used to lavish spending. Once the money runs out and the business must run on its own earnings, it fails.

Starting with the bare minimum forces a business to watch its expenses and be frugal. It necessitates finding the least expensive solutions to problems that crop up and creative ways to be productive.

BORROWING MONEY

It is extremely tempting to look to others to get the money to start a business. The risk of failure is less worrisome and the pressure is lower, but that is a problem with borrowing. If it is others' money you don't have quite the same incentive to succeed as if everything you own is on the line.

Actually, you should be even more concerned when using the money of others. Your reputation should be more valuable than money which can always be replaced. Yet that is not always the case. How many people borrow again and again from their parents for failed business ventures?

FAMILY
Depending on how much money your family can spare it may be the most comfortable or most uncomfortable source of funds for you. If you have been assured a large inheritance and your parents have more funds than they need to live on, you may be able to borrow against your inheritance without worry. It will be your money anyway and you need it much more now than you will ten, twenty, or more years from now. If you lose it all, it's your own loss anyway.

However, if you are borrowing your widowed mother's source of income, asking her to cash in a CD she lives on to finance your get-rich-quick scheme, you should have second thoughts about it. Stop and consider all the real reasons your business might not take off and what your mother would do without the income.

FRIENDS
Borrowing from friends is like borrowing from family members. If you know they have the funds available and could survive a loss, you may want to risk it, but if they would be loaning you their only resources, don't chance it.

Financial problems can be the worst thing for a relationship, whether it is a casual friendship or a long term romantic involvement. Before you borrow from a friend, try to imagine what would happen if you couldn't pay it back and how you would feel if it caused the end of your relationship.

The ideal situation is if your friend were a co-venturer in your business and the burden would not be totally on you to see how the funds were spent. Still, realize that such a venture will put extra strain on the relationship.

BANKS In a way, a bank can be a more comfortable party from which to borrow. You don't have a personal relationship with a bank, a friend or family member, you do. If you fail, a bank will write your loan off rather than disown you. But a bank can also be the least comfortable party from which to borrow--they will demand realistic projections and be on top of you to perform. If you don't meet their expectations, they may call your loan just when you need it most.

The best thing about a bank loan is that they will require you to do your homework: you must have plans that make sense to a banker. If they approve your loan, you know that your plans are at least reasonable.

Bank loans aren't cheap or easy. You'll be paying a good interest rate, and you'll have to put up collateral. If your business does not have equipment or receivables, they may require you to put up your house and other personal property to guarantee the loan.

Banks are a little easier to deal with when you get a Small Business Administration (SBA) loan. That is because the SBA guarantees that it will pay the bank if you default on the loan. SBA loans are obtained through local bank branches.

CREDIT CARDS Borrowing against a credit card is one of the fastest growing ways of financing a business, but it can be one of the most expensive ways. The rates can go higher than twenty percent, but many cards offer lower rates and some people are able to get numerous cards. Some successful businesses have used the partners' credit cards to get off the ground or to weather through a cash crunch, but if the business doesn't begin to generate the cash to make the payments, you could soon end up in bankruptcy. A good strategy is to only use credit cards for a long term asset like a computer or for something that will quickly generate cash, like buying inventory to fill an order. Don't use credit cards to pay expenses that aren't generating revenue.

A Rich Partner

One of the best business combinations is a young entrepreneur with ideas and ambition and a retired investor with business experience and money. Together they can supply everything the business needs.

How to find such a partner? Be creative. You should have investigated the business you are starting and know others who have been in such businesses. Have any of them had partners retire over the last few years? Are any of them planning to phase out of the business?

Selling Shares of Your Business

Silent investors are the best source of capital for your business. You retain full control of the business and if it happens to fail you have no obligation to them. Unfortunately, few silent investors are interested in a new business. It is only after you have proved your concept to be successful, and built up a rather large enterprise that you will be able to attract such investors.

The most common way to obtain money from investors is to issue stock to them. The best type of business entity for this is the corporation. It gives you almost unlimited flexibility in the number and kinds of shares of stock you can issue.

SECURITIES LAWS

There is one major problem with selling stock in your business and that is all of the federal and state regulations with which you must comply. Both the state and federal governments have long and complicated laws dealing with the sales of "securities." There are also hundreds of court cases attempting to explain the meaning of these laws. A thorough explanation of this area of law is obviously beyond the scope of this book.

Basically, securities have been held to exist in any case in which a person provides money to someone with the expectation that he will get a profit through the efforts of that person. This can apply to any situation where someone buys stock in, or makes a loan to your business. What the laws require is disclosure of the risks involved, and in some cases, registration of the securities with the government. There are some exemptions, such as for small amounts of money and for limited numbers of investors.

Penalties for violation of securities laws are severe, including triple damages and prison terms, so you should consult a specialist in securities laws before issuing any security. You can often get an introductory consultation at a reasonable rate to explain your options. A limited explanation of the exemptions is contained in the book *How to Form Your Own Corporation*, available from your local bookstore or from Sphinx Publishing by calling 1-800-432-7444.

USING THE INTERNET TO FIND CAPITAL

In 1995, the owners of Wit Beer made headlines in all the business magazines by successfully raising $1.6 million for their business on the internet. It seemed so easy; every business wanted to try. What wasn't made clear in most of the stories was that the owner was a corporate securities lawyer, and he did all of the necessary legal work to prepare a prospectus and properly register the stock-- something which would have cost anyone else over $100,000 in legal fees. Also, most of the interest in the stock came from the articles, not from the internet promotion. Today, a similar effort would probably not be nearly as successful.

Before attempting to market your company's shares on the internet, be sure to get an opinion from a securities lawyer or do some serious research into securities laws. The lawyer who marketed Wit Beer's shares on the internet has started a business to advise businesses in raising capital. It is Wit Capital, located at 826 Broadway, 6th Floor, New York, NY 10003.

The internet does have some sources of capital listed. The following sites may be helpful.

America's Business Funding Directory:
http://www.businessfinance.com

Angel Capital Electronic Network (SBA): http://www.sba.gov

FinanceHub: http://www.financehub.com

NVST: http://www.nvst.com

Private Capital Clearinghouse: http://www.pricap.com

LOCATING YOUR BUSINESS 5

The right location for your business will be determined by what type of business it is, and how fast you expect to grow. For some types of businesses, the location will not be important to your success or failure in others it will be crucial.

WORKING OUT OF YOUR HOME

Many small businesses get started out of the home. Chapter 6 discusses the legalities of home businesses. This section discusses the practicalities.

Starting a business out of your home can save you the rent, electricity, insurance, and other costs of setting up at another location. For some people this is ideal, and they can combine their home and work duties easily and efficiently, but for other people it is a disaster. A spouse, children, neighbors, television, and household chores can be so distracting that no other work gets done.

Many people use their residential telephone line to conduct business, or add a second residential line, since residential rates are usually lower than business lines. However, if you wish to be listed in the yellow pages, you will need to have a business line in your home. If you are running two or more types of businesses, you can probably add their names as additional listings on the original number and avoid paying for another business line.

You also should consider whether the type of business you are starting is compatible with a home office. For example, if your business mostly consists of making phone calls or calling clients, then the home may be an ideal place to run it. If your clients need to visit you or you will need daily pickups and deliveries by truck, the home may not be a good location. This is discussed in more detail in the next chapter.

CHOOSING A RETAIL SITE

For most types of retail stores, the location is of prime importance. Such things to consider are how close it is to your potential customers, how visible it is to the public, and how easily accessible it is to both autos and pedestrians. The attractiveness and safety should also be considered.

Location would be less important for a business which was the only one of its kind in the area. For example, the only moped parts dealer or Armenian restaurant in a metropolitan area, people would have to come to wherever you are if they want your products or services. However, even with such businesses, keep in mind that there is competition. People who want moped parts can order them by mail and restaurant customers can choose another type of cuisine.

You should look up in the phone book all the businesses like the one you're planning and mark them on a map. For some businesses, like a cleaners, you would want to be far from the others. But for other businesses, like antique stores, you would want to be near the others. Since antique stores usually do not carry the same things, they don't compete and people like to go to an "antique district" and visit all the shops.

Choosing Office, Manufacturing, or Warehouse Site

If your business will be the type where customers will not come to you, then of course locating it near customers is not as much of a concern and you can probably save money by locating away from the high traffic, central business districts. However, you should consider the convenience for employees and not locate in an area which would be unattractive to them, or too far from where they would likely live.

For manufacturing or warehouse operations, you should consider your proximity to a post office, trucking company or rail line. Where several sites are available you might consider which one has the earliest or most convenient pick-up schedule for the carriers you plan to use.

Leasing a Site

A lease of space can be one of the biggest expenses of a small business so you should do a lot of homework before signing one. There are a lot of terms in a commercial lease which can make or break your business. These are the most critical:

ZONING
Before signing a lease, you should be sure that everything that your business will need to do is allowed by the zoning of the property.

RESTRICTIONS
In some shopping centers, existing tenants have guarantees that other tenants do not compete with them. For example, if you plan to open a restaurant and bakery, you may be forbidden to sell carry out baked goods if the supermarket has a bakery and a non-compete clause.

SIGNS
Business signs are regulated by zoning laws, sign laws and property restrictions. If you rent a hidden location with no possibility for adequate signage, your business will have a smaller chance of success than with a more visible site or much larger sign.

ADA COMPLIANCE	The Americans with Disabilities Act requires that reasonable accommodations be made to make businesses accessible to the handicapped. When a business is remodeled, many more changes are required than if no remodeling is done. When renting space you should be sure that it complies with the law, or the landlord will be responsible for compliance, or you are aware of the full costs you will bear.
EXPANSION	As your business grows, you may need to expand your space. The time to find out about your options is before you sign the lease. Perhaps you you can take over adjoining units when those leases expire.
RENEWAL	Location is a key to success for some businesses. If you spend five years building up a clientele, you don't want someone to take over at the end of your lease. Therefore, you should have a renewal clause on your lease. Usually this allows an increase in rent based on inflation.
GUARANTEE	Most landlords of commercial space will not rent to a small corporation without a personal guaranty of the lease. This is a very risky thing for a new business owner to do. The lifetime rent on a long term commercial lease can be hundreds of thousands of dollars and if your business fails the last thing you want to do is be personally responsible for five years of rent.
	Where space is scarce or a location is hot, a landlord can get the guarantees he demands and there is nothing you can do about it (except perhaps set up an asset protection plan ahead of time). But where several units are vacant or the commercial rental market is soft, you can often negotiate around the personal guaranty. If the lease is five years, maybe you can get away with a guaranty of just the first year. Give it a try.
DUTY TO OPEN	Some shopping centers have rules requiring all shops to be open certain hours. If you can't afford to staff it the whole time required, or if you have religious or other reasons which make this a problem, you should negotiate it out of the lease or find another location.
SUBLEASE	At some point you may decide to sell your business, and in many cases the location is the most valuable aspect. For this reason you should be

sure that you have the right to either assign your lease or to sublease the property. If this is impossible, one way around a prohibition is to incorporate your business before signing the lease and when you sell the business, sell the stock. But some lease clauses prohibit transfer of "any interest" in the business, so read the lease carefully.

For more information about leasing you should see the book *How to Negotiate Real Estate Leases* by Mark Warda, also published by Sphinx Publishing. It is available at your local bookstore, or by calling the publisher at 1-800-432-7444.

BUYING A SITE

If you are experienced with owning rental property, you will probably be more inclined to buy a site for your business. If you have no experience with real estate, you should probably rent and not take on the extra cost and responsibility of property ownership.

One reason to buy your site is that you can build up equity. Rather than pay rent to a landlord, you can pay off a mortgage and eventually own the property.

SEPARATING THE OWNERSHIP
One risk in buying a business is that if the business gets into financial trouble, the creditors may go after the building as well. For this reason, most people who buy a site for their business keep the ownership out of the business. For example, the business will be a corporation and the real estate will be owned by the owner or by a trust unrelated to the business.

EXPANSION
Before buying a site, you should consider the growth potential of your business. If it grows quickly will you be able to expand at that site or will you have to move? What are the odds that the property next door will be available for sale in the future? Can you get an option on it?

If the site is a good investment whether you have your business or not, then by all means, buy it. But if its main use is for your business, think twice.

ZONING   Some of the concerns when buying a site are the same as when renting. You will want to make sure that the zoning permits the type of business you wish to start, or that you can get a variance without a large expense or delay. Be aware that just because a business is now using the site does not mean that you can expand or remodel the business at that site. Some zoning laws allow businesses to be grandfathered in, but not expanded. Check with the zoning department and find out exactly what is allowed.

SIGNS   Signs are another concern. Some cities have regulated signs and do not allow new ones, or require them to be smaller. Some businesses have used these laws to get publicity. A car dealer who was told to take down a large number of American flags on his lot filed a federal lawsuit and rallied the community behind him. It couldn't have hurt business except for a few over-controlling public officials.

ADA COMPLIANCE   ADA compliance is another concern when buying a commercial building. Find out from the building department if the building is in compliance or what needs to be done to put it in compliance. If you remodel, the requirements may be more strict.

> *Note:* When dealing with public officials always keep in mind that they do not always know what the law is, or honestly tell you what it is. They are often overzealous and try to intimidate people into doing things which are not required by law. Read the requirements yourself and question them if they seem to be interpreting it wrong. Seek legal advice if they refuse to budge from a clearly erroneous position. But also consider that keeping them happy may be worth the price. If you are already getting away with something they have overlooked, don't make a big deal over a little thing they want changed or they may subject you to a full inspection or audit.

CHECK GOVERNMENTAL REGULATIONS

When looking for a site for your business, you should investigate the difference between governmental regulations in your area. For example, a location just outside the city or county limits might have a lower licensing fee, a lower sales tax rate, and less strict sign requirements.

LICENSING YOUR BUSINESS 6

OCCUPATIONAL LICENSES AND ZONING

Some Texas counties and cities require you to obtain an occupational license. If you are in a city you may need both a city and a county license. Businesses which do work in several cities, such as builders, must obtain a license from each city in which they do work. This does not have to be done until you actually begin a job in a particular city.

County occupational licenses can be obtained from the tax collector in the county courthouse. City licenses are usually available at city hall. Be sure to find out whether zoning laws permit your type of business before buying or leasing property. The licenseing departments will check the zoning before issuing your license.

If you will be preparing or serving food, you will need to check with the local health department to be sure that the premises complies with their regulations. In some areas, if food has been served on the premises in the past, there is no problem getting a license. If food has never been served on the premises, then the property must comply with all the newest regulations, which can be very costly.

HOME
BUSINESSES

Problems occasionally arise when persons attempt to start a business in their home. Small new businesses cannot afford to pay rent for commercial space and cities often try to forbid business in residential areas. Getting a county occupational license or advertising a fictitious name often gives notice to the city that a business is being conducted in a residential area.

Some people avoid the problem by starting their businesses without occupational licenses, figuring that the penalties for not having a license (if they are caught) are less expensive than the cost of office space. Others get the county license and ignore the city rules. If a person regularly parks commercial trucks and equipment on his property, or has delivery trucks coming and going, or employee cars parked along the street, there will probably be complaints from neighbors and the city will probably take legal action. But if a person's business consists merely of making phone calls out of the home and keeping supplies there, the problem may never become an issue.

If a problem does arise regarding a home business which does not disturb the neighbors, a good argument can be made that the zoning law which prohibits the business is unconstitutional. When zoning laws were first instituted, they were not meant to stop people from doing things in a residence which had historically been part of the life in a residence. Consider an artist. Should a zoning law prohibit a person from sitting in his home and painting pictures? If he sells them for a living is there a difference? Can the government force him to rent commercial space just because he decides to sell the paintings he paints?

Similar arguments can be made for many home businesses. For hundreds of years people performed income-producing activities in their homes. (One of the authors is waiting for his city fathers to tell him to stop writing books in his home office.) But court battles with a city are expensive and probably not worth the effort for a small business. The best course of action is to keep a low profile. Using a post office box for the business is sometimes helpful in diverting attention away from the residence.

STATE REGULATED PROFESSIONS

Many professionals must hold special state licenses. You may be called upon to produce such a license when applying for an occupational license.

If you are in a regulated profession, you should be aware of the laws which apply to your profession. The following pages contain a list of many professions and the state laws and regulations covering them. You can make copies of these laws at your local public library or county law library. If you do not think your profession is regulated, you should read through the list anyway. Some of those included may surprise you.

REGULATED PROFESSIONS IN TEXAS

The following is a list of regulated professions in Texas along with the phone number of the division which regulates them, and the Texas Civil Statutes (C.S.) and to various Texas Codes.

Accountancy	C.S. 41a-1
Acupuncture	C.S. 4495b
Adjusters	Ins. 21.07-4
Adult Day Care	Human Resources Code 103.001 et seq.
Aircraft, Pilots & Airports	Transporation Code 24.001 et seq.
Alarm Systems	Local Govt. Code 237.003, 237.004
Architecture	C.S. 249a
Athletic Trainers	C.S. 4512d
Attorneys	Govt. Code 82.001, State Bar Rules
Auctioneers	C.S. 8700
Barbering	C.S. 8402, et. seq.
Career Counseling Services	C.S. 5221a-8
Cemeteries	Health & Safety Code, Chap. 711
Chiropractic	C.S. 4512b
Child Care Facilities	Human Resources Code Chaps. 42, 43

Clinical Social Workers	Human Resources Code 50.001 et. seq.
Commerical Driver	TransportationCode Ch. 522
Community Homes, Disabled Persons	Human Resources Code 123.007
Cosmetology	C.S. 8451a
Counseling	C.S. 4512g
Dentistry	C.S. 4543 et. seq.
Driver Training Instructors	C.S. 4413(29c)
Engineering	C.S. 3271a
Funeral Directors & Embalmers	C.S. 4582b
Hearing Aid Dispensers & Fillers	C.S. 4566-1.01 et. seq.
Home & Community Support Services	Health & Safety Code Ch. 142
Investigative Services	C.S. 4413(29bb)
Land Surveying	C.S. 5282c
Landscape Architects	C.S. 249c
Marriage & Family Therapist	C.S. 4512c-1
Massage Therapy	C.S. 4512e
Medical Doctors	C.S. 4495b
Midwifery	C.S. 4512i
Nursing	C.S.4519 et. seq.
Nursing Homes	Health & Safety Code Chap. 232
Occupational Therapists	C.S. 4512e-1
Opticians	C.S. 4551-1
Optometry	C.S. 4552-3.02 et. seq.
Osteopathy	C.S. 4495b
Outdoor Advertising	Alcoholic Beverage Code Ch. 108, Transportation Code Ch. 391
Personal Employment Service	C.S. 5221a-7
Pest Control	C.S. 135b-6
Pharmacy	C.S. 4542a-1
Plumbing	C.S. 6243-101
Podiatry	C.S. 4567 et. seq.
Physical Therapy	C.S. 4512e-1
Physcian's Assistant	C.S. 4495b-1
Psychologists	C.S. 4512c
Radiologic Technologists	C.S. 4512m

Real Estate Appraisers	C.S. 6573a.2
Real Estate Brokerage, Sales	C.S. 6573a
Real Estate Inspectors	C.S. 6573a, sec. 23
Sanitarians	C.S. 4477-3
Speech Pathology & Audiology	C.S. 4512j
Talent Agency	C.S. 5221a-9
Veterinary Medicine	C.S. 8890
Youth Camps	Health & Safey Code 141.003

FEDERAL LICENSES

So far there are few businesses that require federal registration. If you are in any of the types of businesses listed below, you should check with the federal agency beside it.

Radio or television stations or manufacturers of equipment emitting radio waves:

> Federal Communications Commission
> 1919 M Street, NW
> Washington, DC 20550

Manufacturers of alcohol, tobacco or fire arms:

> Bureau of Alcohol, Tobacco and Firearms,
> Treasury Department
> 1200 Pennsylvania Ave., NW
> Washington, DC 20226

Securities brokers and providers of investment advice:

> Securities and Exchange Commission
> 450 - 5th Street NW
> Washington, DC 20549

Manufacturers of drugs and processors of meat:

Food and Drug Administration
5600 Fishers Lane
Rockville, MD 28057

Interstate carriers:

Interstate Commerce Commission
12th St. & Constitution Ave.
Washington, DC 20423

Exporting:

Bureau of Export Administration
Department of Commerce
14th St. & Constitution Ave., NW
Washington, DC 20220

CONTRACT LAWS 7

As a business owner you will need to know the basics of forming a simple contract for your transactions with both customers and vendors. There is a lot of misunderstanding about what the law is and people may give you erroneous information. Relying on it can cost you money. This chapter will give you a quick overview of the principles which apply to your transactions and pitfalls to avoid. If you face more complicated contract questions, you should consult a law library or an attorney familiar with small business law.

TRADITIONAL CONTRACT LAW

One of the first things taught in law school is that a contract is not legal unless three elements are present: offer, acceptance, and consideration. The rest of the semester dissects exactly what may be a valid offer, acceptance, and consideration. For your purposes, the important things to remember are:

- ☛ If you make an offer to someone, it may result in a binding contract, even if you change your mind or find out it was a bad deal for you.

- ☛ Unless an offer is accepted and both parties agree to the same terms, there is no contract.

☞ A contract does not always have to be in writing. Some laws require certain contracts to be in writing, but as a general rule an oral contract is legal. The problem is proving that the contract existed.

☞ Without consideration (the exchange of something of value or mutual promises), there is not a valid contract.

As mentioned above, an entire semester is spent analyzing each of the three elements of a contract. The most important rules for the business owner are:

☞ An advertisement is not an offer. Suppose you put an ad in the newspaper offering "New IBM computers only $1995!" but there is a typo in the ad and it says $19.95? Can people come in, say "I accept, here's my $19.95" and create a legal contract? Fortunately, no. Courts have ruled that the ad is not an offer which a person can accept. It is an invitation to come in and make offers which the business can accept or reject.

☞ The same rule applies to the price tag on an item. If someone switches price tags on your merchandise, or if you accidentally put the wrong price on it, you are not required by law to sell it at that price. If you intentionally put the wrong price you may be liable under the "bait and switch" law. Many merchants honor a mistaken price just because refusing to would constitute bad will and probably lose a customer.

☞ When a person makes an offer, several things may happen. It may be accepted, creating a legal contract. It may be rejected. It may expire before it has been accepted. Or, it may be withdrawn before acceptance. A contract may expire either by a date made in the offer ("This offer remains open until noon on January 29, 2000") or after a reasonable amount of time. What is reasonable is a legal question which a court must decide. If someone makes you an offer to sell goods, clearly you cannot come back five years later and accept. Can you accept a week later or a month later and create a legal contract? That depends on the type of goods and the circumstances.

☛ A person accepting an offer cannot add any terms to it. If you offer to sell a car for $1,000, and the other party says they accept as long as you put new tires on it, there is no contract. An acceptance with changed terms is considered a rejection and a counteroffer.

☛ When someone rejects your offer and makes a counteroffer, a contract can be created by your acceptance of the counteroffer.

These rules can affect your business on a daily basis. Suppose you offer to sell something to one customer over the phone and five minutes later another customer walks in and offers you more for it. To protect yourself you should call the first customer and withdraw your offer before accepting the offer of the second customer. If the first customer accepts before you have withdrawn your offer, you may be sued if you have sold the item to the second customer.

There are a few exceptions to the basic rules of contracts, these are:

☛ Consent to a contract must be voluntary. If it is made under a threat, the contract is not valid. If a business refuses to give a person's car back unless they pay $200 for changing the oil, the customer could probably sue and get the $200 back.

☛ Contracts to do illegal acts or acts "against public policy" are not enforceable. If an electrician signs a contract to put some wiring in a house that is not legal, the customer could probably not force him to do it because the court would refuse to require an illegal act.

☛ If either party of an offer dies, then the offer expires and cannot be accepted by the heirs. If a painter is hired to paint a portrait, and dies before completing it, his wife cannot finish it and require payment. However, a corporation does not die, even if its owners die. If a corporation is hired to build a house and the owner dies, his heirs may take over the corporation, finish the job, and require payment.

☛ Contracts made under misrepresentation are not enforceable. For example, if someone tells you a car has 35,000 miles on it and you later discover it has 135,000 miles, you may be able to rescind the contract for fraud and misrepresentation.

☛ If there was a mutual mistake a contract may be rescinded. For example, if both you and the seller thought the car had 35,000 miles on it and both relied on that assumption, the contract could be rescinded. However, if the seller knew the car has 135,000 miles on it, and you assumed it had 35,000 but didn't ask, you probably could not rescind the contract.

STATUTORY CONTRACT LAW

The previous section discussed the basics of contract law. These are not usually stated in the statutes, but are the legal principles decided by judges over the past hundreds of years. In recent times the legislatures have made numerous exceptions to these principles. In most cases, these laws have been passed when the legislature felt that traditional law was not fair. The important laws which affect contracts are the following.

Statutes of fraud state that a contract must be in writing to be valid. Some people believe a contract isn't valid unless it's in writing, but that is not so. Only those types of contracts mentioned in the statutes of fraud must be in writing. Of course an oral contract is much harder to prove in court than one that is in writing.

STATUTES OF FRAUD

In Texas, some of the contracts which must be in writing are spelled out in §26.01 of the Business and Commercial Code. The statutes are as follows:

☛ sales of any interest in real estate

☛ leases of real estate over one year

☛ agreements to pay commissions on sales of oil, gas or minerals

☛ warranties or contracts regarding results relating to medical care

☛ promises to pay another's debts

Technically, failure to get the above types of agreements in writing means that a court will not enforce the agreement, even if one party has paid. However, where a court finds that a party has taken advantage, it may allow other types of evidence, such as receipts or cancelled checks to constitute the written agreement.

Due to alleged unfair practices by some types of businesses, laws have been passed controlling the types of contracts they may use. Most notable among these are health clubs and door-to-door solicitations. The laws covering these businesses usually give the consumer a certain time to cancel the contract. These laws are described in chapter 11 on "Advertising and Promotion Laws."

Preparing Your Contracts

CONSUMER PROTECTION LAW

Before you open your business, you should obtain or prepare the contracts or policies you will use in your business. In some businesses such as a restaurant, you will not need much. Perhaps you will want a sign near the entrance stating "shirt and shoes required" or "diners must be seated by 10:30 p.m."

However, if you are a building contractor or a similar business, you will need detailed contracts to use with your customers. If you do not clearly spell out your rights and obligations, you may end up in court and lose thousands of dollars in profits.

Of course, the best way to have an effective contract is to have an attorney, who is experienced in the subject, prepare one to meet the needs of your business. Since this may be too expensive for your new operation, you may desire to go elsewhere. Three sources for the contracts you will need: other businesses like yours, trade associations and legal form books. You should obtain as many different contracts as possible. Compare them, and decide which terms are most useful to you.

INSURANCE 8

There are few laws requiring you to have insurance, but if you do not have insurance you may face liability which would ruin your business. You should be aware of the types of insurance available and weigh the risks of a loss against the cost of a policy.

Be aware there can be a wide range of prices and coverage in insurance policies. You should get at least three quotes from different insurance agents and ask each one to explain the benefits of his or her policy.

WORKERS' COMPENSATION

Workers' compensation insurance covers workers for injuries and illnesses which are related to their jobs. Unlike many states, Texas does not require businesses to carry such insurance. However, such insurance offers valuable protection to a business. If a business does not carry workers' compensation insurance, it can face unlimited liability for a worker's injury resulting from the employer's negligence, including pain and suffering and punitive damages. A company without insurance also is not allowed to use such defenses as contributory negligence of the employee, negligence of another employee, or the employee's assumption of the risk.

By carrying such insurance, a business transfers all of its potential liability to the insurance company and is protected against lawsuits. The problem is that such insurance can be expensive, especially for jobs with high risk of injury, such as in the construction industry.

Some companies choose to self-insure but to qualify for all the protections under the law, a company must strictly comply with all of the rules including an initial security deposit of $300,000. Other companies choose to get cheaper medical insurance policies, but these do not protect against lawsuits or damages for losses such as pain and suffering.

There are many requirements of the workers' compensation law such as reporting wages and injuries and posting notices. The laws in this area change regularly (more than a dozen workers' compensation reform laws were passed by the Texas legislature in 1997 alone). So, to get the latest information, you should contact the Texas Department of Insurance. Their phone number is 800-252-3439, their web site is at http://www.tdi.state.tx.us/consumer/consum79.html and their address is:

Texas Workers' Compensation Commission
Public Information Office
4000 South IH35
Austin, TX 78704-7491

LIABILITY INSURANCE

Although it may be a good idea, Texas businesses are not required to carry liability insurance.

Liability insurance can be divided into two main areas: coverage for injuries on your premises and by your employees, and coverage for injuries caused by your products or services.

Coverage for the first type of injury is usually very reasonably priced. Injuries in your business or by your employees (an auto accident for example) are covered by standard premises or auto policies. But coverage for injuries by products may be harder to find and more expensive. In the current liability crisis, juries have awarded ridiculously high judgments for accidents involving products which had little if any impact on the accident. The situation has become so bad that some industries have gone out of business or moved overseas.

ASSET
PROTECTION

Hopefully, laws will soon be passed to protect businesses from these unfair awards. For now, if insurance is unavailable or unaffordable, you can go without and use a corporation and other asset protection devices to protect yourself from liability. Sphinx Publishing has a specialized manual on asset protection titled, *Simple Ways to Protect Yourself from Lawsuits* by Mark Warda. It is available through your local bookstore, or by calling the publisher at 1-800-432-7444.

The best way to find out if insurance is available for your type of business is to check with other businesses. If there is a trade group for your industry, their newsletter or magazine may contain ads for insurers.

UMBRELLA
POLICY

As a business owner, you will be a more visible target for lawsuits even if there is little merit to them. Lawyers know that a *nuisance suit* is often settled for thousands of dollars. Due to your greater exposure, you should consider getting a personal umbrella policy. This is a policy which covers you for claims of up to a million, or even two or five million dollars, and is very reasonably priced.

HAZARD INSURANCE

One of the worst things that can happen to your business is a fire, flood, or other disaster. With lost customer lists, inventory, and equipment, many businesses have been forced to close after such a disaster.

The premium for such insurance is usually reasonable and could protect you from the loss of your business. You can even get business interruption insurance. This will cover your losses while your business gets back on its feet.

HOME BUSINESS INSURANCE

There is a special insurance problem for home businesses. Most home-owner and tenant insurance policies do not cover business activities. In fact under some policies, you may be denied coverage if you used your home for a business.

If you merely use your home to make business phone calls and send letters, you will probably not have a problem and not need extra coverage. Nonetheless, you could have a problem if you own equipment or have dedicated a portion of your home exclusively to the business. Check with your insurance agent for the options that are available to you.

If your business is a sole proprietorship, and you have, say, a computer which you use both personally and for your business, it would probably be covered under your homeowners' policy. Coverage may be denied, however, if you incorporated your business and bought the computer in the name of the corporation If a computer is your main business asset, you could get a special insurance policy in the company name covering just the computer. One company which offers such a policy is Safeware at 1-800-723-9273 or 1-800-800-1492.

AUTOMOBILE INSURANCE

If you or any of your employees will be using an automobile for business purposes, be sure that such use is covered. Sometime a policy may include an exclusion for business use. Check to be sure your liability policy covers you if one of your employees causes an accident while running a business errand.

HEALTH INSURANCE

While new businesses can rarely afford health insurance for their employees, the sooner they can obtain it, the better chance they'll have to find and keep good employees. Those starting a business usually need insurance for themselves (unless they have a working spouse who can cover the family); they can sometimes get a better rate if they select a small business package.

EMPLOYEE THEFT

If you fear employees may be able to steal from your business, you may want to have them bonded. This can cover all existing and new employees.

HEALTH AND SAFETY LAWS 9

FEDERAL LAWS

OSHA   The Occupational Safety and Health Administration (OSHA) is a good example of government regulation so severe it strangles businesses out of existence. It is government run amok. Robert D. Moran, a former chairman of the committee that hears appeals from OSHA rulings once said that "there isn't a person on earth who can be certain he is in full compliance with the requirements of this standard at any point in time." The point of the law is to place the duty on the employer to see that the workplace is free from recognized hazards that are likely to cause death or serious bodily injury to workers.

For example, OSHA decided to take a look at repetitive-strain injuries, or "RSI" (such as carpal tunnel syndrome). The Bureau of Labor Statistics estimated that 7% of workplace illnesses are RSI and the National Safety Council estimated 4%. OSHA, however, determined that 60% is a more accurate figure and produced a 600 page list of proposed regulations, guidelines, and suggestions. These regulations would have affected over one-half of all businesses in America and cost billions of dollars. After an outcry from businesses, these regulations were shot down by Congress in 1995. Shortly thereafter OSHA officials ignored Congress' sentiment and promised to launch a new effort.

Fortunately for small businesses, the regulations are not as cumbersome as for larger enterprises. If you have ten or fewer employees or if you are in certain types of businesses, you do not have to keep a record of illnesses, injuries, and exposure to hazardous substances of employees. If you have eleven or more employees, you do have to keep this record, which is called *Log 200*. All employers are required to display a poster that you can get from OSHA.

Within forty-eight hours of an on-the-job death of an employee or injury of five or more employees on the job, the area director of OSHA must be contacted.

For more information you should write or call an OSHA office:

U.S. Department of Labor
200 Constitution Avenue, NW, Room N-3101
Washington, DC 20210
Tel. 202-219-4667

Austin (512) 916-5783
Corpus Christi (512) 888-3420
Dallas (214) 320-2400
El Paso (915) 534-7004
Fort Worth (817) 428-2470
Houston North (281) 591-2438
Houston South (281) 286-0583
Lubbock (806) 472-7681

or visit their web site (http://www.osha-slc.gov) and obtain copies of their publications, *OSHA Handbook for Small Business* (OSHA 2209), and *OSHA Publications and Audiovisual Programs Catalog* (OSHA 2019). They also have a poster that is required to be posted in the workplace (http://www.osha-slc.gov/OshDoc/Additional.html).

HAZARD COMMUNICATION STANDARD

The Hazard communication standard requires that employees be made aware of the hazards in the workplace (29 CFR 1910.1200). It is especially applicable to those working with chemicals, but can include offices using copy machines. Businesses utilizing hazardous chemicals must have a comprehensive program for informing employees of the hazards and for protecting them from contamination.

For more information, you can contact OSHA at the previously-mentioned addresses, phone numbers, or web sites. They can supply a copy of the regulation and a booklet called *OSHA 3084* which explains the law.

EPA   The Worker Protection Standard for Agricultural Pesticides requires safety training, decontamination sites, and of course, posters. The Environmental Protection Agency will provide information on compliance with this law. They can be reached at 1-800-490-9198, or via their website: http://www.epa.gov, or by mail:

> Environmental Protection Agency
> 401 M St., SW
> Washington, DC 20460

FDA   The Pure Food and Drug Act of 1906 prohibits the misbranding or adulteration of food and drugs. It also created the Food and Drug Administration (FDA) which has promulgated tons of regulations and which must give permission before a new drug can be brought into the market. You should keep abreast of their policies, if you will be dealing with any food or drugs. Their website is http://www.fda.gov, and their small business site is http://www.fda.gov/opacom/morechoices/smallbusiness/toc.html. Their local small business representative is:

> FDA, Southwest Region
> Small Business Representative, Brenda C. Cox
> 7920 Elmbrook Dr., Suite 102
> Dallas, TX 75247-4982
> Phone 214-655-8100 ext. 133
> Fax 214-655-8114

HAZARDOUS MATERIALS TRANSPORTATION   There are regulations which control the shipping and packing of hazardous materials. For more information contact the Office of Hazardous Materials Transportation at 400 Seventh St., S.W., Washington, DC 20590 or at 202-426-0656.

CPSC The Consumer Product Safety Commission (CPSC) has a set of rules which covers the safety of products. The commission feels that because its rules cover products, rather than people or companies, they apply to everyone producing such products. However, federal laws do not apply to small businesses which do not affect interstate commerce. Whether a small business would fall under a CPSC rule would depend on the size and nature of your business.

The CPSC rules are contained in Title 16 CFR in the following parts. These can be found at most law libraries, some public libraries, and on the internet at http://www.access.gpo.gov/nara/cfr/cfr-table-search.html. The CPSC's site is at: http://cpsc.gov/index.html.

PRODUCT	PART
Antennas, CB and TV	1402
Architectural Glazing Material	1201
Articles Hazardous to Children Under 3	1501
Baby Cribs-Full Size	1508
Baby Cribs-Non-Full Size	1509
Bicycle Helmets	1203
Bicycles	1512
Carpets and Rugs	1630, 1631
Cellulose Insulation	1209, 1404
Cigarette Lighters	1210
Citizens Band Base Station Antennas	1204
Coal and Wood Burning Appliances	1406
Consumer products Containing Chlorofluorocarbons	1401
Electrically Operated Toys	1505
Emberizing Materials Containing Asbestos (banned)	1305
Extremely Flammable Contact Adhesives (banned)	1302
Fireworks	1507
Garage Door Openers	1211
Hazardous Lawn Darts (banned)	1306
Hazardous Substances	1500
Human Subjects	1028
Lawn Mowers, Walk-Behind	1205
Lead-containing Paint (banned)	1303

Matchbooks	1202
Mattresses	1632
Pacifiers	1511
Patching Compounds Containing Asbestos (banned)	1304
Poisons	1700
Rattles	1510
Self-Pressurized Consumer Products	1401
Sleepwear-Childrens	1615, 1616
Swimming Pool Slides	1207
Toys, Electrical	1505
Unstable Refuse Bins (banned)	1301

ADDITIONAL
REGULATIONS

Every day there are proposals for new laws and regulations. It would be impossible to include every conceivable one in this book. To be up to date on the laws that affect your type of business, you should belong to a trade association for your industry and subscribe to newsletters which cover your industry. Attending industry conventions is a good way to learn more and to discover new ways to increase your profits.

TEXAS LAWS

SMOKING

Smoking is prohibited in public places such as schools, elevators, theaters, libraries, museums, hospitals, buses, planes, and trains. Public places must have prominently displayed a notice that smoking is prohibited by law and that an offense is punishable by a fine not to exceed $500. Smoking areas can be designated. (Penal Code, Section 48.01)

It is illegal to sell cigarettes or tobacco products to minors. It is a defense to prosecution if the motif presents an apparently valid proof of age issued by governmental agencies which bears a photograph and physical description consistent with the person's age. It is also illegal to sell or give cigarettes or tobacco products to someone younger than 27 years of age unless the person presents an apparently valid proof of identification. Each person who sells cigarettes or tobacco products at retail, or by vending machine, must post a conspicuous notice close to the place where the cigarettes or tobacco products may be purchased that says:

"PURCHASING OR ATTEMPTING TO PURCHASE TOBACCO PRODUCTS BY A MINOR UNDER 18 YEARS OF AGE IS PROHIBITED BY LAW. SALE OR PROVISION OF TOBACCO PRODUCTS TO A MINOR UNDER 18 YEARS OF AGE IS PROHIBITED BY LAW. UPON CONVICTION, A CLASS C MISDEMEANOR, INCLUDING A FINE UP TO $500.00, MAY BE IMPOSED. VIOLATIONS MAY BE REPORTED TO THE TEXAS COMPTROLLERS OFFICE BY CALLING 1-800-388-2883."

These warning notices are available from the comptroller's office.

Employees who are engaged in the retail sale of cigarettes or tobacco products must be notified of the above laws within 72 hours of the date the employee begins to sell tobacco products. The employee must sign a form indicating that he has received the notice and that the law has been fully explained, he understands the law, and he agrees to comply with the law.

Vending machine sales are not permitted except in a facility or business that is not open to persons younger than 18 years of age at any time. (Health and Safety Codes section 161.081-161.089)

EMPLOYMENT AND LABOR LAWS 10

HIRING AND FIRING LAWS

For small businesses, there are not many rules regarding whom you may hire or fire. Fortunately, the ancient law that an employee can be fired at any time (or may quit at any time) still prevails for small businesses. But in certain situations, and as you grow, you will come under a number of laws which affect your hiring and firing practices.

One of the most important things to consider when hiring someone is that if you fire them they may be entitled to unemployment compensation. If so, your unemployment compensation tax rate will go up and it can cost you a lot of money. Therefore, you should only hire people you are sure you will keep and you should avoid situations where your former employees can make claims against your company.

One way this can be done is by hiring only part time employees. The drawback to this is that you may not be able to attract the best employees. When hiring dishwashers or busboys this may not be an issue, but when hiring someone to develop a software product, you do not want them to leave halfway through the development.

A better solution is to screen applicants from the beginning and only hire those whom you feel certain will succeed. This is easier said than done. Some people interview well but are incompetent at the job.

The best record to look for is someone who has stayed a long time at each of their previous jobs. Next best is someone who has not stayed as long (for good reasons), but has always been employed. The worst type of hire would be someone who is or has been collecting unemployment compensation.

Those who have collected compensation are a bad risk. The reasoning behind the theory is this: if they collect in the future, even if it is not your fault, your employment of them could make you chargeable for their claim. For example, you hire someone who has been on unemployment compensation and they work out well for a year, quit to take another job, and are fired after a few weeks. In this situation, you would be chargeable for most of their claim because their last twelve quarters of work are analyzed. Look for a steady job history.

In the author's experience, the intelligence of an employee is more important than his or her experience. An employee with years of typing experience may be fast, but unable to figure out how to use your new computer. Whereas an intelligent employee can learn the equipment quickly and eventually gain speed. Of course, common sense is important in all situations.

The bottom line is that you cannot know if an employee will be able to fill your needs from a resume and interview. Once you have found someone whom you think will work out, offer them a job with a ninety day probationary period. If you are not completely satisfied with them after the ninety days, offer to extend the probationary period for ninety additional days rather than end the relationship immediately. Of course, all of this should be in writing.

BACKGROUND CHECKS

Checking references is important, but beware that a former boss may be a good friend, or even a relative. It has always been considered acceptable to exaggerate on resumes, but in recent years, some applicants have been found to be completely fabricating sections of their education and experience.

POLYGRAPH
TESTS

Under the federal Employee Polygraph Protection Act you cannot require an employee or prospective employee to take a polygraph test unless you are in the armored car, guard, or pharmaceutical business.

DRUG TESTS

Under the ADA drug testing can only be required of applicants who have been offered jobs conditioned upon passing the drug test. Under §21.120 of the Texas Labor Code, an employer may discriminate against those who use or possess drugs. A Texas employer with 15 or more employees and who has worker's compensation insurance must adopt a policy designed to eliminate drug abuse and its effect on the workplace, and distribute a written copy of the policy to each employee. (Labor Code, Section 411.091) You can contact the Texas Drug-Free Workplace Initiative at 800-343-3822 or 512-328-1144 for more information.

FIRING

In most cases unless you have a contract with an employee for a set time period, you can fire him or her at any time. This is only fair since the employee can quit at any time. The exceptions to this are if you fired someone based on some illegal discrimination (see page 95), or for filing some sort of health or safety complaint (see page 81), or for refusing your sexual advances (see page 99).

NEW HIRE REPORTING

In order to track down parents who do not pay child support, a federal law was passed in 1996 which requires reporting of new hires. The Personal Responsibility and Work Opportunity Reconciliation Act of

1996 (PRWORA) provides that such information must be reported by employers to their state government.

Within twenty days of hiring a new employee an employer must provide the state with information about the employee including the name, social security number and address. This information can be submitted in several ways including mail, fax, magnetic tape, or over the internet. There is a special form which can be used for this reporting, however, an employer can use the W-4 form for this purpose. Since this form must be filled out for all employees anyway, it would be pointless to use a separate form for the new hire reporting. A copy of the W-4 is included in the appendix and this may be faxed to the Texas toll-free number, 1-800-732-5015 or mailed to:

Texas New Hire Reporting Program
PO Box 149224
Austin, TX 78714-9224

For more information about the program you can call them at 1-888-839-4473 or visit their web site: http://www.texasnewhire.state.tx.us/.

EMPLOYMENT AGREEMENTS

To avoid misunderstanding with employees you should use an employment agreement or an employee handbook. These can spell out in detail the policies of your company and the rights of your employees. They can protect your trade secrets and spell out clearly that employment can be terminated at any time by either party.

While it may be difficult or awkward to ask an existing employee to sign such an agreement, an applicant hoping you will hire them will usually sign whatever is necessary to obtain the job. However, because of the unequal bargaining position, you should not use an agreement which would make you look bad if the matter ever went to court.

If having an employee sign an agreement is awkward, you can usually obtain the same rights by putting the company policies in an employee manual. Each existing and new employee should be given a copy along with a letter stating that the rules apply to all employees and that by accepting or continuing employment at your company they agree to abide by the rules. Having an employee sign a receipt for the letter and manual is proof that they received it.

One danger of an employment agreement or handbook is that it may be interpreted to create a long term employment contract. To avoid this, be sure that you clearly state in the agreement or handbook that the employment is "at will" and can be terminated at any time by either party.

Some other things to consider in an employment agreement or handbook are:

☞ what the salary and other compensation will be,

☞ what the hours of employment will be,

☞ what the probationary period will be,

☞ that the employee cannot sign any contracts binding the employer, and

☞ that the employee agrees to arbitration rather than filing a lawsuit.

An employment agreement, as well as a confidentiality agreement, and a non-competition agreement are included in the book *The Most Valuable Business Legal Forms You'll Ever Need* by James C. Ray, published by Sphinx Publishing. It is available at your local bookstore, or by calling the publisher at 1-800-432-7444.

INDEPENDENT CONTRACTORS

One way to avoid problems with employees and taxes at the same time is to have all of your work done through independent contractors. This can relieve you of most of the burdens of employment laws and the obligation to pay social security and medicare taxes for the workers.

An independent contractor is, in effect, a separate business which you pay to do a job. You pay them just as you pay any company from which you buy products or services. If the amount paid exceeds $600 at the end of the year, you will issue a 1099 from instead of a W-2.

This may seem too good to be true; and in some situations it is. The IRS does not like independent contractor (IC) arrangements because it is too easy for the ICs to cheat on their taxes. To limit the use of ICs, the IRS has strict regulations on who may and may not be classified as an independent contractor. Also, companies who do not appear to pay enough in wages for their field of business are audited.

The highest at-risk jobs are those not traditionally done by independent contractors. For example, you could not get away with hiring a secretary as an independent contractor. One of the most important factors considered in determining if a worker can be an independent contractor is the amount of control the company has over his or her work. If you need someone to paint your building and you agree to pay them a certain price to do it according to their own methods and schedule, you can pay them as an independent contractor. But if you tell them when to work, how to do the job, and provide them with the tools and materials, they will be classified as an employee.

If you just need some typing done and you take it to a typing service and pick it up when it is ready, you will be safe in treating them as independent contractors. But if you need someone to come into your office to type on your machine at your schedule, you will probably be required to treat that person as an employee for tax purposes.

The IRS has a form you can use in determining if a person is an employee or an independent contractor. It is form SS-8 and is included in the appendix of this book.

INDEPENDENT CONTRACTORS V. EMPLOYEES

In deciding whether to make use of independent contractors or employees, you should weigh the following advantages and disadvantages.

Advantages.

☛ Lower taxes. You do not have to pay social security, medicare, unemployment, or other employee taxes

☛ Less paperwork. You do not have to handle federal withholding deposits or the monthly employer returns to the state or federal government.

☛ Less insurance. You do not have to pay workers' compensation insurance and since the workers are not your employees, you do not have to insure against their possible liabilities.

☛ More flexibility. You can use ICs when you need them and not pay them when business is slow.

Disadvantages.

☛ The IRS and state tax offices are strict concerning when workers may be qualified as ICs, and they will audit companies whose use of them does not appear to be legitimate.

☛ If your use of ICs is found to be improper, you may have to pay back taxes and penalties and have problems with your pension plan.

☛ While employees usually cannot sue you for their injuries (if you have covered them with workers' compensation), ICs can sue you if their injuries were your fault.

☛ If you are paying someone to produce a creative work (writing, photography, artwork), you receive less rights to the work of an IC. (See *How to Register Your Own Copyright* by Mark Warda, published by Sphinx Publishing. Available by calling 1-800-432-7444.)

☛ You have less control over the work of an IC and less flexibility in terminating them if you are not satisfied that the job is being done the way you require.

☞ You have less loyalty from an IC who works sporadically for you and possibly others than from your own full time employees.

For some businesses the advantages outweigh the disadvantages but for others they do not. Consider your business plans and the consequences from each type of arrangement. Keep in mind that it will be easier to start with ICs and switch to employees than to fire employees and have to fire them to hire ICs.

TEMPORARY WORKERS

Another way to avoid the hassles of hiring employees is to get workers from a temporary agency. In this arrangement you may pay a higher amount per hour for the work, but the agency will take care of all of the tax and insurance requirements. Since these can be expensive and time-consuming, the extra cost may be well worth it.

Whether or not temporary workers will work for you depends upon your type of business, and the tasks you need performed. For jobs like sales management, you would probably want someone who will stay with you long term and develop relationships with the buyers; but for order fulfillment, temporary workers might work out well.

Another advantage of temporary workers is that you can easily stop using those who do not work out well for you, but if you find one who is ideal you may be able to hire him or her on a full time basis.

In recent years a new wrinkle has developed in the temporary worker area. Many large companies are beginning to use them because they are so much cheaper than paying the benefits demanded by full time employees. For example, Microsoft Corp. has had as many as 6,000 temporary workers, some of whom work for them for years. Some of the temporary workers recently won a lawsuit declaring that they are really employees and are entitled to the same benefits of other employees (such as pension plans).

The law is not yet settled in this area as to what arrangements will result in a temporary worker being declared an employee. That will take several more court cases, some of which have already been filed. A few things you can do to protect yourself are:

☛ Be sure that any of your benefit plans make it clear that they do not apply to workers obtained through temporary agencies

☛ Do not keep the same temporary workers for longer than a year

☛ Do not list temporary workers in any employee directories or hold them out to the public as your employees

☛ Do not allow them to use your business cards or stationery

DISCRIMINATION LAWS

FEDERAL LAW   There are numerous federal laws forbidding discrimination based upon race, sex, pregnancy, color, religion, national origin, age, or disability. The laws apply to both hiring and firing, and to employment practices such as salaries, promotions and benefits. Most of these laws only apply to an employer who has fifteen or more employees for twenty weeks of a calendar year or has federal contracts or subcontracts. Therefore, you most likely will not be required to comply with the law immediately upon opening your business. However, there are similar state laws which may apply to your business.

One exception is the Equal Pay Act which applies to employers with two or more employees and requires that women be paid the same as men in the same type of job.

Employers with fifteen or more employees are required to display a poster regarding discrimination. This poster is available from the Equal Employment Opportunity Commission, 2401 E. Street, N.W., Washington, DC 20506. Employers with 100 or more employees are required to file an annual report with the EEOC.

When hiring employees, some questions are illegal or inadvisable to ask. The following questions should not be included on your employment application, or in your interviews, unless the information is somehow directly tied to the duties of the job:

☛ Don't ask about an applicant's citizenship or place of birth. But after hiring an employee, you must ask about his or her right to work in this country.

☛ Don't ask a female applicant her maiden name. However, you can ask if she has been known by any other name in order to do a background check.

☛ Don't ask if applicants have children, plan to have them, or have child care. You can ask if an applicant will be able to work the required hours.

☛ Don't ask if the applicant has religious objections for working Saturday or Sunday. You can mention if the job requires such hours and ask whether the applicant can meet this job requirement.

☛ Don't ask an applicant's age. You can ask if an applicant is eighteen or over, or for a liquor-related job, if they are at least twenty-one.

☛ Don't ask an applicant's weight.

☛ Don't ask if an applicant has AIDS or is HIV positive.

☛ Don't ask if the applicant has filed a workers' compensation claim.

☛ Don't ask about the applicant's previous health problems.

☛ Don't ask if the applicant is married or whether their spouse would object to the job, hours, or duties.

☛ Don't ask if the applicant owns a home, furniture, car, as it is considered racially-discriminatory.

☛ Don't ask if the applicant was ever arrested. You can ask if the applicant was ever convicted of a crime.

The most recent, and perhaps most onerous, law is the Americans with Disabilities Act of 1990. Under this law employers who do not make "reasonable accommodations for disabled employees" will face fines of up to $100,000, as well as other civil penalties and civil damage awards.

While the goal of creating more opportunities for people with disabilities is a good one, the result of this law is to place all of the costs of achieving this goal on businesses that are faced with disabled applicants. For example, it has been suggested that the requirement of "reasonable accommodation" will require some companies to hire blind applicants for jobs which require reading and then to hire second employees to read to the blind employees. We will only know the extent to which this law can be applied after some unlucky employers have been taken to court. (Some lawyers love this law.)

A study released by two MIT economists in late 1998 indicated that since the ADA was passed employers have hired less rather than more disabled people. It is theorized that this may be due to the expense of the "reasonable accommodations" or the fear of lawsuits by disabled employees.

The ADA currently applies to employers with fifteen or more employees. Employers who need more than fifteen employees might want to consider contracting with independent contractors to avoid problems with this law, particularly if the number of employees is only slightly larger than fifteen.

To find out how this law affects your business, you might want to pay the government $25 for their *ADA Technical Assistance Manual.* You can order it from The Superintendent of Documents, P. O. Box 371954, Pittsburgh, PA 15250-7954, or you can fax your credit card order to (202) 512-2233.

Tax benefits. There are three types of tax credits to help small businesses with the burden of these laws.

☛ Businesses can deduct up to $15,000 a year for making their premises accessible to the disabled and can depreciate the rest. (IRC §190)

- Small businesses (under $1,000,000 in revenue and under 30 employees) can get a tax credit each year for 50% of the cost of making their premises accessible to the disabled, but this only applies to the amount between $250 and $10,500.

- Small businesses can get a credit of up to 40% of the first $6,000 of wages paid to certain new employees who qualify. See IRS form 8850 and instructions.

Records. To protect against potential claims of discrimination, all employers should keep detailed records showing reasons for hiring or not hiring applicants and for firing employees.

TEXAS LAW

Discrimination. Texas has its own laws regarding discrimination. They are contained in Chapter 21 of the Labor Code and apply to Texas businesses which affect commerce and have 15 or more employees who work at least 20 weeks a year. Section 21.051 of the Texas Labor Code Statutes prohibits discrimination or classification based upon race, color, disability, religion, sex, national origin, or age. Conversely, Section 21.115 permits an employment practice that has a discriminatory effect if it is justified by business necessity.

Under §21.124 of the Texas Labor Code, it is illegal to adjust test scores of job applicants based on race, color, sex, national origin, religion, age, or disability. Under subchapter H of Chapter 21 of the Texas Labor Code, it is illegal to use genetic testing to discriminate against employees.

Evacuations. Under Chapter 22 of the Texas Labor Code employer may not discharge or in any other manner discriminate against an employee who leaves the employee's place of employment to participate in a general public evacuation ordered under an emergency evacuation order.

SEXUAL HARASSMENT

FEDERAL LAW   What began as protection for employees who were fired or not pro-
moted for failing to succumb to sexual advances of their superiors has
been expanded to outlaw nearly any sexual comments or references in
the workplace. As an example of how far this has gone, one university
was forced to take down a painting by Goya depicting a nude because
a teacher felt sexually harassed by its presence!

In the 1980s, the Equal Employment Opportunity Commission interpreted the Title VII of the Civil Rights Act of 1964 to forbid sexual
harassment. After that, the courts took over and reviewed all types of
conduct in the workplace. The numerous lawsuits that followed began
a trend toward expanding the definition of sexual harassment and
favoring employees.

Some of the actions which have been considered harassment are:

☞ displaying sexually explicit posters in the workplace;

☞ requiring female employees to wear revealing uniforms;

☞ rating of sexual attractiveness of female employees as they passed
   male employees' desks

☞ continued sexual jokes and innuendos.

In 1993, the United States Supreme Court ruled that an employee can
make a claim for sexual harassment even without proof of a specific
injury. However, lower federal courts in more recent cases (such as the
Paula Jones case against President Clinton) have dismissed cases where
no specific injury was shown (although these cases may be overruled by
a higher court). These new cases may indicate that the pendulum has
stopped moving toward expanded rights for the employee.

On the other hand another recent case ruled that an employer can be
liable for the harassment of an employee by a supervisor, even if the
employer was unaware of the supervisor's conduct, if the employer did
not have a system in place to allow complaints against harassment. This

area of law is still developing and to avoid a possible lawsuit you should be aware of the things which could potentially cause liability and avoid them.

Some things a business can do to protect against claims of sexual harassment are:

☛ Distribute a written policy against all kinds of sexual harassment to all employees

☛ Encourage employees to report all incidents of sexual harassment

☛ Insure there is no retaliation against those who complain

COMMON LAW
Although the federal civil rights laws only apply to businesses with fifteen or more employees, it is possible for an employee to sue for sexual harassment in civil court. However, this is difficult and expensive and would only be worthwhile where there were substantial damages.

WAGE AND HOUR LAWS

FEDERAL LAW
Businesses covered. The Fair Labor Standards Act (FLSA) applies to all employers who are engaged in "interstate commerce" or in the production of goods for interstate commerce (anything which will cross the state line), and all employees of hospitals, schools, residential facilities for the disabled or aged, or public agencies. It also applies to all employees of enterprises that gross $500,000 or more per year.

While many small businesses might not think they are engaged in interstate commerce, the laws have been interpreted broadly so that nearly any use of the mails, interstate telephone service, or other interstate services, however minor, is enough to bring a business under the law. The authors of our Constitution clearly intended for most rights to be reserved to the states, but the *commerce clause* has been used to expand federal control to many unintended areas.

Minimum wage. The federal wage and hour laws are contained in the Federal Fair Labor Standards Act. In 1996, Congress passed and President Clinton signed legislation raising the minimum wage to $5.15 an hour beginning September 1, 1997.

In certain circumstances a wage of $3.62 may be paid to employees under twenty years of age for a ninety day training period.

For employees who regularly receive more than $30 a month in tips, the minimum wage is $2.13 per hour. But if the employee's tips do not bring him up to the full $5.15 minimum wage, the employer must make up the difference.

Overtime. Workers who work over forty hours in a week must be paid time-and-a-half for the time worked over forty hours.

Exempt employees. While nearly all businesses are covered, certain employees are exempt from the FLSA. Exempt employees include employees that are considered executives, administrative and managerial, professionals, computer professionals, and outside salespeople.

Whether or not one of these exceptions applies to a particular employee is a complicated legal question. Thousands of court cases have been decided on this issue but they have given no clear answers. In one case a person could be determined to be exempt because of his duties, but in another a person with the same duties could be found not exempt.

One thing that is clear is that the determination is made on the employee's function, and not just the job title. You can't make a secretary exempt by calling her a manager if most of her duties are clerical.

For more information contact:

Wage and Hour Division
U. S. Department of Labor
200 Constitution Ave., N.W. Room S-3325
Washington, DC 20210

Or call the closest office:

> Dallas 214-767-6294
> Houston 713-339-5500
> San Antonio 308-229-4515

On the internet you can obtain information on the Department of Labor's *Small Business Handbook* at:

> http://www.dol.gov/dol/asp/public/programs/handbook/main.htm

TEXAS LAWS
Texas has a minimum wage law, Chapter 62 of the Labor Standards Act. Chapter 61, Labor Code, regulates payment of wages, such as paydays, deductions, and intentional failure to pay wages. Wages must be paid at least twice a month in most cases. Section 52.001 of the Labor Code prohibits requiring retail employees to work 7 consecutive days without at least one 24 hour break.

PENSION AND BENEFIT LAWS

FEDERAL LAW
There are no laws requiring small businesses to provide any types of special benefits to employees. Such benefits are given to attract and keep good employees. With pension plans the main concern is if you do start one it must comply with federal tax laws.

HOLIDAYS
There are no federal or Texas laws which require that employees be given holidays off. You can require them to work Thanksgiving and Christmas and dock their pay or fire them for failing to show. Of course you will not have much luck keeping employees with such a policy.

Most companies give full time employees a certain number of paid holidays, such as New Year's Day (January 1), Memorial Day (last Monday in May), Fourth of July, Labor Day (first Monday in September), Thanksgiving (fourth Thursday in November) and Christmas (December 25). Some, but not many, employers include other holidays such as Martin Luther King, Jr.'s birthday (January 15), President's Day, and Columbus Day. If one of the holidays falls on a Saturday or Sunday, many employers give the preceding Friday or following Monday off.

SICK DAYS
There is no federal or Texas law mandating that an employee be paid for time that he or she is home sick. The situation seems to be that the larger the company, the more paid sick leave is allowed. Part time workers rarely get sick leave and small business sick leave is usually limited for the simple reason that they cannot afford to pay for time that employees do not work.

Some small companies have an official policy of no paid sick leave, but when an important employee misses a day because he or she is clearly sick, it is paid.

BREAKS
There are no federal or Texas laws requiring coffee breaks or lunch breaks. However, it is common sense that employees will be more productive if they have reasonable breaks for nourishment or to use the toilette facilities.

PENSION PLANS AND RETIREMENT ACCOUNTS
Few small new businesses can afford to provide pension plans for their employees. The first concern of a small business is usually how the owner can shelter income in a pension plan without having to set up a pension plan for an employee. Under most pension plans this is not allowed.

IRA. Anyone with $2,000 of earnings can put up to that amount in an Individual Retirement Account. Unless the person or his or her spouse are covered by a company pension plan and have income over a certain amount, the amount put into the account is fully tax deductible.

ROTH IRA. Contributions to a Roth IRA are not tax deductible but when the money is taken out, it is not taxable. People who expect to still have taxable income when they withdraw from their IRA can benefit from these.

SEP IRA, SAR-SEP IRA, SIMPLE IRA. With these types of retirement accounts, a person can put a much greater amount into a retirement plan and deduct it from their taxable income. Employees must also be covered by such plans, but certain employees are exempt so it is some-times possible to use these for the owners alone. The best source for more information is a mutual fund company (such as Vanguard, Fidelity, Dreyfus, etc.), or a local bank which can set up the plan and provide you with all of the rules. These have an advantage over quali-fied plans (discussed below) since they do not have the high annual fees. One internet site which contains some useful information on these accounts is: http://www.retirement-information.com/iraaccts.htm.

Qualified Retirement Plans. Qualified retirement plans are 401(k) plans, Keough plans, and corporate retirement plans. These are covered by ERISA, the Employee Retirement Income Security Act which is a complicated law meant to protect employee pension plans. Congress did not want employees who contributed to pension plans all their lives ending up with nothing when the plan goes bankrupt. The law is so complicated and the penalties so severe that some companies are can-celling their pension plans. Applications for new plans are a fraction of what they previously were. However, many banks and mutual funds have created "canned plans" which can be used instead of drafting one from scratch. Still the fees for administering them are steep. Check with a bank or mutual fund for details.

FAMILY AND MEDICAL LEAVE LAW

FEDERAL LAW   Since Congress thinks business owners are not capable of deciding what type of leave to offer their employees, it passed the Family and Medical Leave Act of 1993. This law requires an employee to be given up to twelve weeks of unpaid leave when:

☛ The employee or employee's spouse has a child

☛ The employee adopts a child or takes in a foster child

☛ The employee needs to care for an ill spouse, child, or parent

☛ The employee becomes seriously ill

Fortunately, the law only applies to employers with fifty or more employees. Also, the top ten percent of an employer's salaried employees can be denied this leave because of the disruption in business their loss could cause.

CHILD LABOR LAWS

FEDERAL LAW   The Federal Fair Labor Standards Act also contains rules regarding the hiring of children. The basic rules are that children under sixteen years old may not be hired at all except in a few jobs such as acting and newspaper delivery, and those under eighteen may not be hired for dangerous jobs. Children may not work more than three hours a day/eighteen hours a week in a school week or more than eight hours a day/forty hours a week in a non-school week. If you plan to hire children, you should check the Federal Fair Labor Standards Act which is in Chapter 29, United States Code (29 USC) and also the related regulations which are in Chapter 29 of the Code of Federal Regulations (29 CFR).

TEXAS LAW   Texas also has a set of child labor laws as follows:

Child labor (Chapter 51, Labor Code). The following rules apply to child labor in Texas in addition to federal laws:

☛ Minors of any age may work as performers in movies, TV, or radio; in business for their parents, on a paper route; in agriculture when not required to be in school; in school or court supervised programs; or in nonhazardous, casual employment consented to by the parent.

☛ No child under fourteen years of age may be employed in any gainful occupation at any time except as described above.

☛ No person under eighteen years of age may work where alcoholic beverages are sold at retail unless excepted by Texas Alcoholic Beverage Commission.

- ☞ mining occupations,

- ☞ operation of power-driven bakery, metalforming, woodworking, paper products, printing, or hoisting machines, and

- ☞ manufacturing of brick, tile, or similar materials.

Proof of child's age. A person who employs a child must keep on file proof of the child's age, such as a photocopy of a birth certificate, driver's license, school age certificate, passport, or visa.

Children's hours Children 14 and 15 cannot be employed for more than 8 hours per day, 48 hours per week, and cannot work between 10 p.m. and 5 a.m. on a school night or after midnight at any time. The Texas Workforce Commission may grant a hardship exemption. (Section 51.013, Labor Code)

IMMIGRATION LAWS

FEDERAL LAW

In 1986 a law was passed by Congress which imposes stiff penalties for any business which hires aliens who are not eligible to work. Under this law, you must verify both the identity and the employment eligibility of anyone you hire by using form I-9. Both you and the employee must fill out the form and you must check an employee's identification cards or papers. Fines for hiring illegal aliens range from $250 to $2,000 for the first offense and up to $10,000 for the third offense. Failure to maintain the proper paperwork may result in a fine of up to $1,000. The law does not apply to independent contractors with whom you may contract and it does not penalize you if the employee used fake identification.

There are also penalties which apply to employers of four or more persons for discriminating against eligible applicants because they appear foreign or because of their national origin or citizenship status.

The following pages include a list of acceptable documentation, a sample filled-in Form I-9, and instructions. A blank form is in the appendix. The blank form can also be downloaded from the following web site:

http://www.ins.usdoj.gov/forms/download/i-9.htm

For more information call 1-202-514-2000 for the *Handbook for Employers and Instructions for Completing Form I-9*, check the INS web site (http://www.ins.usdoj.gov) or write to the following address:

> U. S. Department of Justice
> Immigration and Naturalization Service
> 425 I Street, NW
> Washington, DC 20536

The Illegal Immigration Reform and Immigrant Responsibility Act of 1996 (IIRIRA) required changes in the rules, but as of early 1999 the INS had not yet promulgated final versions of the rules. The interim rule made the following changes to the requirements:

☞ Remove documents 2, 3, 8 and 9 from column A

☞ Allow document 4 only for aliens authorized to work for a specific employer

☞ New rules for employees who do not have their original documents

However, no new forms or instructions have been made available and employers are not yet being prosecuted for violations of these changes. Employers can receive updates to these laws by fax. To receive them, send your name, address and fax number to 202-305-2523.

HIRING "OFF THE BOOKS"

Because of the taxes, insurance, and red tape involved with hiring employees, some new businesses hire people "off the books." They pay them in cash and never admit they are employees. While the cash paid in wages would not be deductible, they consider this a smaller cost than compliance. Some even use "off the books" receipts to cover it.

Except when your spouse or child is giving you some temporary help this is a terrible idea. Hiring people off the books can result in civil fines, loss of insurance coverage, and even criminal penalties. When engaged in dangerous work like roofing or using power tools you are risking millions of dollars in potential liability if a worker is killed or seriously injured.

It may be more costly and time consuming to comply with the employment laws, but if you are concerned with long term growth with less risk, it's the wiser way to go.

FEDERAL CONTRACTS

Companies which do work for the federal government are subject to several laws.

DAVIS-BACON ACT

The Davis-Bacon Act requires contractors engaged in U.S. government construction projects to pay wages and benefits which are equal to or better than the prevailing wages in the area.

McNAMARA-O'HARA SERVICE CONTRACT ACT

The McNamara-O'Hara Service Contract Act sets wages and other labor standards for contractors furnishing services to agencies of the U.S. government.

WALSH-HEALEY PUBLIC CONTRACTS ACT

The Walsh-Healey Public Contracts Act requires the Department of labor to settle disputes regarding manufacturers supplying products to the U.S. government.

MISCELLANEOUS LAWS

FEDERAL LAW

Affirmative action. In most cases, the federal government does not yet tell employers who they must hire. This would be especially true for small new businesses. The only situation where a small business would need to comply with affirmative action requirements would be if it accepted federal contracts or subcontracts. These requirements could include the hiring of minorities or of Vietnam veterans.

Layoffs. Companies with 100 or more full-time employees at one location are subject to the Worker Adjustment and Retraining Notification Act. This law requires a sixty-day notification prior to certain lay-offs and has other strict provisions.

Unions. The National Labor Relations Act of 1935 (29 U.S.C. §§151 and following) gives employees the right to organize a union or to join one. There are things employers can do to protect themselves, but you should consult a labor attorney or a book on the subject before taking action which might be illegal and result in fines.

Poster laws. Yes, there are laws regarding what posters you may or may not display in the workplace. A previous edition of this book stated that nothing forbids Playboy or Playgirl-type posters, but a "politically correct" federal judge in 1991 ruled that Playboy posters in a workplace were sexual harassment. This ruling is being appealed by the American Civil Liberties Union (ACLU). However, there are other poster laws which require certain posters to be displayed to inform employees of their rights. Not all businesses are required to display all posters, but the following list should be of help.

☛ All employers must display the wage and hour poster available from:

> U. S. Department of Labor
> 200 Constitution Ave., NW
> Washington, DC 20210

☛ Employers with fifteen or more employees for twenty weeks of the year must display the sex, race, religion, and ethnic discrimination poster and the age discrimination poster available from:

> EEOC
> 2401 E Street NW
> Washington, DC 20506

☞ Employers with federal contracts or subcontracts of $10,000 or more must display the sex, race, etc. discrimination poster mentioned above plus a poster regarding Vietnam Era Veterans available from the local federal contracting office.

☞ Employers with government contracts subject to the Service Contract Act or the Public Contracts Act must display a notice to employees working on government contracts available from:

Employment Standards Division
U. S. Department of Labor
200 Constitution Ave., NW
Washington, DC 20210

TEXAS LAW

Right to Work. Texas is a right to work state. That means that in Texas a person may not be denied a job because of membership or nonmembership in a labor union. (Labor Code, Section 101.052)

Right to Organize. In Texas, workers can organize into labor unions and collectively bargain. (Labor Code, Section 101.001, et. seq.)

Blacklisting. It is illegal to blacklist a former employee, but an employer can provide a truthful written statement of the reason for discharge to the employee or a prospective employer. (Labor Code, Section 52.031)

Coercion of Employee Trade with Particular Firm. An employer may not coerce an employee to trade with a particular company. Nor can the employee be fired, punished, or blacklisted for failing to do so. (Labor Code, Section 52.031)

Checks and Drafts. Any payment for labor by check, draft, note, memorandum or other acknowledgement on indebtedness must be paid in cash on demand.

Farm Labor. Employers who hire farm labor should read Labor Code sections 62.101 through 62.114 regarding minimum wage for agricultural pieceworkers.

Drug-free Workplace. A Texas employer with 15 or more employees who has workers' compensation insurance must adopt a policy designed to eliminate drug abuse and its effect upon the workplace. A written copy of this policy must be distributed to each employee. Labor Code §411.091. You can contact the Texas Drug-Free Workplace Initiative at 1-800-343-3822 or 512-328-1144.

Please read instructions carefully before completing this form. The instructions must be available during completion of this form. **ANTI-DISCRIMINATION NOTICE.** It is illegal to discriminate against work eligible individuals. Employers **CANNOT** specify which document(s) they will accept from an employee. The refusal to hire an individual because of a future expiration date may also constitute illegal discrimination.

Section 1. Employee Information and Verification. To be completed and signed by employee at the time employment begins

Print Name: Last	First	Middle Initial	Maiden Name
REDDENBACHER	MARY	J	HASSENFUSS

Address (Street Name and Number)	Apt. #	Date of Birth (month/day/year)
1234 LIBERTY LANE		1/26/69

City	State	Zip Code	Social Security #
FORT WORTH	TEXAS	73000	123-45-6789

I am aware that federal law provides for imprisonment and/or fines for false statements or use of false documents in connection with the completion of this form.

I attest, under penalty of perjury, that I am (check one of the following):

[X] A citizen or national of the United States

[ ] A Lawful Permanent Resident (Alien # A _____)

[ ] An alien authorized to work until ___/___/___

(Alien # or Admission # _____)

Employee's Signature	Date (month/day/year)
Mary Reddenbacher	1/29/00

Preparer and/or Translator Certification. (To be completed and signed if Section 1 is prepared by a person other than the employee.) I attest, under penalty of perjury, that I have assisted in the completion of this form and that to the best of my knowledge the information is true and correct.

Preparer's/Translator's Signature	Print Name

Address (Street Name and Number, City, State, Zip Code)	Date (month/day/year)

Section 2. Employer Review and Verification. To be completed and signed by employer. Examine one document from List A OR examine one document from List B and one from List C as listed on the reverse of this form and record the title, number and expiration date, if any, of the document(s).

List A	OR	List B	AND	List C
Document title: PASSPORT				
Issuing authority: PASSPORT AGN. FT. WTH.				
Document #: 123456789				
Expiration Date (if any): 10/5/06		___/___/___		___/___/___
Document #:				
Expiration Date (if any): ___/___/___				

CERTIFICATION - I attest, under penalty of perjury, that I have examined the document(s) presented by the above-named employee, that the above-listed document(s) appear to be genuine and to relate to the employee named, that the employee began employment on (month/day/year) 01/29/00 and that to the best of my knowledge the employee is eligible to work in the United States. (State employment agencies may omit the date the employee began employment).

Signature of Employer or Authorized Representative	Print Name	Title
Xavier Y. Zork	XAVIER Y. ZORK	OWNER

Business or Organization Name	Address (Street Name and Number, City, State, Zip Code)	Date (month/day/year)
XYZ PRODUCTS, INC, 2431 S. DALLAS ST., FT. WORTH, TX 73000		01 29 00

Section 3. Updating and Reverification. To be completed and signed by employer

A. New Name (if applicable)	B. Date of rehire (month/day/year) (if applicable)

C. If employee's previous grant of work authorization has expired, provide the information below for the document that establishes current employment eligibility.

Document Title: _____ Document #: _____ Expiration Date (if any): ___/___/___

I attest, under penalty of perjury, that to the best of my knowledge, this employee is eligible to work in the United States, and if the employee presented document(s), the document(s) I have examined appear to be genuine and to relate to the individual.

Signature of Employer or Authorized Representative	Date (month/day/year)

Form I-9 (Rev. 11-21-91) N

INSTRUCTIONS
PLEASE READ ALL INSTRUCTIONS CAREFULLY BEFORE COMPLETING THIS FORM.

Anti-Discrimination Notice. It is illegal to discriminate against any individual (other than an alien not authorized to work in the U.S.) in hiring, discharging, or recruiting or referring for a fee because of that individual's national origin or citizenship status. It is illegal to discriminate against work eligible individuals. Employers **CANNOT** specify which document(s) they will accept from an employee. The refusal to hire an individual because of a future expiration date may also constitute illegal discrimination.

Section 1 - Employee. All employees, citizens and noncitizens, hired after November 6, 1986, must complete Section 1 of this form at the time of hire, which is the actual beginning of employment. **The employer is responsible for ensuring that Section 1 is timely and properly completed.**

Preparer/Translator Certification. The Preparer/Translator Certification must be completed if Section 1 is prepared by a person other than the employee. A preparer/translator may be used only when the employee is unable to complete Section 1 on his/her own. However, the employee must still sign Section 1 personally.

Section 2 - Employer. For the purpose of completing this form, the term "employer" includes those recruiters and referrers for a fee who are agricultural associations, agricultural employers, or farm labor contractors.

Employers must complete Section 2 by examining evidence of identity and employment eligibility within three (3) business days of the date employment begins. If employees are authorized to work, but are unable to present the required document(s) within three business days, they must present a receipt for the application of the document(s) within three business days and the actual document(s) within ninety (90) days. However, if employers hire individuals for a duration of less than three business days, Section 2 must be completed at the time employment begins. **Employers must record: 1)** document title; **2)** issuing authority; **3)** document number, **4)** expiration date, if any; and **5)** the date employment begins. Employers must sign and date the certification. Employees must present original documents. Employers may, but are not required to, photocopy the document(s) presented. These photocopies may only be used for the verification process and must be retained with the I-9. **However, employers are still responsible for completing the I-9.**

Section 3 - Updating and Reverification. Employers must complete Section 3 when updating and/or reverifying the I-9. Employers must reverify employment eligibility of their employees on or before the expiration date recorded in Section 1. Employers **CANNOT** specify which document(s) they will accept from an employee.

- If an employee's name has changed at the time this form is being updated/ reverified, complete Block A.

- If an employee is rehired within three (3) years of the date this form was originally completed and the employee is still eligible to be employed on the same basis as previously indicated on this form (updating), complete Block B and the signature block.

- If an employee is rehired within three (3) years of the date this form was originally completed and the employee's work authorization has expired **or** if a current employee's work authorization is about to expire (reverification), complete Block B and:
  - examine any document that reflects that the employee is authorized to work in the U.S. (see List A **or** C),
  - record the document title, document number and expiration date (if any) in Block C, and
  - complete the signature block.

Photocopying and Retaining Form I-9. A blank I-9 may be reproduced provided both sides are copied. The Instructions must be available to all employees completing this form. Employers must retain completed I-9s for three (3) years after the date of hire **or** one (1) year after the date employment ends, whichever is later.

For more detailed information, you may refer to the INS Handbook for Employers, (Form M-274). You may obtain the handbook at your local INS office.

Privacy Act Notice. The authority for collecting this information is the Immigration Reform and Control Act of 1986, Pub. L. 99-603 (8 U.S.C. 1324a).

This information is for employers to verify the eligibility of individuals for employment to preclude the unlawful hiring, or recruiting or referring for a fee, of aliens who are not authorized to work in the United States.

This information will be used by employers as a record of their basis for determining eligibility of an employee to work in the United States. The form will be kept by the employer and made available for inspection by officials of the U.S. Immigration and Naturalization Service, the Department of Labor, and the Office of Special Counsel for Immigration Related Unfair Employment Practices.

Submission of the information required in this form is voluntary. However, an individual may not begin employment unless this form is completed since employers are subject to civil or criminal penalties if they do not comply with the Immigration Reform and Control Act of 1986.

Reporting Burden. We try to create forms and instructions that are accurate, can be easily understood, and which impose the least possible burden on you to provide us with information. Often this is difficult because some immigration laws are very complex. Accordingly, the reporting burden for this collection of information is computed as follows: 1) learning about this form, 5 minutes; 2) completing the form, 5 minutes; and 3) assembling and filing (recordkeeping) the form, 5 minutes, for an average of 15 minutes per response. If you have comments regarding the accuracy of this burden estimate, or suggestions for making this form simpler, you can write to both the Immigration and Naturalization Service, 425 I Street, N.W., Room 5304, Washington, D. C. 20536; and the Office of Management and Budget, Paperwork Reduction Project, OMB No. 1115-0136, Washington, D.C. 20503.

Form I-9 (Rev. 11-21-91) N

EMPLOYERS MUST RETAIN COMPLETED I-9
PLEASE DO NOT MAIL COMPLETED I-9 TO INS

LISTS OF ACCEPTABLE DOCUMENTS

LIST A		LIST B		LIST C
Documents that Establish Both Identity and Employment Eligibility	**OR**	**Documents that Establish Identity**	**AND**	**Documents that Establish Employment Eligibility**

LIST A — Documents that Establish Both Identity and Employment Eligibility

1. U.S. Passport (unexpired or expired)

2. Certificate of U.S. Citizenship (INS Form N-560 or N-561)

3. Certificate of Naturalization (INS Form N-550 or N-570)

4. Unexpired foreign passport, with I-551 stamp or attached INS Form I-94 indicating unexpired employment authorization

5. Alien Registration Receipt Card with photograph (INS Form I-151 or I-551)

6. Unexpired Temporary Resident Card (INS Form I-688)

7. Unexpired Employment Authorization Card (INS Form I-688A)

8. Unexpired Reentry Permit (INS Form I-327)

9. Unexpired Refugee Travel Document (INS Form I-571)

10. Unexpired Employment Authorization Document issued by the INS which contains a photograph (INS Form I-688B)

OR

LIST B — Documents that Establish Identity

1. Driver's license or ID card issued by a state or outlying possession of the United States provided it contains a photograph or information such as name, date of birth, sex, height, eye color, and address

2. ID card issued by federal, state, or local government agencies or entities provided it contains a photograph or information such as name, date of birth, sex, height, eye color, and address

3. School ID card with a photograph

4. Voter's registration card

5. U.S. Military card or draft record

6. Military dependent's ID card

7. U.S. Coast Guard Merchant Mariner Card

8. Native American tribal document

9. Driver's license issued by a Canadian government authority

For persons under age 16 who are unable to present a document listed above:

10. School record or report card

11. Clinic, doctor, or hospital record

12. Day-care or nursery school record

AND

LIST C — Documents that Establish Employment Eligibility

1. U.S. social security card issued by the Social Security Administration (other than a card stating it is not valid for employment)

2. Certification of Birth Abroad issued by the Department of State (Form FS-545 or Form DS-1350)

3. Original or certified copy of a birth certificate issued by a state, county, municipal authority or outlying possession of the United States bearing an official seal

4. Native American tribal document

5. U.S. Citizen ID Card (INS Form I-197)

6. ID Card for use of Resident Citizen in the United States (INS Form I-179)

7. Unexpired employment authorization document issued by the INS (other than those listed under List A)

Illustrations of many of these documents appear in Part 8 of the Handbook for Employers (M-274)

ADVERTISING AND PROMOTION LAWS

11

ADVERTISING LAWS AND RULES

FEDERAL LAWS

The federal government regulates advertising through the Federal Trade Commission (FTC). The rules are contained in the Code of Federal Regulations (CFR). You can find these rules in most law libraries and many public libraries. , You might want to check the rules if you plan any advertising which you think may be questionable. If you uncertain about it, most likely the Washington bureaucrats have forbidden it. As you read the rules below, you will probably think of many violations you see every day.

Federal rules do not apply to every business; and small businesses that operate only within the state and do not use the postal service may be exempt. However, many of the federal rules have been adopted into law by the state of Texas. Therefore, a violation could be prosecuted by the state rather than the federal government.

Some of the important rules are summarized below. If you wish to learn more details about the rules you should obtain copies from your library.

Deceptive pricing (16 CFR Ch. I Part 233). When prices are being compared, it is required that actual and not inflated prices are used. For example, if an object would usually be sold for $7, you should not first offer it for $10 and then start offering it at 30% off. It is considered misleading to suggest that a discount from list price is a bargain if the item is seldom actually sold at list price. If most surrounding stores sell an item for $7 it is considered misleading to say it has a "retail value of $10" even if there are some stores elsewhere selling it at that price.

Bait advertising (16 CFR Ch. I Part 238). Bait advertising is placing an ad when you don't really want the respondents to buy the product offered but to switch to another item. The factors used to determine if there was a violation are similar to those used by Texas.

Use of "free," "half-off," and similar words (16 CFR Ch. I Part 251). Use of words such as "free," "1¢ sale" and the like must not be misleading. This means that the "regular price" must not include a mark-up to cover the "free" item. The seller must expect to sell the product without the free item at some time in the future. (How many violations of this rule can you find in today's paper?)

Substantiation of claims (16 CFR 3.40; 48 FR 10471, March 11, 1983). The FTC requires that advertisers be able to substantiate their claims. Some information on this policy is contained on the internet at http://www.ftc.gov/bcp/guides/ad3subst.htm.

Endorsements (16 CFR Ch. I Part 255). This rule forbids endorsements which are misleading. An example is a quote from a film review which is used in such a way as to change the substance of the review. It is not necessary to use the exact words of the person endorsing the product as long as the opinion is not distorted. If a product is changed, an endorsement which does not apply to the new version cannot be used. For some items, such as drugs, claims cannot be used without scientific proof. Endorsements by organizations cannot be used unless one is sure that the membership holds the same opinion.

Unfairness (15 USC 45). Any advertising practices which can be deemed to be "unfair" are forbidden by the FTC. An explanation of this policy is located on the internet at http://www.ftc.gov/bcp/policy stmt/ad-unfair.htm.

Negative option plans (16 CFR Ch. I Part 425). When a seller uses a sales system in which the buyer must notify the seller if he does not want the goods, the seller must provide the buyer with a form to decline the sale and at least ten days in which to decline. Bonus merchandise must be shipped promptly and the seller must promptly terminate any who so request after completion of the contract.

Laser eye surgery (15 USC §§45, 52-57). Under the laws governing deceptive advertising the FTC and the FDA are regulating the advertising of laser eye surgery. Anyone involved in this area should obtain a copy of these rules. The are located on the internet at http://www.ftc.gov/bcp/guides/eyecare2.htm.

Food and dietary supplements (21 USC §§343). Under the Nutritional Labeling Education Act of 1990, the FTC and the FDA regulate the packaging and advertising of food and dietary products. Anyone involved in this area should obtain a copy of these rules. The are located on the internet at http://www.ftc.gov/bcp/guides/ad4diet.htm and http://www.ftc.gov/bcp/guides/ad-food.htm.

Jewelry and precious metals (61 FR 27212). The FTC has numerous rules governing the sale and advertising of jewelry and precious metals. Anyone in this business should obtain a copy of these rules. The are located on the internet at http://www.ftc.gov/bcp/guides/jewel-gd.htm.

TEXAS LAWS   Texas has many laws regulating advertisements within the state. Such laws and regulations cover advertisements in specific industries from auctioneers and alcoholic beverages to chiropractors, pharmacists, and physical therapists. Billboards and outdoor advertising are heavily regulated. Transportation Code Chapter 391 and Alcoholic Beverage Code, Chapter 108.

Texas law provides civil and criminal penalties for deceptive advertising. It is illegal for a person to intentionally, knowingly, recklessly, or with criminal negligence:

☞ provide false weights or measures,

☞ sell less than the represented quantity of a good,

☞ sell adulterated or mislabeled commodities,

☞ pass off property or services as that of another,

☞ represent that good are original or new if they are not,

☞ represent that good or services are of a particular style, grade or model if they are another,

☞ make a false or misleading statement concerning the reason for a price reduction, conduct a deceptive sales contest, or

☞ make a materially false or misleading statement in an advertisement for the purchase or sale of property or service (Penal Code, Section 32.42). Offenses under this Section are Class A or C misdemeanors.

Misleading advertising. It is illegal to willfully misrepresent a business by using the words manufacturer, wholesaler, or retailer and to misrepresent the ownership of a business for the purpose of holding a liquidation sale, auction sale, or going out of business sale. (Texas Business and Commerce Code, Section 17.11)

Going out of business sale. A person may not advertise a sale as going out of business or closeout, etc., unless the business is closing all of its operations in that county and all adjacent counties, files an original inventory with the County Clerk of that county, and obtains a permit from the County Clerk to conduct the sale. Sale inventories must be filed each thirty days and a final inventory within thirty days after the sale ends. An item offered for sale under the Going Out of Business Permit cannot be sold at retail after the sale ends. A business may not conduct another going out of business sale for two years following the end of the previous going out of business sale. (Texas Business and Commerce Code, Sec. 17.81 et seq.)

Business opportunities. Texas regulates the advertisement and offering of certain franchise type business opportunities. Sellers of such opportunities must register with the Secretary of State, and provide potential purchasers written disclosure statements containing detailed information. Sellers of a business opportunity may not represent that the business opportunity provides or will provide earning potential of any kind unless the seller has documented data to substantiate the claims of earning potential and discloses this data to the prospective buyer. These laws apply to those opportunities where the initial consideration is more than $500 worth of products, equipment, supplies, or services. It does not apply to the sale or lease of an established and ongoing business, consignment type arrangements, and other exceptions. (Business and Commerce Code, Chapter 41)

Contests and Gift Giveaways. Texas has recently enacted laws regulating the use of contests and gift giveaways in any advertising plan or program, or the use of any type of gift to solicit prospective purchasers to attend sales presentations. The laws do not prohibit gifts and contests but require detailed disclosures. Advertisers are also required to keep extensive records and lists of winners. (Business & Commerce Code, Chapter 40) This law does not apply to a sales presentation conducted in connection with a business seminar, trade show, convention or other similar gathering.

Names and Photographs. It is unlawful to use a deceased person's name, voice, signature, photograph or likeness without the consent of the owner of the property right in such name, voice, signature, photograph or likeness until after the 50th anniversary of that person's death. (Chapter 26, Property Code)

INTERNET SALES LAWS

FEDERAL LAWS There are not yet specific laws governing internet transactions which are different from laws governing other transactions. The FTC feels that its current rules regarding deceptive advertising, substantiation, disclaimers, refunds, and related matters must be followed by internet businesses and that consumers are adequately protected by them. See the first three pages of this chapter for that information.

For some specific guidelines on internet advertising, see the FTC's site at http://ftc.gov/bcp/conline/pubs/buspubs/ruleroad.htm.

HOME SOLICITATION LAWS

The Federal Trade Commission has rules governing door-to-door sales. In any such sale it is a deceptive trade practice to fail to furnish a receipt explaining the sale (in the language of the presentation) and giving notice that there is a three day right of recision. The notice must be supplied in duplicate, must be in at least 10-point type, and must be captioned either "Notice of Right to Cancel" or "Notice of Cancellation." The notice must be worded as follows in the form on the next page:

NOTICE OF CANCELLATION

_____
Date

YOU MAY CANCEL THIS TRANSACTION, WITHOUT ANY PENALTY OR OBLIGATION, WITHIN THREE BUSINESS DAYS FROM THE ABOVE DATE.

IF YOU CANCEL, ANY PROPERTY TRADED IN, ANY PAYMENTS MADE BY YOU UNDER THE CONTRACT OR SALE, AND ANY NEGOTIABLE INSTRUMENT EXECUTED BY YOU WILL BE RETURNED TO YOU WITHIN 10 BUSINESS DAYS FOLLOWING RECEIPT BY THE SELLER OF YOUR CANCELLATION NOTICE, AND ANY SECURITY INTEREST ARISING OUT OF THE TRANSACTION WILL BE CANCELLED.

IF YOU CANCEL, YOU MUST MAKE AVAILABLE TO THE SELLER AT YOUR RESIDENCE, IN SUBSTANTIALLY AS GOOD CONDITION AS WHEN RECEIVED, ANY GOODS DELIVERED TO YOU UNDER THIS CONTRACT OR SALE; OR YOU MAY IF YOU WISH, COMPLY WITH THE INSTRUCTIONS OF THE SELLER REGARDING THE RETURN SHIPMENT OF THE GOODS AT THE SELLER'S EXPENSE AND RISK.

IF YOU DO MAKE THE GOODS AVAILABLE TO THE SELLER AND THE SELLER DOES NOT PICK THEM UP WITHIN 20 DAYS OF THE DATE OF YOUR NOTICE OF CANCELLATION, YOU MAY RETAIN OR DISPOSE OF THE GOODS WITHOUT ANY FURTHER OBLIGATION. IF YOU FAIL TO MAKE THE GOODS AVAILABLE TO THE SELLER, OR IF YOU AGREE TO RETURN THE GOODS AND FAIL TO DO SO, THEN YOU REMAIN LIABLE FOR PERFORMANCE OF ALL OBLIGATIONS UNDER THE CONTRACT.

TO CANCEL THIS TRANSACTION, MAIL OR DELIVER A SIGNED AND DATED COPY OF THIS CANCELLATION NOTICE OR ANY OTHER WRITTEN NOTICE, OR SEND A TELEGRAM, TO [name of seller], AT [address of seller's place of business] NOT LATER THAN MIDNIGHT OF _____ (date).

I HEREBY CANCEL THIS TRANSACTION.

(DATE) _____

_____
(Buyer's signature)

The seller must complete the notice and orally inform the buyer of the right to cancel. He cannot misrepresent the right to cancel, assign the contract until the fifth business day, nor include a confession of judgment in the contract. For more specific details see the rules contained in 16 CFR Ch. I Part 429.

TEXAS LAW   Texas Business and Commerce Code Chapter 39 covers home solicitation transactions. This chapter applies to a consumer transaction where the merchant or his agent makes a personal solicitation of a sale to a consumer at a place other than the merchant's place of business and the consumer's agreement or offer to purchase is given to the merchant or at a place other than a merchant's place of business and:

☞ It is a purchase of goods or services for more than $25.00; or

☞ It is a purchase of real property for more than $100.00.

This chapter does not apply to the sale of farm equipment; insurance sales; sales made under a pre-existing revolving charge account or retail charge agreement; a sale made after negotiations between the parties at the merchant's business establishment or a fixed location; and a sales of real property if the purchaser is either represented by an attorney, or the transaction is negotiated by the owner at a place other than the consumer's residence.

Written Agreement. The seller must furnish the consumer with a completed receipt or copy of the contract in the same language used in the solicitation (such as Spanish), showing the date and name and address of the seller, and containing in the immediate proximity (such as next to or right above) the signature block, or on the front page of the receipt, in at least 10-point boldface type, the following:

YOU THE BUYER, MAY CANCEL THIS TRANSACTION AT ANY TIME PRIOR TO MIDNIGHT OF THE THIRD BUSINESS DAY AFTER THE DATE OF THIS TRANSACTION. SEE THE ATTACHED NOTICE OF CANCELLATION FORM FOR AN EXPLANATION OF THIS RIGHT.

Right to cancel. Any such sale may be cancelled by the consumer until midnight of the third business day after the day the agreement is signed. While no particular form of notice is required, the seller must furnish the buyer, at the time the buyer signs the agreement, a completed form easily detachable from the contract. The form must state, in 10-point boldface type, in the same language used in the contract, the following:

NOTICE OF CANCELLATION

_____
Date

YOU MAY CANCEL THIS TRANSACTION, WITHOUT ANY PENALTY OR OBLIGATION, WITHIN THREE BUSINESS DAYS FROM THE ABOVE DATE.

IF YOU CANCEL, ANY PROPERTY TRADED IN, ANY PAYMENTS MADE BY YOU UNDER THE CONTRACT OR SALE, AND ANY NEGOTIABLE INSTRUMENT EXECUTED BY YOU WILL BE RETURNED TO YOU WITHIN 10 BUSINESS DAYS FOLLOWING RECEIPT BY THE MERCHANT OF YOUR CANCELLATION NOTICE, AND ANY SECURITY INTEREST ARISING OUT OF THE TRANSACTION WILL BE CANCELLED.

IF YOU CANCEL, YOU MUST MAKE AVAILABLE TO THE MERCHANT AT YOUR RESIDENCE, IN SUBSTANTIALLY AS GOOD CONDITION AS WHEN RECEIVED, ANY GOODS DELIVERED TO YOU UNDER THIS CONTRACT OR SALE; OR YOU MAY IF YOU WISH, COMPLY WITH THE INSTRUCTIONS OF THE SELLER REGARDING THE RETURN SHIPMENT OF THE GOODS AT THE SELLER'S EXPENSE AND RISK.

IF YOU DO NOT AGREE TO RETURN THE GOODS TO THE MERCHANT OR IF THE MERCHANT DOES NOT PICK THEM UP WITHIN 20 DAYS OF THE DATE OF YOUR NOTICE OF CANCELLATION, YOU MAY RETAIN OR DISPOSE OF THE GOODS WITHOUT ANY FURTHER OBLIGATION.

TO CANCEL THIS TRANSACTION, MAIL OR DELIVER A SIGNED AND DATED COPY OF THIS CANCELLATION NOTICE OR ANY OTHER WRITTEN NOTICE, OR SEND A TELEGRAM, TO [name of merchant], AT [address of seller's place of business] NOT LATER THAN MIDNIGHT OF _____ (date).

I HEREBY CANCEL THIS TRANSACTION.

(DATE) _____

_____
(Buyer's signature)

Refund. The refund must be made to the Buyer within ten days.

Buyer's duty. The buyer may keep the goods until the seller makes the refund. Within a reasonable time after cancellation and demand, the buyer must return any goods received under contract. If the seller has made no demand within 20 days, the buyer may keep the goods without obligation to pay for them. The buyer must take reasonable care of the goods but is not required to deliver them except at the buyer's residence.

Seller's duty. In addition to the requirements described above, the seller must:

☞ complete the notice of cancellation form

☞ orally inform the consumer of the right to cancel.

Prohibitions. The seller may not:

☞ include a waiver in the contract or receipt of the right to cancel

☞ misrepresent the consumer's right to cancel

☞ fail to honor a valid notice of cancellation or fail to make the refund

TELEPHONE SOLICITATION LAWS

FEDERAL LAWS

Phone calls. Telephone solicitations are governed by the Telephone Consumer Protection Act (47 USC 227) and the Federal Communications Commission rules implementing the act 47 CFR 64.1200). Violators of the act can be sued for $500 damages by consumers and can be fined $10,000 by the FCC. Some of the requirements under the law are:

☞ Calls can only be made between 8 A.M. and 9 P.M.

☞ Solicitors must keep a "do not call" list and honor requests to not call.

☞ There must be a written policy that the parties called are told the name of the caller, the callers business name and phone number or address. They must also be told that the call is a sales call and the nature of the goods or services.

☞ Personnel must be trained in the policies.

☞ Recorded messages cannot be used to call residences.

Faxes. It is illegal under the act to send advertising faxes to anyone who has not consented to receiving such faxes or is an existing customer.

TEXAS LAWS

Texas telephone solicitation law (Business and Commerce Code Chapters 37 and 38) prohibits any telephone solicitation from this state, or to a person in this state, without filing a certificate of registration with the Secretary of State for the business location from where the call is originated.

The act contains many exemptions such as persons selling magazines, newspapers, cable TV services, certain catalogs, banks, repair services to former customers, and calls to businesses.

The registration certificate must contain certain information and disclosures regarding the business and those in charge including convictions, judgements and bankruptcies, and include extensive information and documents regarding items offered, sales literature, and contest premium awards. To obtain the registration application, call the Secretary of State at (512) 475-0775.

Postings. The seller must post the certificate of registration at its business location and have copies available for inspection by government agencies or purchasers, along with the name of the person in charge of the location.

Disclosure. Before completing the sale, a seller is required to disclose to purchasers certain information including the calling location, actual numbers of gifts or premium awards given, and if the item is being offered at a price lower than usually charged by the manufacturer.

Anyone interested in using telephone solicitation should obtain the rules and regulations from the Secretary of State.

Prohibitions. A seller may not represent or imply that a purchaser will receive a gift or prize, or request a credit card number or checking account number to charge or debit against as a precondition to the purchaser receiving the gift or prize.

Deceptive Trade Practice. A violation of this act is a deceptive trade practice, and the violator is subject to being sued under the Deceptive Trade Practices Act described previously as well as by the Attorney General for up to $5,000 per violation.

Chapter 37 of the Texas Business and Commerce Code also regulates telephone solicitation.

It requires any telephone solicitor who calls a consumer to:

☛ immediately identify himself and his company,

☛ call only between 9:00 a.m. and 9:00 p.m. on weekdays and Saturday,

☛ call only between 12:00 noon and 9:00 p.m. on Sunday.

If an automated dial announcing device is used, it must disconnect with the consumer's phone within 30 seconds after the consumer hangs up.

Credit cards. A seller using telephone solicitation cannot charge a consumer's credit card unless:

☛ The consumer can get a full refund for return of the goods or cancellation of services if he gives notice within seven days after receipt, and the seller processes the refund within 30 days; or

☛ The seller provides the consumer with a written contract.

Automatic Dial Announcing Devices (ADAD). A person may not use an ADAD system to make telephone solicitations unless he obtains a permit from the Public Utility Commission. The permissible time, identification, and disconnect requirements described above apply. (C.S., Article 1446c, Sections 111 through 120)

PRICING, WEIGHTS AND LABELING

FEDERAL LAW   ***Food products.*** Beginning in 1994, all food products were required to have labels with information on the product's nutritional values such as calories, fat, and protein. For most products, the label must be in the required format so that consumers can easily compare products. However, if such a format will not fit on the product label, the information may be in another format which is easily readable.

Metric measures. In 1994, federal rules requiring metric measurement of products took effect. Some federal agencies, such as the federal highway department, indefinitely postponed implementation of the rules, but the Federal Trade Commission (FTC) and the Food and Drug Administration intend to enforce the rules against businesses.

Under these rules, metric measures do not have to be the first measurement on the container, but they must be included. Food such as delicatessen items, which are packaged as they are sold, do not have to contain metric labels.

TEXAS LAW The Texas Department of Agriculture supervises and enforces all weights and measures sold or offered for sale. (Agricultural Code, Chapter 13).

Misrepresentation. It is a Class C misdemeanor to:

☛ Use a false weight or measure in buying, selling, or computing charges for services.

☛ Misrepresent the price of an item or service offered for sale or sold, or represent the price in a way that tends to mislead or deceive a customer.

☛ Offer for sale or sell a quantity of a commodity or service that is less than represented.

☛ Use the buyer's weight or measure in order to take more than requested.

Method of sale. This statute specifies the legal standards for weights, length, liquid capacity, and solid capacity, including standard weight for a "bushel" of certain commodities.

If a commodity is sold by weight, it must be by net weight. A liquid commodity must be sold by liquid measure, unless sold for immediate consumption on the premises or if there is a general consumer usage that expresses the quantity by weight and is accurate. Special rules require sale of milk in standard liquid measure containers and sale of cheese and meat by standard net weight, unless sold for immediate consumption on the premises.

Information required on packages. Generally, all packages of commodities for sale must bear a conspicuous statement of:

☞ the net quantity in terms of weight, measure, or numerical count

☞ the name and place of business of the manufacturer, packer, or distributor

DECEPTIVE PRACTICES

TEXAS LAW

Of great importance to anyone doing business is Texas is the Texas Deceptive Trade Practices-Consumer Protection Act (Business & Commerce Code, Section 17.41 et. seq.). This makes any false, misleading, or deceptive acts or practices in the conduct of any trade or commerce with consumers unlawful. This includes misrepresentations as to:

☞ the source and sponsorship of goods,

☞ characteristics and ingredients,

☞ reasons for price reductions,

☞ false or misleading statements concerning the need for parts, replacement, or repair service,

☞ turning back the odometer on an automobile,

☞ fraudulently advertising that a person is going out of business,

☞ representing that a guaranty or warranty has rights or remedies that it does not have, and many others

The definition of "consumer" is very broad and can include a business which "consumes" your goods or services. Under the Act, a consumer can sue a person, who committed a deceptive trade practice, for economic damages the consumer suffered, without needing to prove that the businessman knew his advertisement was false or intended to mislead. If the consumer can prove the deceptive act was committed knowingly, he can recover damages for mental anguish and not more than three times the amount of economic damages. If the consumer can prove the deceptive conduct was committed intentionally, he may recover economic damages, mental anguish damages, and up to three times the total amount of economic and mental anguish damages.

Fraud in Real Estate and Stock Transactions. A person who makes a false representation in a transaction involving real estate or stock in a corporation commits fraud in Texas. He is then liable to the person defrauded for actual damages, even without proof that the person knew that the statement was false or intended to mislead or deceive. A person who makes false representation with actual awareness that it is false is also liable for exemplary damages. (Section 27.01, Texas Business and Commerce Code)

PAYMENT AND COLLECTION 12

Depending on the business you are in, you may be paid by cash, checks, credit cards, or some sort of financing arrangement such as a promissory note and mortgage. Both state and federal laws affect the type of payments you collect, and failure to follow the laws can cost you considerably.

CASH

Cash is probably the easiest form of payment and it is subject to few restrictions. The most important restriction is that you keep an accurate accounting of your cash transactions and that you report all of your cash income on your tax return. Recent efforts to stop the drug trade have resulted in some serious penalties for failing to report cash transactions and for money laundering. The laws are so sweeping that even if you deal in cash in an ordinary business you may violate the law and face huge fines and imprisonment. One member of Congress even stated that he thought a grocer selling food to drug dealers should be subject to forfeiture laws!

The most important law to be concerned with is the one requiring the filing of IRS Form 8300 for cash transactions of $10,000 or more. A transaction does not have to happen in one day. If a person brings you smaller amounts of cash that add up to $10,000 and the government can construe them as one transaction, the form must be filed. Under this law, "cash" also includes travelers' checks, and money orders, but not cashier's checks or bank checks. For more information, obtain Form 8300 and instructions from the IRS.

CHECKS

ACCEPTING
CHECKS

It is important to accept checks in your business. While there is a small percentage which will be bad, most checks will be good, and you will be able to accommodate more customers. To avoid having problems with checks, you should obey the following rules.

BAD CHECKS

Under Texas Statutes, art. 9022, a holder of a bad check can charge a service charge of $25. Tho procedure is to send the maker of the check a notice by certified mail and then file suit (usually in small claims court) on the check.

There is also a criminal law against writing a bad check. (Texas Penal Code §32.41) Usually you can go to the district attorney's bad check division, and they may prosecute the maker for you. This would be easier for you than filing a civil case and might get you the funds quicker.

It is important that you be able to identify the person who gave you the check. To do this, you should require identification and write down the sources of identification on the face of the check. Another rule is that they will not prosecute someone for a bad check if it was post-dated.

REFUNDS AFTER
CASHING CHECKS

A popular scam is for a person to purchase something by using a check and then come back the next day demanding a refund. After making the refund, the business discovers the initial payment check bounced. Do not make refunds until checks clear!

CREDIT CARDS

In our buy-now, pay-later society, charge cards can add greatly to your sales potential especially with large, discretionary purchases. For MasterCard, Visa, and Discover, the fees are about 2%, and this amount is easily paid for by the extra purchases which the cards allow. American Express charges 4% to 5% and you may decide this is not worth paying, since almost everyone who has an American Express card also has another card. You will find that affluent purchasers prefer to use American Express. (And, if ordering by phone, the insecure among them will mention to you if it is a gold card.)

For businesses which have a retail outlet, there is usually no problem getting merchant status. Most commercial banks can handle it. Discover can also set you up to accept their card as well as MasterCard and Visa, and they will wire the money into your bank account daily.

For mail order businesses, especially those operating out of the home, it is much harder to get merchant status. This is because of the number of scams in which large amounts are charged, no products are shipped and the company folds. At one point, even a business offering to post a large cash bond and let the bank hold the charges for six months was refused.

Today things are a little better. Some companies are even soliciting merchants. But beware of those which charge exorbitant fees (such as $5 or $10 per order for "processing"). One good thing about American Express is that they will accept mail order companies operating out of the home. However, not as many people have their cards as others.

Some companies open a small storefront (or share one) to get merchant status, then process mostly mail orders. The processors usually do not want to accept you if you will do more than fifty percent mail order; but if you do not have many complaints, you may be allowed to process mostly mail orders. Whatever you do, keep your charge customers happy so that they do not complain!

You might be tempted to try to run your charges through another business. This may be okay if you actually sell your products through them, but if you run your business charges through their account the other business may lose its merchant status. People who bought a book by mail from you and then have a charge on their statement from a florist shop will probably call the credit card company saying that they never bought anything from the florist shop. Too many of these and the account will be closed.

FINANCING LAWS

Some businesses can make sales more easily if they finance the purchases themselves. If the business has enough capital to do this it can earn extra profits on the financing terms. However, because of abuses, many consumer protection laws have been passed by both the federal and state governments.

FEDERAL LAW **Reg. Z.** Two important federal laws regarding financing are called the *Truth in Lending Act* and the *Fair Credit Billing Act*. These are implemented by what is called *Regulation Z* (commonly known as *Reg. Z*), issued by the Board of Governors of the Federal Reserve System. It is contained in Volume 12 of the Code of Federal Regulations, page 226 (cited by lawyers as 12 CFR 226). This is a very complicated law and some believe that no business can be sure to be in compliance with it.

The regulation covers all transactions in which four conditions are met:

1. credit is offered,

2 the offering of credit is regularly done,

3. there is a finance charge for the credit or there is a written agreement with more than four payments, and

4. the credit is for personal, family, or household purposes.

It also covers credit card transactions where only the first two conditions are met. It applies to leases if the consumer ends up paying the full value and keeping the item leased. It does not apply to the following transactions:

- ☞ transactions with businesses or agricultural purposes,

- ☞ transactions with organizations such as corporations or the government,

- ☞ transactions of over $25,000 which are not secured by the consumer's dwelling,

- ☞ credit involving public utilities,

- ☞ credit involving securities or commodities, and

- ☞ home fuel budget plans.

The way for a small business to avoid Reg. Z violations is to avoid transactions which meet the conditions or to make sure all transactions fall under the exceptions. For many businesses this is easy. Instead of extending credit to customers, accept credit cards and let the credit card company extend the credit. However, if your customers usually do not have credit cards or if you are in a business which often extends credit, such as used car sales, you should consult a lawyer knowledgeable about Reg. Z or, if you dare, get a copy for yourself.

TEXAS LAW Texas also has laws regarding financing arrangements. Anyone engaged in retail installment selling should get a copy of the laws applicable to their type of business and be sure that their procedures comply. The laws covering these transactions are contained in Texas Finance Code:

Revolving Credit Accounts (Finance Code Chapter 346)

Retail installment sales (Finance Code Chapter 345)

Manufactures home sales (Finance Code Chapter 347)

Second mortgage loans (Finance Code Chapter 344)

Motor vehicle sales (Finance Code Chapter 348)

In addition, certain consumer credit businesses must be licensed by the Consumer Credit Commission.

USURY

Usury is the charging, demanding, or receipt of an illegally high rate of interest. In Texas, if you have a written agreement the maximum rate you may charge is 18% per year. Where there is no agreement as to the rate of interest, the rate is set by law at 6% per year beginning 30 days after the bill is due. In an oral agreement, the maximum rate of interest that can be agreed to is 10% per annum. In order to charge more than 6% per year interest on accounts receivable, you must have an agreement to pay interest (which should be in writing before goods are delivered). You can be subject to the stiffest usury penalty if you indicate an interest greater than 6% per year (or 1/2% per month) on your invoice without a prior written agreement. (C.S. 5069-1c.001 et seq., Finance Code Chapters 302, 303, 304 & 305)

A person who contracts for, charges, demands, or receives interest greater than the legal rate is liable to the borrower for the greater of either three times the illegal interest or the lesser of $2,000.00 or 20% of the principal. If the lender contracts for, charges, demands, or receives twice the legal rate of interest, he must pay the borrower the principal amount of the debt as well.

Anyone charging or receiving interest at a rate double the legal interest is guilty of a misdemeanor as subject to a fine of up to $1,000.

COLLECTIONS

FEDERAL LAW

Fair Debt Collection Practice Act. The Fair Debt Collection Practices Act of 1977 bans the use of deception, harassment, and other unreasonable acts in the collection of debts. It has strict requirements whenever someone is collecting a debt for someone else. If you are in the collection business, you must get a copy of this law.

The Federal Trade Commission has issued some rules which prohibit deceptive representations such as pretending to be in the motion picture industry, the government, or a credit bureau and/or using questionnaires which do not say that they are for the purpose of collecting a debt (16 CFR Ch I Part 237).

Soldiers and Sailors Relief Act. Under the Soldiers and Sailors Relief Act, persons in the armed services, including the Reserves and national Guard, are protected in certain financial situations. For example, those on active duty may be entitled to reduce interest rates.

TEXAS LAW   Texas law (Finance Code Chapter 392) protects people who owe a debt created primarily for personal, family, or household purposes from certain activities by bill collectors, including:

☛ threatening violence

☛ falsely accusing a person of fraud or other crime

☛ representing or threatening to represent any other person that the consumer is refusing to pay a nondisputed debt when the debt is, in fact, disputed and the collector knows it

☛ threatening arrest for nonpayment without proper court proceedings

☛ threatening to file criminal charges when no criminal laws have been broken

☛ threatening seizure or repossession of property unless the creditor has the right to do so

☛ using profane or obscene language intended to abuse the consumer

☛ making harassing or annoying phone calls without identifying the caller

☛ making repeated and continuous calls intending to harass

☛ using false names

- failing to disclose that the collector is to collect a debt, unless the communication is for the purpose of determining the whereabouts of the debtor

- falsely representing government affiliation, bonding, or approval

- representing that a debt is being collected by an attorney when it is not

- using communication that pretends to be from an attorney when it is not

- representing that a debt may be increased by attorney's fees, interest, or other charges unless an agreement or statute authorizes it.

A debtor who is a victim of the above may sue the creditor in civil court for injunction, attorney's fees, and $100 per violation. If a debtor brings a suit in bad faith or for harassment, he may have to pay the creditor's attorney fees and court costs.

BUSINESS RELATIONS LAWS 13

THE UNIFORM COMMERCIAL CODE

The Uniform Commercial Code (Texas Business and Commerce Code) is a set of laws regulating numerous aspects of doing business. A national group drafted this set of uniform laws to avoid having a patchwork of different laws around the fifty states. Although some states modified some sections of the laws, the code is basically the same in most of the states. In Texas, the "UCC," as it is called, is contained in the Texas Business and Commerce Code, Chapters 1-9. Each chapter is concerned with a different aspect of commercial relations such as sales, warranties, bank deposits, commercial paper, and bulk transfers.

Businesses that wish to know their rights in all types of transactions should obtain a copy of the UCC and become familiar with it. It is especially useful in transactions between merchants. However, the meaning is not always clear from a reading of the statutes. In law school, students usually spend a full semester studying each chapter of this law.

COMMERCIAL DISCRIMINATION

FEDERAL LAW The Robinson-Patman Act of 1936, prohibits businesses from injuring competition by offering the same goods at different prices to different buyers. This means that the large chain stores should not be getting a better price than your small shop. It also requires that promotional allowances must be made on proportionally the same terms to all buyers.

As a small business, you may be a victim of Robinson-Patman Act violations. A good place to look for information on the act is the following web site: http://www.lawmall.com/rpa/.

RESTRAINING TRADE

FEDERAL LAW One of the earliest federal laws affecting business is the Sherman Antitrust Act of 1890. The purpose of the law was to protect competition in the marketplace by prohibiting monopolies. For example, one large company might buy out all of its competitors and then raise prices to astronomical levels. In recent years, this law was used to break up AT&T.

Examples of some things that are prohibited are:
- ☞ agreements between competitors to sell at the same prices,
- ☞ agreements between competitors on how much will be sold or produced,
- ☞ agreements between competitors to divide up a market,
- ☞ refusing to sell one product without a second product,
- ☞ exchanging information among competitors which results in similarity of prices.

As a new business you probably won't be in a position to violate the act, but you should be aware of it in case a larger competitor tries to put you out of business. A good place to find information on the act is the following internet site:

http://www.lawmall.com/sherman.act/index.html

TEXAS LAW Under the Texas Business and Commerce Code, Chapter 15, it is unlawful to have any contract, combination, or conspiracy to restrain trade or to monopolize, attempt to monopolize, or combine or conspire with any other person to monopolize any part of trade or commerce.

☞ The civil penalty for any violation is up to $100,000 for a natural person, and up to $1,000,000 for a corporation.

☞ Anyone violating this law can be guilty of a felony and sentenced for up to three years in prison.

☞ A person whose business is hurt by a violation can collect triple his damages in a suit against a violator.

COMMERCIAL BRIBERY

TEXAS LAW Since 1973, Texas law has enforced the crime of commercial bribery. It applies to persons in positions of trust, such as employees, agents, trustees, guardians, executors, attorneys, accountants, doctors, corporate directors and officers, and business partners. A "fiduciary" is guilty of a third degree felony if he knowingly or intentionally accepts or agrees to accept a benefit from someone with the understanding that the benefit will influence his conduct in the affairs of his beneficiary. A person who offers or confers such a benefit to a fiduciary is also guilty of a felony.

INTELLECTUAL PROPERTY PROTECTION

As a business owner, you should know enough about intellectual property law to protect your own creations and to keep from violating the rights of others. Intellectual property is that which is the product of human creativity, such as writings, designs, inventions, melodies, and processes. They are things which can be stolen without being physically taken. For example, if you write a book, someone can steal the words from your book without stealing a physical copy of it.

As the internet grows, intellectual property is becoming more valuable. Smart business owners are those who will take the action necessary to protect their company's intellectual property. Additionally, business owners should know intellectual property law to be sure that they do not violate the rights of others. Even an unknowing violation of the law can result in stiff fines and penalties.

The following are the types of intellectual property and the ways to protect them.

PATENT   A patent is protection given to new and useful inventions, discoveries and designs. To be entitled to a patent, a work must be completely new and "unobvious." A patent is granted to the first inventor who files for the patent. Once an invention is patented, no one else can make use of that invention, even if they discover it independently after a lifetime of research. A patent protects an invention for seventeen years; for designs it is three and a half, seven, or fourteen years. Patents cannot be renewed. The patent application must clearly explain how to make the invention so that when the patent expires, others will be able to freely make and use the invention. Patents are registered with the United States Patent and Trademark Office (USPTO). Examples of things which would be patentable would be mechanical devices or new drug formulas.

COPYRIGHT   A copyright is protection given to "original works of authorship," such as written works, musical works, visual works, performance works or computer software programs. A copyright exists form the moment of creation, but one cannot register a copyright until it has been fixed in tangible form. Also, one cannot copyright titles, names, or slogans. A copyright currently gives the author and his heirs exclusive right to his work for the life of the author plus seventy years. Copyrights first registered before 1978 last for ninety-five years. This was previously seventy-five. but was extended twenty years to match the European system. (Perhaps because copyrights owned by Disney and Warner Brothers were due to expire?) Copyrights are registered with the Register of Copyrights at the Library of Congress. Examples of works which would be copyrightable are books, paintings, songs, poems, plays, drawings, and films.

TRADEMARK

A trademark is protection given to a name or symbol which is used to distinguish one person's goods or services from those of others. It can consist of letters, numerals, packaging, labeling, musical notes, colors or a combination of these. If a trademark is used on services as opposed to goods, it is called a service mark. A trademark lasts indefinitely if it is used continuously and renewed properly. Trademarks are registered with the United States Patent and Trademark Office and with individual states. This is explained further in chapter 3. Examples of trademarks are the "Chrysler" name on automobiles, the red border on TIME magazine, and the shape of the Coca-Cola bottle.

TRADE SECRET

A trade secret is some information or process that provides a commercial advantage which is protected by keeping a secret. Examples of trade secrets may be list of successful distributors, the formula for Coca-Cola, or some unique source code in a computer program. Trade secrets are not registered anywhere, they are protected by the fact that they are not disclosed. They are protected only for as long as they are kept secret. If you independently discover the formula for Coca-Cola tomorrow, you can freely market it. (But you can't use the trademark "Coca-Cola" on your product to market it.)

NON-PROTECTABLE
CREATIONS

Some things just are not protectable. Such things as ideas, systems and discoveries are not allowed any protection under any law. If you have a great idea, such as selling packets of hangover medicine in bars, you can't stop others from doing the same thing. If you invent a new medicine, you can patent it; if you pick a distinctive name for it, you can register it as a trademark; if you create a unique picture or instructions for the package, you can copyright them. But you cannot stop others from using your basic business idea of marketing hangover medicine in bars.

Notice the subtle differences between the protective systems available. If you invent something two days after someone else does, and that person patented it, you cannot even use it yourself. But, if you write the same poem as someone else and neither of you copied the other, both of you can copyright the poem. If you patent something, you can have the exclusive rights to it for the term of the patent, but you must disclose how others can make it after the patent expires. However, if you keep it a trade secret, you have exclusive rights as long as no one learns the secret.

We are in a time of transition of the law of intellectual property. Every year new changes are made in the laws and new forms of creativity win protection. For more information, you should consult a new edition of a book on these types of property. Some are listed in the section of this book "for further reading."

ENDLESS LAWS 14

The state of Texas and the federal government have numerous laws and rules which apply to every aspect of every type of business. There are laws governing even such things as fence posts, hosiery, rabbit raising, refund policies, frozen desserts, and advertising. Every business is affected by one or another of these laws.

Some activities are covered by both state and federal laws. In such cases, you must obey the stricter of the rules. In addition, more than one agency of the state or federal government may have rules governing your business. Each of these may have the power to investigate violations and impose fines or other penalties.

Penalties for violations of these laws can range from a warning to a criminal fine and even jail time. In some cases, employees can sue for damages. Recently, employees have been given awards of millions of dollars from employers who violated the law. Since "ignorance of the law is no excuse," it is your duty to learn which laws apply to your business, or to risk these penalties.

Very few people in business know the laws that apply to their businesses. If you take the time to learn them, you can become an expert in your field and avoid problems with regulators. You can also fight back if one of your competitors uses an illegal method to compete with you.

The laws and rules which affect the most businesses are explained in this section. Following that is a list of more specialized laws. You should read through this list and see which ones may apply to your business. Then go to your public library or law library and read them. Some may not apply to your phase of the business, but if any of them do apply, you should make copies to keep on hand.

No one could possibly know all the rules that affect business, much less comply with them all. The Interstate Commerce Commission alone has 40 trillion (that is 40 million million or 40,000,000,000,000) rates on its books telling the transportation industry what it should charge! But if you keep up with the important rules, you will stay out of trouble and have more chance of success.

Federal Laws

The federal laws which are most likely to affect small businesses are rules of the Federal Trade Commission (FTC). The FTC has some rules which affect many businesses such as the rules about labeling, warranties, and mail order sales. Other rules affect only certain industries.

If you sell goods by mail you should send for their booklet, *A Business Guide to the Federal Trade Commission's Mail Order Rule*. If you are going to be involved in a certain industry such as those listed below, or using warranties or your own labeling, you should ask for their latest information on the subject. The address is:

Federal Trade Commission
Washington, DC 20580

The rules of the FTC are contained in the Code of Federal Regulations (CFR) in Chapter 16. Some of the industries covered are:

INDUSTRY	PART
Adhesive Compositions	235
Aerosol Products Used for Frosting Cocktail Glasses	417

Shoes	231
Sleeping Bags	400
Tablecloths and Related Products	404
Television Sets	410
Textile Wearing Apparel	423
Textiles	236
Tires	228
Used Automobile Parts	20
Used Lubricating Oil	406
Used Motor Vehicles	455
Waist Belts	405
Watches	245
Wigs and Hairpieces	252

Some other federal laws which affect businesses are as follows:

☛ Alcohol Administration Act (27 U.S.C. §201 et seq.)

☛ Child Protection and Toy Safety Act (1969)

☛ Clean Water Act (U.S.C. Title 33)

☛ Comprehensive Smokeless Tobacco Health Education Act (1986). See also 16 CFR Ch. I, Part 307 for rules.

☛ Consumer Credit Protection Act (1968)

☛ Consumer Product Safety Act (1972)

☛ Energy Policy and Conservation Act. See also 16 CFR Ch. I, Part 305 for rules about energy cost labeling.

☛ Environmental Pesticide Control Act of 1972

☛ Fair Credit Reporting Act (1970)

☛ Fair Packaging and Labeling Act (1966). See also 16 CFR Ch. I, Parts 500-503 for rules.

☛ Flammable Fabrics Act (1953). See also 16 CFR Ch. II, Parts 1602-1632 for rules.

☛ Food, Drug, and Cosmetic Act (21 U.S.C. §301 et seq.)

☛ Fur Products Labeling Act (1951). See also 16 CFR Ch. I, Part 301 for rules.

☛ Hazardous Substances Act (1960)

☛ Hobby Protection Act. See also 16 CFR Ch. I, Part 304 for rules.

☛ Insecticide, Fungicide, and Rodenticide Act (7 U.S.C. §136 et seq.)

☛ Magnuson-Moss Warranty Act. See also 16 CFR Ch. I, Part 239 for rules.

☛ Poison Prevention Packaging Act of 1970. See also 16 CFR Ch. II, Parts 1700-1702 for rules.

☛ Solid Waste Disposal Act (42 U.S.C. §6901 et seq.)

☛ Textile Fiber Products Identification Act. See also 16 CFR Ch. I, Part 303 for rules.

☛ Toxic Substance Control Act (U.S.C. Title 15)

☛ Wool Products Labeling Act (1939). See also 16 CFR Ch. I, Part 300 for rules.

☛ Nutrition Labeling and Education Act of 1990

☛ Food Safety Enforcement Enhancement Act of 1997

TEXAS LAWS

Texas has numerous laws regulating specific types of businesses or certain activities of businesses. The following is a list of those laws that are most likely to affect small businesses.

Citations refer to Civil Statutes (CS) or Various Texas Codes

Adult day care facilities	Hum. Resources Code Chap. 103
Air conditioning	C.S. 8861
Alcoholic beverages	Alcoholic Beverage Code
Ambulance service contracts	Health & Safety Code, Chapter 773
Anatomical gifts	Health & Safety Code, Chapter 692
Aquaculture	Agriculture Code, Chapter 134
Auctions	C.S. 8700
Bail bondsmen	C.S. 2372p-3
Banking	Finance Code
Boiler safety	Health & Safety Code, Chapter 755

Boxing & wrestling	C.S. 8501-1
Burial contracts	Finance Code, Chapter 154
Cemeteries	Health & Safety Code, Chapter 711-712
Charitable telephone solicitation	C.S. 9023
Citrus	Agriculture Code
Condominiums	Property Code, Chapters 81- 82
Cosmetics	Health & Safety Code, Chapter 431
Credit cards	Finance Code
Credit service organizations	Finance Code, Chapter 393
Dairies	Food, Drug & Commodities Act Health & Safety Code, Chapter 431
Dog racing & horseracing	C.S. 179e
Drinking water	Health & Safety Code, Chapter 341
Drugs	Health & Safety Code, chapters 431, 481
Eggs & poultry	Health & Safety Code, Chapter 431
Electrical	Utilities Code
Elevators	Health & Safety Code, Chapter 754
Energy conservation standards	Government Code, Chapter 2166
Explosives	Local Govt. Code, Chapter 236
Fences and livestock at large	Agriculture Code, 143.028, 143.077
Fireworks	Insurance Code, Sec. 5.34-4 Local Govt. Code 240.904
Food	Health & Safety Code, Chapter 431
Frozen desserts	Health & Safety Code, Chapter 440
Fruits & vegetables	Health & Safety Code, Chapter 431 Agriculture Code
Gambling	Penal Code 47.01 & 47.02
Gas, liquefied petroleum	Natural Resources Code, Chapter 113
Hazardous waste	Health & Safety Code, Chapter 361
Health care	Health & Safety Code, Chapter 221, 161, 105, 241
Health spas	C.S. 52211
Home health agencies	Health & Safety Code, Chapter 142
Honey	Agriculture Code, Chapter 131
Hospices	Health & Safety Code, Chapter 142
Insurance	Insurance Code
Invention development	C.S. 9020

Landfills	Health & Safety 361.531 et seq.
Landlord & Tenant	Property Code, Chapter 91,92
Lead acid batteries	Health & Safety Code, Chapter 361, 451
Legal Services	See Attorneys
Liquor	See Alcoholic Beverages
Livestock Caretakers	Agriculture Code, Chapter 161
Lottery	Govt. Code, Chapter 466
Meats	Health & Safety Code, Chapter 431
Mental Health	Health & Safety Code, Chapter 531, 571
Metal Recyclers	C.S. 9009b
Milk & Milk Products	Health & Safety Code, Chapter 431
Mines & Minerals	Natural resources Code, Chapter 53
Mobile homes	C.S. 5221f, 5069-6A, 6686, 6687-1
Money orders	Finance Code Chapter 152
Motor vehicle lemon law	C.S. 4413(36) Section 6.07
Motor vehicles	C.S. 4413(36), Transportation Code
Multi-level marketing	Business & Commerce Code, Section 17.461
Newsprint recycling	Health & Safety Code 361.430
Nursing homes	Health & Safety Code, Chapter 242
Obscene language	Penal Code 21.08, 43.21
Oil & Gas	Natural Resources Code, Title 3
Outdoor Advertising	Transportation Code, Chapter 391, Local Ordinances
Pari-mutual Wagering	C.S. 179e (Texas Racing Act)
Plants & Nurseries	Agriculture Code, Chapter 71
Plumbing	C.S. 6243-101, et seq.
Prostitution	Penal Code 43.02
Pyramid schemes	Penal Code 32.48 Business & Commerce Code, Sect. 17.461
Radiation	Health & Safety Code Chapter 401
Real estate sales	Property Code & C.S. 6573a
Rental housing	C.S. 5221f, Prop. Code, Chapter 92, 301
Restaurants	Health & Safety Code 437, Local Ordinances
Secondhand Dealers	C.S. 9009, 9024
Securities Transactions	C.S. 581-1 et seq.

Swimming & Bathing Places	Health & Safety Code, 341.064
Timber and Lumber	Natural resources Code, Chapter 151
Time Shares	Property Code, Chapter 221
Tires	Health & Safety Code, Chap. 361
Tobacco	Hlth. & Safety Code, Sect. 161.081 et seq.
Tourism	Government Code 481
Sound & Film, Copying	Business & Comm. Code Sec. 35.91 et seq.
Viticulture	Agriculture Code, Chapter 41
Watches, Used	Business & Commerce Code, Sec. 17.18
Weapons and Firearms	Penal Code, Chapter 46
	Local Govt. Code, Sect. 250.001
	Hlth. & Safety Code, Sect. 756.041 et seq.

BOOKKEEPING AND ACCOUNTING 15

It is beyond the scope of this book to explain all the intricacies of setting up a business's bookkeeping and accounting systems. But the important thing to realize is that if you do not set up an understandable bookkeeping system, your business will undoubtedly fail.

Without accurate records of where your income is coming from and where it is going you will be unable to increase your profits, lower your expenses, obtain needed financing, or make the right decisions in all areas of your business. The time to decide how you will handle your bookkeeping is when you open your business, not a year later when it is tax time.

INITIAL BOOKKEEPING

If you do not understand business taxation you should pick up a good book on the subject, as well as the IRS tax guide for your type of business (proprietorship, partnership, or corporation). A few good books on the subject are *The Small Business Survival Guide* by Robert Fleury (Sourcebooks), *Small Time Operator* by Bernard Kamoroff (Bell Springs), and *Tax Savvy for Small Business* by Frederick Daily (Nolo Press).

The IRS tax book for small businesses is Publication 334, *Tax Guide for Small Businesses*. There are also instruction booklets for each type of business's form, Schedule C for proprietorships, Form 1120 or 1120S for C corporations and S corporations, and 1165 for partnerships and businesses which are taxed like partnerships (LLCs, LLPs).

Keep in mind that the IRS doesn't give you the best advice for saving on taxes and does not give you the other side of contested issues. For that you need a private tax guide or advisor.

The most important thing to do is to set up your bookkeeping so that you can easily fill out your monthly, quarterly, and annual tax returns.

The best way to do this is to get copies of the returns, not the totals that you will need to supply and set up your bookkeeping system to group those totals.

For example, for a sole proprietorship you will use "Schedule C" to report business income and expenses to the IRS at the end of the year. Use the categories on that form to sort your expenses. To make your job especially easy, every time you pay a bill, put the category number on the check.

ACCOUNTANTS

Most likely your new business will not be able to afford hiring an accountant right off to handle your books. That is good. Doing the books yourself will force you to learn about business accounting and taxation. The worst way to run a business is to know nothing about the tax laws and turn everything over to an accountant at the end of the year to find out what is due.

You should know the basics of tax law before making basic decisions such as whether to buy or rent equipment or premises. You should understand accounting so you can time your financial affairs appropriately. If you were a boxer who only needed to win fights, you could turn everything over to an accountant. If your business needs to buy supplies, inventory, or equipment and provides goods or services throughout the year, you need to at least have a basic understanding of the system within which you are working.

Once you can afford an accountant you should weigh the cost against your time and the risk that you will make an error. Even if you think you know enough to do your own corporate tax return, you should still take it to an accountant one year to see if you have been missing any deductions. You might decide that the money saved is worth the cost of the accountant's services.

COMPUTER PROGRAMS

Today every business should keep its books by computer. There are inexpensive programs such as Quicken which can instantly provide you with reports of your income and expenses and the right figures to plug into your tax returns.

Most programs even offer a tax program each year which will take all of your information and print it out on the current year's tax forms. It sure beats sorting through shoe boxes of receipts with an adding machine!

TAX TIPS

Here are a few tax tips for small businesses which will help you save money:

- Usually when you buy equipment for a business you must amortize the cost over several years. That is, you don't deduct it all when you buy it, you take, say, twenty-five percent of the cost off your taxes each year for four years. (The time is determined by the theoretical usefulness of the item.) However, small businesses are allowed to write off the entire cost of a limited amount of items under Internal Revenue Code §179. If you have income to shelter, use it.

☛ Owners of S corporations do not have to pay social security or medicare taxes on the part of their profits that is not considered salary. As long as you pay yourself a reasonable salary, other money you take out is not subject to these taxes.

☛ You should not neglect to deposit withholding taxes for your own salary or profits. You will not only be forced to produce a large amount of money in April, but there are penalties which must also be paid for the failure to do so.

☛ Do not fail to keep track of and remit your employees' withholding. You will be personally liable for them even if you are a corporation.

☛ If you keep track of your use of your car for business you can deduct 31.5¢ per mile (this may go up or down each year). If you use your car for business a considerable amount of time you may be able to depreciate it.

☛ If your business is a corporation and you designate the stock as "section 1244 stock," and the business fails, you are able to get a much better deduction for the loss.

☛ By setting up a retirement plan you can exempt up to twenty percent of your salary from income tax. See chapter 10. But don't use money you might need later. There are penalties for taking it out of the retirement plan.

☛ When you buy things which will be resold or made into products which will be resold, you do not have to pay sales taxes on those purchases. See chapter 17.

PAYING FEDERAL TAXES 16

FEDERAL INCOME TAX

The manner in which each type of business pays taxes is as follows:

PROPRIETORSHIP
A proprietor reports profits and expenses on Schedule C attached to the usual Form 1040 and pays tax on all of the net income of the business. Each quarter Form ES-1040 must be filed along with payment of one-quarter of the amount of income tax and social security taxes estimated to be due for the year.

PARTNERSHIP
The partnership files a return showing the income and expenses but pays no tax. Each partner is given a form showing his share of the profits or losses and reports these on Schedule E of Form 1040. Each quarter, Form ES-1040 must be filed by each partner along with payment of one-quarter of the amount of income tax and social security taxes estimated to be due for the year.

C CORPORATION
A regular corporation is a separate taxpayer, and pays tax on its profits after deducting all expenses, including officers' salaries. If dividends are distributed, they are paid out of after-tax dollars, and the shareholders pay tax a second time when they receive the dividends. If a corporation needs to accumulate money for investment, it may be able to do so at lower tax rates than the shareholders. But if all profits will be

distributed to shareholders, the double-taxation may be excessive unless all income is paid as salaries. A C corporation files Form 1120.

S CORPORATION

A small corporation has the option of being taxed like a partnership. If Form 2553 is filed by the corporation and accepted by the Internal Revenue Service, the S corporation will only file an informational return listing profits and expenses. Then each shareholder will be taxed on a proportional share of the profits (or be able to deduct a proportional share of the losses). Unless a corporation will make a large profit that will not be distributed, S-status is usually best in the beginning. An S corporation files Form 1120S and distributes Form K-1 to each shareholder. If any money is taken out by a shareholder that is not listed as wages subject to withholding, then the shareholder will usually have to file form ES-1040 each quarter along with payment of the estimated withholding on the withdrawals.

LIMITED LIABILITY
COMPANIES AND
PARTNERSHIPS

Limited liability companies and limited liability partnerships are allowed by the IRS to elect to be taxed either as a partnership or a corporation. To make this election you file Form 8832, Entity Classification Election with the IRS.

TAX WORKSHOPS
AND BOOKLETS

The IRS conducts workshops to inform businesses about the tax laws. (Don't expect in-depth study of the loopholes.) For more information call or write to the IRS at the following addresses:

Austin	***Houston***	***Dallas***
300 E. 8th St.	8701 S. Gessner	1100Commerce St.
Stop 6610-AUS	Stop 6610-HOU	Stop 6610-DAL
Austin, TX 78701	Houston, TX 77074	Dallas, TX 75242
512-499-5439	281-721-7070	214-767-1428

Or call 1-800-829-1040, or visit their website at:
  http://www.irs.ustreas.gov

FEDERAL WITHHOLDING, SOCIAL SECURITY, AND MEDICARE TAXES

If you need basic information on business tax returns, the IRS publishes a rather large booklet that answers most questions and is available free of charge. Call or write them and ask for Publication No. 334. If you have any questions, look up their toll-free number in the phone book under United States Government/Internal Revenue Service. If you want more creative answers and tax saving information, you should find a good local accountant. But to get started you will need the following:

EMPLOYER IDENTIFICATION NUMBER

If you are a sole proprietor with no employees, you can use your social security number for your business. If you are a corporation, a partnership or a proprietorship with employees, you must obtain an "Employer Identification Number." This is done by filing form SS-4. It usually takes a week or two to receive. You will need this number to open bank accounts for the business, so you should file this form a soon as you decide to go into business. A sample filled-in form and instructions are at the end of this chapter.

EMPLOYEE'S WITHHOLDING ALLOWANCE CERTIFICATE

You must have each employee fill out a W-4 form to calculate the amount of federal taxes to be deducted and to obtain their social security numbers. (The number of allowances on this form is used with IRS Circular E, Publication 15, to figure out the exact deductions.) A sample filled-in form is at the end of this chapter.

FEDERAL TAX DEPOSIT COUPONS

After making withholdings from employees' wages, you must deposit them at a bank which is authorized to accept such funds. If at the end of any month you have over $1000 in withheld taxes (including your contribution to FICA), you must make a deposit prior to the 15th of the following month. If on the 3rd, 7th, 11th, 15th, 19th, 22nd, or 25th of any month you have over $3,000 in withheld taxes, you must make a deposit within three banking days. The deposit is made using the coupons in the Form 8109 booklet. A sample 8109-B coupon, which you will use to order your booklet, is shown at the end of this chapter.

ELECTRONIC
FILING

Businesses which make $50,000 or more a year in federal tax deposits are required to begin electric filing by June 30, 1999. However, this deadline had been extended in the past and may be again. (It was originally scheduled for July 1, 1997, but faced strong business opposition.)

ESTIMATED TAX
PAYMENT
VOUCHER

Sole proprietors and partners usually take draws from their businesses without the formality of withholding. However, they are still required to make deposits of income and FICA taxes each quarter. If more than $500 is due in April on a person's 1040 form, then not enough money was withheld each quarter and a penalty is assessed unless the person falls into an exception. The quarterly withholding is submitted on Form 1040-ES on April 15th, June 15th, September 15th, and January 15th each year. If these days fall on a weekend then the due date is the following Monday. The worksheet with Form 1040-ES can be used to determine the amount to pay. *Important Note*: One of the exceptions to the rule is that if you withhold the same amount as last year's tax bill, then you do not have to pay a penalty. This is usually a lot easier than filling out the 1040-ES worksheet.

EMPLOYER'S
QUARTERLY TAX
RETURN

Each quarter you must file Form 941 reporting your federal withholding and FICA taxes. If you owe more than $1000 at the end of a quarter, you are required to make a deposit at the end of any month that you have $1000 in withholding. The deposits are made to the Federal Reserve Bank or an authorized financial institution on Form 501. Most banks are authorized to accept deposits. If you owe more than $3,000 for any month, you must make a deposit at any point in the month in which you owe $3,000. After you file form SS-4, the 941 forms will be sent to you automatically if you checked the box saying that you expect to have employees.

WAGE AND TAX
STATEMENT

At the end of each year, you are required to issue a W-2 Form to each employee. This form shows the amount of wages paid to the employee during the year as well as the amounts withheld for taxes, social security, medicare, and other purposes. A sample W-2 is at the end of this chapter.

MISCELLANEOUS   If you pay at least $600 to a person other than an employee (such as independent contractors), you are required to file a Form 1099 for that person. Along with the 1099s, you must file a form 1096 which is a summary sheet.

Many people are not aware of this law and fail to file these forms, but they are required for such things as services, royalties, rents, awards and prizes which you pay to individuals (but not corporations). The rules for this are quite complicated so you should either obtain "Package 1099" from the IRS or consult your accountant. Sample forms 1099 and 1096 are at the end of this chapter.

EARNED
INCOME CREDIT   Persons who are not liable to pay income tax may have the right to a check from the government because of the "Earned Income Credit." You are required to notify your employees of this. You can satisfy this requirement with one of the following:

☛ a W-2 Form with the notice on the back;

☛ a substitute for the W-2 Form with the notice on it;

☛ a copy of Notice 797; or

☛ a written statement with the wording from Notice 797.

A Notice 797 can be obtained by calling 800-829-3676.

FEDERAL EXCISE TAXES

Excise taxes are taxes on certain activities or items. Most federal excise taxes have been eliminated since World War II, but a few remain.

Some of the things which are subject to federal excise taxes are tobacco and alcohol, gasoline, tires and inner tubes, some trucks and trailers, firearms, ammunition, bows, arrows, fishing equipment, the use of highway vehicles of over 55,000 pounds, aircraft, wagering, telephone and teletype services, coal, hazardous wastes, and vaccines. If you are involved with any of these, you should obtain from the IRS publication No. 510, *Information on Excise Taxes.*

UNEMPLOYMENT COMPENSATION TAXES

You must pay federal unemployment taxes if you paid wages of $1,500 in any quarter, or if you had at least one employee for twenty calendar weeks. The federal tax amount is 0.8% of the first $7,000 of wages paid each employee. If more than $100 is due by the end of any quarter (if you paid $12,500 in wages for the quarter), then Form 508 must be filed with an authorized financial institution or the Federal Reserve Bank in your area. You will receive Form 508 when you obtain your employer identification number.

At the end of each year, you must file Form 940 or Form 940EZ. This is your annual report of federal unemployment taxes. You will receive an original form from the IRS.

Form **SS-4**

(Rev. February 2000)

Department of the Treasury
Internal Revenue Service

Application for Employer Identification Number

(For use by employers, corporations, partnerships, trusts, estates, churches,
government agencies, certain individuals, and others. See instructions.)

▶ Keep a copy for your records.

EIN
OMB No. 1545-0003

Please type or print clearly.

1 Name of applicant (legal name) (see instructions)

Doe Company

2 Trade name of business (if different from name on line 1)	**3** Executor, trustee, "care of" name

4a Mailing address (street address) (room, apt., or suite no.) 123 Main Street	**5a** Business address (if different from address on lines 4a and 4b)
4b City, state, and ZIP code Abilene, TX 75123	**5b** City, state, and ZIP code

6 County and state where principal business is located

Taylor County, Texas

7 Name of principal officer, general partner, grantor, owner, or trustor—SSN or ITIN may be required (see instructions) ▶ 123-45-6789

John Doe

8a Type of entity (Check only one box.) (see instructions)

Caution: *If applicant is a limited liability company, see the instructions for line 8a.*

☐ Sole proprietor (SSN) _____

☒ Partnership   ☐ Personal service corp.

☐ REMIC   ☐ National Guard

☐ State/local government   ☐ Farmers' cooperative

☐ Church or church-controlled organization

☐ Other nonprofit organization (specify) ▶ _____

☐ Other (specify) ▶

☐ Estate (SSN of decedent) _____

☐ Plan administrator (SSN) _____

☐ Other corporation (specify) ▶ _____

☐ Trust

☐ Federal government/military

(enter GEN if applicable) _____

8b If a corporation, name the state or foreign country
(if applicable) where incorporated

State	Foreign country

9 Reason for applying (Check only one box.) (see instructions)

☒ Started new business (specify type) ▶_____

☐ Hired employees (Check the box and see line 12.)

☐ Created a pension plan (specify type) ▶

☐ Banking purpose (specify purpose) ▶ _____

☐ Changed type of organization (specify new type) ▶ _____

☐ Purchased going business

☐ Created a trust (specify type) ▶ _____

☐ Other (specify) ▶

10 Date business started or acquired (month, day, year) (see instructions) 10-15-2000	**11** Closing month of accounting year (see instructions) December

12 First date wages or annuities were paid or will be paid (month, day, year). **Note:** *If applicant is a withholding agent, enter date income will first be paid to nonresident alien. (month, day, year)* . . . . ▶   10-22-2000

13 Highest number of employees expected in the next 12 months. **Note:** *If the applicant does not expect to have any employees during the period, enter -0-. (see instructions)* . . . . ▶	Nonagricultural	Agricultural	Household

14 Principal activity (see instructions) ▶   clothing manufacturing

15 Is the principal business activity manufacturing? . . . .   ☒ Yes   ☐ No

If "Yes," principal product and raw material used ▶   fabric

16 To whom are most of the products or services sold? Please check one box.   ☒ Business (wholesale)

☐ Public (retail)   ☐ Other (specify) ▶   ☐ N/A

17a Has the applicant ever applied for an employer identification number for this or any other business? . . . .   ☐ Yes   ☒ No

Note: *If "Yes," please complete lines 17b and 17c.*

17b If you checked "Yes" on line 17a, give applicant's legal name and trade name shown on prior application, if different from line 1 or 2 above.

Legal name ▶   Trade name ▶

17c Approximate date when and city and state where the application was filed. Enter previous employer identification number if known.

Approximate date when filed (mo., day, year)	City and state where filed	Previous EIN

Under penalties of perjury, I declare that I have examined this application, and to the best of my knowledge and belief, it is true, correct, and complete.

Business telephone number (include area code)
(518) 555-0000
Fax telephone number (include area code)

Name and title (Please type or print clearly.) ▶   John Doe, Partner

Signature ▶   *John Doe*   Date ▶   *10/15/00*

Note: *Do not write below this line. For official use only.*

Please leave blank ▶	Geo.	Ind.	Class	Size	Reason for applying

For Paperwork Reduction Act Notice, see page 4.   Cat. No. 16055N   Form **SS-4** (Rev. 2-98)

General Instructions

Section references are to the Internal Revenue Code unless otherwise noted.

Purpose of Form

Use Form SS-4 to apply for an employer identification number (EIN). An EIN is a nine-digit number (for example, 12-3456789) assigned to sole proprietors, corporations, partnerships, estates, trusts, and other entities for tax filing and reporting purposes. The information you provide on this form will establish your business tax account.

Caution: *An EIN is for use in connection with your business activities only. Do NOT use your EIN in place of your social security number (SSN).*

Who Must File

You must file this form if you have not been assigned an EIN before and:

● You pay wages to one or more employees including household employees.

● You are required to have an EIN to use on any return, statement, or other document, even if you are not an employer.

● You are a withholding agent required to withhold taxes on income, other than wages, paid to a nonresident alien (individual, corporation, partnership, etc.). A withholding agent may be an agent, broker, fiduciary, manager, tenant, or spouse, and is required to file **Form 1042**, Annual Withholding Tax Return for U.S. Source Income of Foreign Persons.

● You file **Schedule C**, Profit or Loss From Business, **Schedule C-EZ**, Net Profit From Business, or **Schedule F**, Profit or Loss From Farming, of **Form 1040**, U.S. Individual Income Tax Return, **and** have a Keogh plan or are required to file excise, employment, or alcohol, tobacco, or firearms returns.

The following must use EINs even if they do not have any employees:

● State and local agencies who serve as tax reporting agents for public assistance recipients, under Rev. Proc. 80-4, 1980-1 C.B. 581, should obtain a separate EIN for this reporting. See **Household employer** on page 3.

● Trusts, except the following:

   1. Certain grantor-owned trusts. (See the **Instructions for Form 1041.**)

   2. Individual Retirement Arrangement (IRA) trusts, unless the trust has to file **Form 990-T**, Exempt Organization Business Income Tax Return. (See the **Instructions for Form 990-T.**)

● Estates

● Partnerships

● REMICs (real estate mortgage investment conduits) (See the **Instructions for Form 1066**, U.S. Real Estate Mortgage Investment Conduit Income Tax Return.)

● Corporations

● Nonprofit organizations (churches, clubs, etc.)

● Farmers' cooperatives

● Plan administrators (A plan administrator is the person or group of persons specified as the administrator by the instrument under which the plan is operated.)

When To Apply for a New EIN

New Business. If you become the new owner of an existing business, **do not** use the EIN of the former owner. IF YOU ALREADY HAVE AN EIN, USE THAT NUMBER. If you do not have an EIN, apply for one on this form. If you become the "owner" of a corporation by acquiring its stock, use the corporation's EIN.

Changes in Organization or Ownership. If you already have an EIN, you may need to get a new one if either the organization or ownership of your business changes. If you incorporate a sole proprietorship or form a partnership, you must get a new EIN. However, **do not** apply for a new EIN if:

● You change only the name of your business,

● You elected on **Form 8832**, Entity Classification Election, to change the way the entity is taxed, or

● A partnership terminates because at least 50% of the total interests in partnership capital and profits were sold or exchanged within a 12-month period. (See Regulations section 301.6109-1(d)(2)(iii).) The EIN for the terminated partnership should continue to be used. This rule applies to terminations occurring after May 8, 1997. If the termination took place after May 8, 1996, and before May 9, 1997, a new EIN must be obtained for the new partnership unless the partnership and its partners are consistent in using the old EIN.

Note: *If you are electing to be an "S corporation," be sure you file Form 2553, Election by a Small Business Corporation.*

File Only One Form SS-4. File only one Form SS-4, regardless of the number of businesses operated or trade names under which a business operates. However, each corporation in an affiliated group must file a separate application.

EIN Applied for, But Not Received. If you do not have an EIN by the time a return is due, write "Applied for" and the date you applied in the space shown for the number. **Do not** show your social security number (SSN) as an EIN on returns.

If you do not have an EIN by the time a tax deposit is due, send your payment to the Internal Revenue Service Center for your filing area. (See **Where To Apply** below.) Make your check or money order payable to Internal Revenue Service and show your name (as shown on Form SS-4), address, type of tax, period covered, and date you applied for an EIN. Send an explanation with the deposit.

For more information about EINs, see **Pub. 583**, Starting a Business and Keeping Records, and **Pub. 1635**, Understanding your EIN.

How To Apply

You can apply for an EIN either by mail or by telephone. You can get an EIN immediately by calling the Tele-TIN number for the service center for your state, or you can send the completed Form SS-4 directly to the service center to receive your EIN by mail.

Application by Tele-TIN. Under the Tele-TIN program, you can receive your EIN by telephone and use it immediately to file a return or make a payment. To receive an EIN by telephone, complete Form SS-4, then call the Tele-TIN number listed for your state under **Where To Apply**. The person making the call must be authorized to sign the form. (See **Signature** on page 4.)

An IRS representative will use the information from the Form SS-4 to establish your account and assign you an EIN. Write the number you are given on the upper right corner of the form and sign and date it.

Mail or fax (facsimile) the signed SS-4 within 24 hours to the Tele-TIN Unit at the service center address for your state. The IRS representative will give you the fax number. The fax numbers are also listed in Pub. 1635.

Taxpayer representatives can receive their client's EIN by telephone if they first send a fax of a completed **Form 2848**, Power of Attorney and Declaration of Representative, or **Form 8821**, Tax Information Authorization, to the Tele-TIN unit. The Form 2848 or Form 8821 will be used solely to release the EIN to the representative authorized on the form.

Application by Mail. Complete Form SS-4 at least 4 to 5 weeks before you will need an EIN. Sign and date the application and mail it to the service center address for your state. You will receive your EIN in the mail in approximately 4 weeks.

Where To Apply

The Tele-TIN numbers listed below will involve a long-distance charge to callers outside of the local calling area and can be used only to apply for an EIN. THE NUMBERS MAY CHANGE WITHOUT NOTICE. Call 1-800-829-1040 to verify a number or to ask about the status of an application by mail.

If your principal business, office or agency, or legal residence in the case of an individual, is located in:	Call the Tele-TIN number shown or file with the Internal Revenue Service Center at:
Florida, Georgia, South Carolina	Attn: Entity Control Atlanta, GA 39901 770-455-2360
New Jersey, New York City and counties of Nassau, Rockland, Suffolk, and Westchester	Attn: Entity Control Holtsville, NY 00501 516-447-4955
New York (all other counties), Connecticut, Maine, Massachusetts, New Hampshire, Rhode Island, Vermont	Attn: Entity Control Andover, MA 05501 978-474-9717
Illinois, Iowa, Minnesota, Missouri, Wisconsin	Attn: Entity Control Stop 6800 2306 E. Bannister Rd. Kansas City, MO 64999 816-926-5999
Delaware, District of Columbia, Maryland, Pennsylvania, Virginia	Attn: Entity Control Philadelphia, PA 19255 215-516-6999
Indiana, Kentucky, Michigan, Ohio, West Virginia	Attn: Entity Control Cincinnati, OH 45999 606-292-5467

Kansas, New Mexico, Oklahoma, Texas	Attn: Entity Control Austin, TX 73301 512-460-7843
Alaska, Arizona, California (counties of Alpine, Amador, Butte, Calaveras, Colusa, Contra Costa, Del Norte, El Dorado, Glenn, Humboldt, Lake, Lassen, Marin, Mendocino, Modoc, Napa, Nevada, Placer, Plumas, Sacramento, San Joaquin, Shasta, Sierra, Siskiyou, Solano, Sonoma, Sutter, Tehama, Trinity, Yolo, and Yuba), Colorado, Idaho, Montana, Nebraska, Nevada, North Dakota, Oregon, South Dakota, Utah, Washington, Wyoming	Attn: Entity Control Mail Stop 6271 P.O. Box 9941 Ogden, UT 84201 801-620-7645
California (all other counties), Hawaii	Attn: Entity Control Fresno, CA 93888 209-452-4010
Alabama, Arkansas, Louisiana, Mississippi, North Carolina, Tennessee	Attn: Entity Control Memphis, TN 37501 901-546-3920
If you have no legal residence, principal place of business, or principal office or agency in any state	Attn: Entity Control Philadelphia, PA 19255 215-516-6999

Specific Instructions

The instructions that follow are for those items that are not self-explanatory. Enter N/A (nonapplicable) on the lines that do not apply.

Line 1. Enter the legal name of the entity applying for the EIN exactly as it appears on the social security card, charter, or other applicable legal document.

Individuals. Enter your first name, middle initial, and last name. If you are a sole proprietor, enter your individual name, not your business name. Enter your business name on line 2. Do not use abbreviations or nicknames on line 1.

Trusts. Enter the name of the trust.

Estate of a decedent. Enter the name of the estate.

Partnerships. Enter the legal name of the partnership as it appears in the partnership agreement. **Do not** list the names of the partners on line 1. See the specific instructions for line 7.

Corporations. Enter the corporate name as it appears in the corporation charter or other legal document creating it.

Plan administrators. Enter the name of the plan administrator. A plan administrator who already has an EIN should use that number.

Line 2. Enter the trade name of the business if different from the legal name. The trade name is the "doing business as" name.

Note: *Use the full legal name on line 1 on all tax returns filed for the entity. However, if you enter a trade name on line 2 and choose to use the trade name instead of the legal name, enter the trade name on all returns you file. To prevent processing delays and errors, always use either the legal name only or the trade name only on all tax returns.*

Line 3. Trusts enter the name of the trustee. Estates enter the name of the executor, administrator, or other fiduciary. If the entity applying has a designated person to receive tax information, enter that person's name as the "care of" person. Print or type the first name, middle initial, and last name.

Line 7. Enter the first name, middle initial, last name, and SSN of a principal officer if the business is a corporation; of a general partner if a partnership; of the owner of a single member entity that is disregarded as an entity separate from its owner; or of a grantor, owner, or trustor if a trust. If the person in question is an alien individual with a previously assigned individual taxpayer identification number (ITIN), enter the ITIN in the space provided, instead of an SSN. You are not required to enter an SSN or ITIN if the reason you are applying for an EIN is to make an entity classification election (see Regulations section 301.7701-1 through 301.7701-3), and you are a nonresident alien with no effectively connected income from sources within the United States.

Line 8a. Check the box that best describes the type of entity applying for the EIN. If you are an alien individual with an ITIN previously assigned to you, enter the ITIN in place of a requested SSN.

Caution: *This is not an election for a tax classification of an entity. See "Limited liability company" below.*

If not specifically mentioned, check the "Other" box, enter the type of entity and the type of return that will be filed (for example, common trust fund, Form 1065). Do not enter N/A. If you are an alien individual applying for an EIN, see the **Line 7** instructions above.

Sole proprietor. Check this box if you file Schedule C, C-EZ, or F (Form 1040) and have a Keogh plan, or are required to file excise, employment, or alcohol, tobacco, or firearms returns, or are a payer of gambling

winnings. Enter your SSN (or ITIN) in the space provided. If you are a nonresident alien with no effectively connected income from sources within the United States, you do not need to enter an SSN or ITIN.

REMIC. Check this box if the entity has elected to be treated as a real estate mortgage investment conduit (REMIC). See the **Instructions for Form 1066** for more information.

Other nonprofit organization. Check this box if the nonprofit organization is other than a church or church-controlled organization and specify the type of nonprofit organization (for example, an educational organization).

If the organization also seeks tax-exempt status, you must file either **Package 1023**, Application for Recognition of Exemption, or **Package 1024**, Application for Recognition of Exemption Under Section 501(a). Get **Pub. 557**, Tax Exempt Status for Your Organization, for more information.

Group exemption number (GEN). If the organization is covered by a group exemption letter, enter the four-digit GEN. (Do not confuse the GEN with the nine-digit EIN.) If you do not know the GEN, contact the parent organization. Get Pub. 557 for more information about group exemption numbers.

Withholding agent. If you are a withholding agent required to file Form 1042, check the "Other" box and enter "Withholding agent."

Personal service corporation. Check this box if the entity is a personal service corporation. An entity is a personal service corporation for a tax year only if:

● The principal activity of the entity during the testing period (prior tax year) for the tax year is the performance of personal services substantially by employee-owners, and

● The employee-owners own at least 10% of the fair market value of the outstanding stock in the entity on the last day of the testing period.

Personal services include performance of services in such fields as health, law, accounting, or consulting. For more information about personal service corporations, see the **Instructions for Form 1120**, U.S. Corporation Income Tax Return, and **Pub. 542**, Corporations.

Limited liability company (LLC). See the definition of limited liability company in the **Instructions for Form 1065**. An LLC with two or more members can be a partnership or an association taxable as a corporation. An LLC with a single owner can be an association taxable as a corporation or an entity disregarded as an entity separate from its owner. See Form 8832 for more details.

● If the entity is classified as a partnership for Federal income tax purposes, check the "partnership" box.

● If the entity is classified as a corporation for Federal income tax purposes, mark the "Other corporation" box and write "limited liability co." in the space provided.

● If the entity is disregarded as an entity separate from its owner, check the "Other" box and write in "disregarded entity" in the space provided.

Plan administrator. If the plan administrator is an individual, enter the plan administrator's SSN in the space provided.

Other corporation. This box is for any corporation other than a personal service corporation. If you check this box, enter the type of corporation (such as insurance company) in the space provided.

Household employer. If you are an individual, check the "Other" box and enter "Household employer" and your SSN. If you are a state or local agency serving as a tax reporting agent for public assistance recipients who become household employers, check the "Other" box and enter "Household employer agent." If you are a trust that qualifies as a household employer, you do not need a separate EIN for reporting tax information relating to household employees; use the EIN of the trust.

QSSS. For a qualified subchapter S subsidiary (QSSS) check the "Other" box and specify "QSSS."

Line 9. Check only **one** box. Do not enter N/A.

Started new business. Check this box if you are starting a new business that requires an EIN. If you check this box, enter the type of business being started. **Do not** apply if you already have an EIN and are only adding another place of business.

Hired employees. Check this box if the existing business is requesting an EIN because it has hired or is hiring employees and is therefore required to file employment tax returns. **Do not** apply if you already have an EIN and are only hiring employees. For information on the applicable employment taxes for family members, see **Circular E**, Employer's Tax Guide (Publication 15).

Created a pension plan. Check this box if you have created a pension plan and need this number for reporting purposes. Also, enter the type of plan created.

Note: *Check this box if you are applying for a trust EIN when a new pension plan is established.*

Banking purpose. Check this box if you are requesting an EIN for banking purposes only, and enter the banking purpose (for example, a bowling league for depositing dues or an investment club for dividend and interest reporting).

Changed type of organization. Check this box if the business is changing its type of organization, for example, if the business was a sole proprietorship and has been incorporated or has become a partnership. If you check this box, specify in the space provided the type of change made, for example, "from sole proprietorship to partnership."

Purchased going business. Check this box if you purchased an existing business. **Do not** use the former owner's EIN. **Do not** apply for a new EIN if you already have one. Use your own EIN.

Created a trust. Check this box if you created a trust, and enter the type of trust created. For example, indicate if the trust is a nonexempt charitable trust or a split-interest trust.

Note: *Do not check this box if you are applying for a trust EIN when a new pension plan is established. Check "Created a pension plan."*

Exception. Do **not** file this form for certain grantor-type trusts. The trustee does not need an EIN for the trust if the trustee furnishes the name and TIN of the grantor/owner and the address of the trust to all payors. See the Instructions for Form 1041 for more information.

Other (specify). Check this box if you are requesting an EIN for any reason other than those for which there are checkboxes, and enter the reason.

Line 10. If you are starting a new business, enter the starting date of the business. If the business you acquired is already operating, enter the date you acquired the business. Trusts should enter the date the trust was legally created. Estates should enter the date of death of the decedent whose name appears on line 1 or the date when the estate was legally funded.

Line 11. Enter the last month of your accounting year or tax year. An accounting or tax year is usually 12 consecutive months, either a calendar year or a fiscal year (including a period of 52 or 53 weeks). A calendar year is 12 consecutive months ending on December 31. A fiscal year is either 12 consecutive months ending on the last day of any month other than December or a 52-53 week year. For more information on accounting periods, see **Pub. 538**, Accounting Periods and Methods.

Individuals. Your tax year generally will be a calendar year.

Partnerships. Partnerships generally must adopt one of the following tax years:
● The tax year of the majority of its partners,
● The tax year common to all of its principal partners,
● The tax year that results in the least aggregate deferral of income, or
● In certain cases, some other tax year.
See the **Instructions for Form 1065**, U.S. Partnership Return of Income, for more information.

REMIC. REMICs must have a calendar year as their tax year.

Personal service corporations. A personal service corporation generally must adopt a calendar year unless:
● It can establish a business purpose for having a different tax year, or
● It elects under section 444 to have a tax year other than a calendar year.

Trusts. Generally, a trust must adopt a calendar year except for the following:
● Tax-exempt trusts,
● Charitable trusts, and
● Grantor-owned trusts.

Line 12. If the business has or will have employees, enter the date on which the business began or will begin to pay wages. If the business does not plan to have employees, enter N/A.

Withholding agent. Enter the date you began or will begin to pay income to a nonresident alien. This also applies to individuals who are required to file Form 1042 to report alimony paid to a nonresident alien.

Line 13. For a definition of agricultural labor (farmwork), see **Circular A**, Agricultural Employer's Tax Guide (Publication 51).

Line 14. Generally, enter the exact type of business being operated (for example, advertising agency, farm, food or beverage establishment, labor union, real estate agency, steam laundry, rental of coin-operated vending machine, or investment club). Also state if the business will involve the sale or distribution of alcoholic beverages.

Governmental. Enter the type of organization (state, county, school district, municipality, etc.).

Nonprofit organization (other than governmental). Enter whether organized for religious, educational, or humane purposes, and the principal activity (for example, religious organization—hospital, charitable).

Mining and quarrying. Specify the process and the principal product (for example, mining bituminous coal, contract drilling for oil, or quarrying dimension stone).

Contract construction. Specify whether general contracting or special trade contracting. Also, show the type of work normally performed (for example, general contractor for residential buildings or electrical subcontractor).

Food or beverage establishments. Specify the type of establishment and state whether you employ workers who receive tips (for example, lounge—yes).

Trade. Specify the type of sales and the principal line of goods sold (for example, wholesale dairy products, manufacturer's representative for mining machinery, or retail hardware).

Manufacturing. Specify the type of establishment operated (for example, sawmill or vegetable cannery).

Signature. The application must be signed by (a) the individual, if the applicant is an individual, (b) the president, vice president, or other principal officer, if the applicant is a corporation, (c) a responsible and duly authorized member or officer having knowledge of its affairs, if the applicant is a partnership or other unincorporated organization, or (d) the fiduciary, if the applicant is a trust or an estate.

How To Get Forms and Publications

Phone. You can order forms, instructions, and publications by phone. Just call 1-800-TAX-FORM (1-800-829-3676). You should receive your order or notification of its status within 7 to 15 workdays.

Personal computer. With your personal computer and modem, you can get the forms and information you need using:
● IRS's Internet Web Site at **www.irs.ustreas.gov**
● Telnet at **iris.irs.ustreas.gov**
● File Transfer Protocol at **ftp.irs.ustreas.gov**

You can also dial direct (by modem) to the Internal Revenue Information Services (IRIS) at 703-321-8020. IRIS is an on-line information service on FedWorld.

For small businesses, return preparers, or others who may frequently need tax forms or publications, a CD-ROM containing over 2,000 tax products (including many prior year forms) can be purchased from the Government Printing Office.

CD-ROM. To order the CD-ROM call the Superintendent of Documents at 202-512-1800 or connect to **www.access.gpo.gov/su_docs**

Privacy Act and Paperwork Reduction Act Notice. We ask for the information on this form to carry out the Internal Revenue laws of the United States. We need it to comply with section 6109 and the regulations thereunder which generally require the inclusion of an employer identification number (EIN) on certain returns, statements, or other documents filed with the Internal Revenue Service. Information on this form may be used to determine which Federal tax returns you are required to file and to provide you with related forms and publications. We disclose this form to the Social Security Administration for their use in determining compliance with applicable laws. We will be unable to issue an EIN to you unless you provide all of the requested information which applies to your entity.

You are not required to provide the information requested on a form that is subject to the Paperwork Reduction Act unless the form displays a valid OMB control number. Books or records relating to a form or its instructions must be retained as long as their contents may become material in the administration of any Internal Revenue law. Generally, tax returns and return information are confidential, as required by section 6103.

The time needed to complete and file this form will vary depending on individual circumstances. The estimated average time is:

Recordkeeping	7 min.
Learning about the law or the form	19 min.
Preparing the form	45 min.
Copying, assembling, and sending the form to the IRS . .	20 min.

If you have comments concerning the accuracy of these time estimates or suggestions for making this form simpler, we would be happy to hear from you. You can write to the Tax Forms Committee, Western Area Distribution Center, Rancho Cordova, CA 95743-0001. **Do not** send this form to this address. Instead, see **Where To Apply** on page 2.

Form W-4 (2000)

Purpose. Complete Form W-4 so your employer can withhold the correct Federal income tax from your pay. Because your tax situation may change, you may want to refigure your withholding each year.

Exemption from withholding. *If you are exempt, complete only lines 1, 2, 3, 4, and 7, and sign the form to validate it.* Your exemption for 2000 expires February 16, 2001.

Note: *You cannot claim exemption from withholding if (1) your income exceeds $700 and includes unearned income (e.g., interest and dividends) and (2) another person can claim you as a dependent on their tax return.*

Basic instructions. If you are not exempt, complete the Personal Allowances Worksheet. The worksheets on page 2 adjust your withholding allowances based on itemized deductions, adjustments to income, or two-earner/two-job situations. Complete all worksheets that apply. They will help you figure the number of withholding allowances you are entitled to claim. However, you may claim fewer allowances.

New—Child tax and higher education credits. For details on adjusting withholding for these and other credits, see **Pub. 919,** Is My Withholding Correct for 2000?

Head of household. Generally, you may claim head of household filing status on your tax return only if you are unmarried and pay more than 50% of the costs of keeping up a home for yourself and your dependent(s) or other qualifying individuals.

Nonwage income. If you have a large amount of nonwage income, such as interest or dividends, you should consider making estimated tax payments using Form 1040-ES. Otherwise, you may owe additional tax.

Two earners/two jobs. If you have a working spouse or more than one job, figure the total number of allowances you are entitled to claim on all jobs using worksheets from only one W-4. Your withholding will usually be most accurate when all allowances are claimed on the W-4 filed for the highest paying job and zero allowances are claimed for the others.

Check your withholding. After your W-4 takes effect, use Pub. 919 to see how the dollar amount you are having withheld compares to your estimated total annual tax. Get Pub. 919 especially if you used the Two-Earner/Two-Job Worksheet and your earnings exceed $150,000 (Single) or $200,000 (Married). To order Pub. 919, call 1-800-829-3676. Check your telephone directory for the IRS assistance number for further help.

Sign this form. Form W-4 is not valid unless you sign it.

Personal Allowances Worksheet

A Enter "1" for **yourself** if no one else can claim you as a dependent . . . . **A** _____

B Enter "1" if:
- You are single and have only one job; or
- You are married, have only one job, and your spouse does not work; or
- Your wages from a second job or your spouse's wages (or the total of both) are $1,000 or less.

. . **B** __1__

C Enter "1" for your **spouse.** But, you may choose to enter -0- if you are married and have either a working spouse or more than one job. (This may help you avoid having too little tax withheld.) . . . . **C** _____

D Enter number of **dependents** (other than your spouse or yourself) you will claim on your tax return . . . . **D** _____

E Enter "1" if you will file as **head of household** on your tax return (see conditions under **Head of household** above) . **E** _____

F Enter "1" if you have at least $1,500 of **child or dependent care expenses** for which you plan to claim a credit . . **F** _____

G **New—Child Tax Credit:** • If your total income will be between $16,500 and $47,000 ($21,000 and $60,000 if married), enter "1" for each eligible child. • If your total income will be between $47,000 and $80,000 ($60,000 and $115,000 if married), enter "1" if you have two or three eligible children, or enter "2" if you have four or more . . . . **G** __1__

H Add lines A through G and enter total here. **Note:** This amount may be different from the number of exemptions you claim on your return. ▶ **H** _____

| For accuracy, complete all worksheets that apply. | • If you plan to **itemize or claim adjustments to income** and want to reduce your withholding, see the Deductions and Adjustments Worksheet on page 2.
• If you are **single,** have **more than one job,** and your combined earnings from all jobs exceed $32,000 OR if you are **married** and have a **working spouse or more than one job,** and the combined earnings from all jobs exceed $55,000, see the Two-Earner/Two-Job Worksheet on page 2 to avoid having too little tax withheld.
• If **neither** of the above situations applies, **stop here** and enter the number from line H on line 5 of Form W-4 below. |

- - - - - - - - **Cut here and give the certificate to your employer. Keep the top part for your records.** - - - - - - - -

Form **W-4** Department of the Treasury Internal Revenue Service	**Employee's Withholding Allowance Certificate** ▶ **For Privacy Act and Paperwork Reduction Act Notice, see page 2.**	OMB No. 1545-0010 2000

1 Type or print your first name and middle initial John A.	Last name Smith	2 Your social security number 123 45 6789

Home address (number and street or rural route) 567 Wharf Blvd.	3 ☒ Single ☐ Married ☐ Married, but withhold at higher Single rate. **Note:** *If married, but legally separated, or spouse is a nonresident alien, check the Single box.*
City or town, state, and ZIP code Austin, TX 78700	4 If your last name differs from that on your social security card, check here and call 1-800-772-1213 for a new card . . . . . ▶ ☐

5 Total number of allowances you are claiming (from line H above or from the worksheets on page 2 if they apply) . **5** | 1

6 Additional amount, if any, you want withheld from each paycheck . . . . **6** $ | 0

7 I claim exemption from withholding for 1998, and I certify that I meet **BOTH** of the following conditions for exemption:
- Last year I had a right to a refund of **ALL** Federal income tax withheld because I had **NO** tax liability **AND**
- This year I expect a refund of **ALL** Federal income tax withheld because I expect to have **NO** tax liability.

If you meet both conditions, enter "EXEMPT" here . . . . ▶ **7**

Under penalties of perjury, I certify that I am entitled to the number of withholding allowances claimed on this certificate or entitled to claim exempt status.

Employee's signature ▶ *John A. Smith*   Date ▶ *June 6* , *2000*

8 Employer's name and address (Employer: Complete 8 and 10 only if sending to the IRS)	9 Office code (optional)	10 Employer identification number

Cat. No. 10220Q

SAMPLE FORM 8109-B: FEDERAL TAX DEPOSIT COUPONS

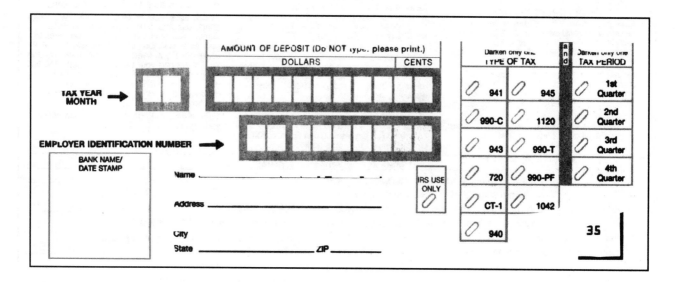

SAMPLE FORM 1040-ES: ESTIMATED TAX PAYMENT VOUCHER

Cat. No. 61900V

OMB No. 1545-0087

Form 1040-ES (OCR)
Department of the Treasury
Internal Revenue Service

2000 Estimated Tax

Payment
Voucher **4**

Calendar year—
Due Jan. 15, 2000

Cross out any errors and print the correct information. Get **Form 8822** to report a new address (see instructions). For Paperwork Reduction Act Notice, see instructions.

0746497

07 234-56-7890 DC 9712

234-56-7890 DC WARD 30 0 9712 430 07

JOHN DOE
123 ANYWHERE STREET
ABILENE, TX 72123

ABILENE, TX 72123-0001

|.||.||I||.....||.||..||.|..|.|||.|..|||..||...||...||..|.|.|

Enter the amount of your payment. File this voucher only if you are making a payment of **estimated** tax.	$	▶ Make your check or money order payable to "**Internal Revenue Service.**" ▶ Write your social security number and "1997 Form 1040-ES" on your payment. ▶ Send your payment and payment voucher to the address above. ▶ Do not send cash. Do not staple your payment to the voucher.

SAMPLE FORM W-2: WAGE AND TAX STATEMENT

a Control number	22222	Void ☐	For Official Use Only ▶ OMB No. 1545-0008		

b Employer's identification number 59-123456			**1** Wages, tips, other compensation 25,650.00	**2** Federal income tax withheld 5,050.00

c Employer's name, address, and ZIP code	**3** Social security wages 25,650.00	**4** Social security tax withheld 1,590.30

Doe Company

123 Main Street

Abilene, TX 75123

5 Medicare wages and tips	**6** Medicare tax withheld
25,650.00	371.93
7 Social security tips 0	**8** Allocated tips 0

d Employee's social security number 123-45-6789	**9** Advance EIC payment 0	**10** Dependent care benefits 0

e Employee's name (first, middle initial, last)	**11** Nonqualified plans 0	**12** Benefits included in box 1 0

John A. Smith

567 Wharf Boulevard

Abilene, TX 75123

13 See Instrs. for box 13	**14** Other

15 Statutory employee ☐	Deceased ☐	Pension plan ☐	Legal rep. ☐	Hshld. emp. ☐	Subtotal ☐	Deferred compensation ☐

f Employee's address and ZIP code

16 State	Employer's state I.D. No.	17 State wages, tips, etc.	18 State income tax	19 Locality name	20 Local wages, tips, etc.	21 Local income tax

Cat. No. 10134D

Department of the Treasury—Internal Revenue Service

Form **W-2** **Wage and Tax Statement** **2000**

For Paperwork Reduction Act Notice, see separate instructions.

Copy A For Social Security Administration

SAMPLE FORMS 1099 AND 1096: MISCELLANEOUS INCOME

9595 ☐ VOID ☐ CORRECTED

PAYER'S name, street address, city, state, and ZIP code		**1** Rents $	OMB No. 1545-0115	**Miscellaneous Income**
Doe Company 123 Main Street Abilene, TX 75123		**2** Royalties $	**2000**	
		3 Other income $	Form **1099-MISC**	
PAYER'S Federal identification number 59-123456	RECIPIENT'S identification number 345-67-8900	**4** Federal income tax withheld $	**5** Fishing boat proceeds $	**Copy A** **For Internal Revenue Service Center**
RECIPIENT'S name Roger Tulliver		**6** Medical and health care payments $	**7** Nonemployee compensation $ 21,000	**File with Form 1096.**
Street address (including apt. no.) 1342 Crockett Avenue		**8** Substitute payments in lieu of dividends or interest $	**9** Payer made direct sales of $5,000 or more of consumer products to a buyer (recipient) for resale ▶ ☐	For Paperwork Reduction Act Notice and instructions for completing this form, see **Instructions for Forms 1099, 1098, 5498, and W-2G.**
City, state, and ZIP code Abilene, TX 75123		**10** Crop insurance proceeds $	**11** State income tax withheld $ 00.00	
Account number (optional)	2nd TIN Not. ☐	**12** State/Payer's state number		

Form **1099-MISC** Cat. No. 14425J Department of the Treasury - Internal Revenue Service

Do NOT Cut or Separate Forms on This Page

DO NOT STAPLE **6969**

Form **1096** Department of the Treasury Internal Revenue Service	**Annual Summary and Transmittal of U.S. Information Returns**		OMB No. 1545-0108 **2000**

ATTACH IRS LABEL HERE

FILER'S name

Doe Company

Street address (including room or suite number)

123 Main Street

City, state, and ZIP code
Abilene, TX 75123

If you are not using a preprinted label, enter in box 1 or 2 below the identification number you used as the filer on the information returns being transmitted. Do not fill in both boxes 1 and 2.	Name of person to contact if the IRS needs more information John Doe Telephone number (518) 5550000	**For Official Use Only** ☐☐☐☐☐☐☐ ☐☐

1 Employer identification number 59-123456	**2** Social security number	**3** Total number of forms 3	**4** Federal income tax withheld $ 0	**5** Total amount reported with this Form 1096 $ $63,000

Enter an "X" in only one box below to indicate the type of form being filed. If this is your FINAL return, enter an "X" here . . ▶ ☒

W-2G 32	1098 81	1099-A 80	1099-B 79	1099-C 85	1099-DIV 91	1099-G 86	1099-INT 92	1099-MISC 95	1099-OID 96	1099-PATR 97	1099-R 98	1099-S 75	5498 28
☐	☐	☐	☐	☐	☐	☐	☐	☒	☐	☐	☐	☐	☐

PAYING TEXAS TAXES 17

SALES AND USE TAX

If you will be selling or renting goods or services at retail, you must collect Texas Sales and Use Tax. Some services such as doctors and lawyers fees and newspaper advertising are not taxed, but most others are. If you have any doubt, check with the Comptroller of Public Accounts.

First, you must obtain a sales and tax permit form the Comptroller. A sample filled-in copy of the permit application form is at the end of this chapter and a blank form is in the appendix. You can obtain this and many other Texas tax forms from the Texas Comptroller of Public Accounts, Post Office Box 13528, Capitol Station, Austin, Texas 78711-3528 or from their web site: http://www.window.texas.gov/

Until you have shown adequate history of payment, you must provide the Comptroller adequate security (usually a bond) for the payment of state, local sales, and use taxes. You can obtain bond information from the above address or web site. If you sell wholesale to a retailer and do not collect sales tax, you must obtain a resale certificate from the retailer. If someone claims to be exempt from sales tax you must have them complete a tax exemption certificate. Sample copies of these forms are at the end of this chapter and blank forms are included in the appendix.

Sale and use taxes are due each month on the 20th of the following month unless taxes are prepaid quarterly. If the tax liability is less than $500 per month, payment is due quarterly.

Returns are due monthly, quarterly, or annually depending on the amount of tax due ($1500 or more per quarter-monthly; less than $1500 per quarter-quarterly; less than $1000 per year-annually). An instruction sheet on preparing the return and sample filled-in form are at the end of this chapter.

Most cities and towns levy local sales and use taxes which must be collected by the retailer and paid to the Comptroller along with the state tax. The Comptroller pays the city its share. No additional permits are required.

UNEMPLOYMENT COMPENSATION TAXES

Unemployment compensation contributions are payable to the Texas Workforce Commission (TWC). You are not liable for contributions to the Unemployment Compensation Fund until you have had an employee work a part of a day in any 20 calender weeks or paid $1500 in wages in a quarter. But once you reach that point you are liable for all back contributions. The "tax" is based on wages paid and claims paid to former employees, and is paid on the first $9,000 of wages for each employee each year. You can obtain an information packet from the TWC by calling 512-463-2826 or 800-832-6279. Some larger cities have local TWC offices.

You will be sent quarterly returns to complete. Filled-in examples are on the following pages.

Some businesses try to keep taxes low by having all work done by independent contractors instead of employees. However, if the TWC determines the person is really an employee for unemployment compensation purposes, the business can be subject to back taxes, interest, and penalties.

Tangible Property Taxes

There is a tax on all tangible personal property used in a business and on inventory. It includes such things as dishes, machinery, furniture, tools, signs, carpeting, appliances, laboratory equipment, and just about everything else. It is imposed by counties, cities, and school districts. Intangible personal property such as promissory notes, stocks, bonds, licenses, and accounts receivable are not taxed. Farm and ranch implements and products of farming, including livestock, are not taxed.

Property is taxed on its value as of January 1st. A tax bill is sent out in October, the same time as the real property tax bill.

A tax notice is sent out each year by the county tax accessor letting taxpayers know the assessed value of their property and the tax rate that will apply. If you feel there is an error in the valuation of your property, you may discuss it with an appraiser or file a petition for a review.

It is not unusual to see the assessed value of personal property remain the same or even go up over the years while the actual value depreciates greatly. Filing a petition protesting the assessment occasionally helps, but for the small amount of money involved it is usually not worth it. For the property assessors this is the easiest way to collect taxes which are not due.

Corporate Franchise Tax

Each Texas corporation and each corporation doing business in Texas (including limited liability companies) must pay franchise taxes. This tax is paid on the greater of the corporation's net taxable capital or net taxable earned in the state of Texas, and is due annually. For a new corporation, the tax and return is due ninety days after the first anniversary of incorporation. Thereafter, the tax and return is due on May 15th of each year. An accountant or other tax professional should be consulted for payment of franchise taxes and preparation of the franchise tax return.

EXCISE TAXES

The following are a sample of the activities or products on which Texas imposes taxes.

- ☛ Cigarettes, cigars, and tobacco products
- ☛ Mixed alcoholic beverages
- ☛ Oil and gas production
- ☛ Utility companies
- ☛ Motor fuels
- ☛ Manufactured housing
- ☛ Cement production

The Comptroller of Public Accounts has information on all such taxes.

TEXAS APPLICATION FOR SALES TAX PERMIT, USE TAX PERMIT, AND/OR TELECOMMUNICATIONS INFRASTRUCTURE FUND ASSESSMENT

JOHN SHARP • COMPTROLLER OF PUBLIC ACCOUNTS

GENERAL INSTRUCTIONS

WHO MUST SUBMIT THIS APPLICATION - You must submit this application if:

- you are an individual, partnership, corporation, or organization engaged in business in Texas; AND
- you are selling tangible personal property or providing taxable services in Texas to customers in Texas; and/or
- you acquire tangible personal property or taxable services from out-of-state suppliers that do not hold a Texas permit;

OR

- you sell or resell telecommunications services, such as electronic transmission of tax returns or other information, the provision of phone service for a charge to tenants or hotel guests, fax services, or paging services, or you are telecommunications utility or a mobile service provider collecting and paying telecommunications receipts under Texas Tax Code, Chapter 151.

DEFINITIONS -

- **SALES TAX PERMIT**: This permit is required for every individual, partnership, corporation, or organization who makes sales, leases or rentals of taxable items in Texas. Permits are issued without charge.

- **SALES TAX BOND:** You may need to post a bond or other security for this permit. To determine the amount of bond or security required, complete a "Texas Sales and Use Tax-Bond-Security Information," Form 01-707. Submit this application and Form 01-707 to avoid delay in receiving your permit.

- **USE TAX PERMIT:** This permit is required for every individual, partnership, corporation, or organization who makes sales, leases or rentals of taxable items in Texas but does NOT have a place of business in Texas, AND for out-of-state contractors improving real property in Texas with tangible personal property purchased outside of Texas.

- **ENGAGED IN BUSINESS:** You are engaged in business in Texas if you or your independent salespersons make sales, leases or rentals, or take orders for tangible personal property, or deliver tangible personal property or perform taxable services; or have lease (personal) property, a warehouse or other location in Texas; or benefit from a location in Texas of authorized installations, servicing or repairing facilities; or allow a franchisee or licensee to operate under your trade name if they are required to collect Texas tax.

- **PLACE OF BUSINESS OR BUSINESS LOCATION:** Any store, office, or location where you receive orders for tangible personal property or taxable services or make sales, leases or rentals of tangible personal property or taxable services at least three times or more in a calender year. *(See Rule 3.286: State Sales and Use Tax Seller's and Purchaser's Responsibilities.)*

NOTE: If you have been making sales and have not applied for a permit, you will need to file returns and pay tax, plus applicable penalty and interest, for the period of time that you have been in business.

FOR ASSISTANCE - If you have any questions about this application or any other telecommunications infrastructure fund or sales tax-related matter, contact your nearest Texas State Comptroller's Office or call us toll free at 1-800-252-5555. The local number in Austin is 512/463-4600. The Tax Help E-mail Address is: tax.help@cpa.state.tx.us

AMERICANS WITH DISABILITIES ACT - In compliance with the Americans with Disabilities Act, this document may be requested in alternative formats by calling toll-free 1-800-252-5555. From a Telecommunications Device for the Deaf (TDD), our hearing impaired taxpayers may call toll-free 1-800-248-4099, or they may call via 1-800-RELAY-TX. The Austin TDD number is 512/463-4621.

FEDERAL PRIVACY ACT - Disclosure of your social security number is required and will be used for tax administration and identification of any individual affected by the law. 42 U.S.C. sec. 405(c)(2)(C)(i).

If you are hiring one or more employees, please contact the Texas Workforce Commission (512/463-2699) or your local TWC tax office to determine if you are liable for payroll taxes under the Texas Unemployment Compensation Act.

Complete this application and mail to: COMPTROLLER OF PUBLIC ACCOUNTS
111 E. 17th Street
Austin, TX 78774-0100

AP-201-1 (2-98)

SPECIFIC INSTRUCTIONS

Item 32 - You WILL be required to report interest earned on sales tax IF:
- you make retail sales of taxable items on an installment purchase plan or deferred payment plan; **AND**
- you charge interest on the entire balance, including sales tax, on the sale of taxable items made on installment purchases or deferred payment plans; **AND**
- you do your own financing on some accounts on which interest is charge; **AND**
- you include installment payments which were received during a reporting period in "TOTAL SALES" on your sales tax return for that period (i.e., you keep your records on a cash basis of accounting).

NOTE: *If any one of the statements above does **NOT** apply to your business, then you will **NOT** be required to report interest earned on sales tax.*

Below is a listing of taxes and fees collected by the Comptroller of Public Accounts. If you are responsible for reporting or paying one of the listed taxes or fees, and you **DO NOT HAVE A PERMIT OR AN ACCOUNT WITH US FOR THIS PURPOSE**, please obtain the proper application by calling toll-free 1-800-252-5555, or by visiting your local Enforcement office.

TAX TYPE(S)

Amusement Tax - If you engage in any business dealing with coin operated machines OR engage in business to own or operate coin-operated machines exclusively on premises occupied by and in connection with the business, you must complete **Form AP-146** or **Form AP-147**.

Automotive Oil Sales Fee - If you manufacture and sell automotive oil in Texas; or you import or cause automotive oil to be imported into Texas for sale, use, or consumption; or you sell more than 25,000 gallons of automotive oil annually and you own warehouse or distribution center located in Texas, you must complete **Form AP-161**.

Battery Sales Fee - If you sell or offer to sell new or used lead acid batteries, you must complete **Form AP-160**.

Cement Production Tax - If you manufacture or produce cement in Texas, or you import cement into Texas and you distribute or sell cement in intrastate commerce or use the cement in Texas, you must complete **Form AP-171**.

Cigarette, Cigar and/or Tobacco Products Tax - If you wholesale, distribute, store, or make retail sales of cigarettes, cigars, and/or tobacco products, you must complete **Form AP-175** or **Form AP-193**.

Coastal Protection Fee - If you transfer crude oil and condensate from or to vessels at a marine terminal located in Texas, you must complete **Form AP-134**.

Direct Payment Permit - If you annually purchase at least $800,000 worth of taxable items for your own use and not for resale, you must complete **Form AP-101** to qualify for the permit.

Franchise Tax - If you are a non-Texas corporation or a non-Texas limited liability company without a certificate of authority, you must complete **Form AP-114**.

Fuels Tax - If you are required to be licensed under Texas Fuels Tax Law for the type and class permit required, you must complete **Form AP-133**.

Gross Receipts Tax - If you provide certain services on oil and gas wells OR are a utility company located in an incorporated city or town having a population of more than 1.000 according to the most recent federal census and intend to do business in Texas, you must complete **Form AP-110**.

Hotel Occupancy Tax - If you provide sleeping accommodations to the public for a cost of $2 or more per day, you must complete **Form AP-102**.

International Fuel Tax Agreement (FTA) - If you operate qualified motor vehicles which require you to be licensed under the International Fuel Tax Agreement, you must complete **Form AP-118**.

Maquiladora Export Permit - If you are a maquiladora enterprise and wish to make tax-free purchases in Texas for export to Mexico, you must complete **Form AP-153**, to receive the permit.

Motor Vehicle Seller-Financed Sales Tax - If you finance sales of motor vehicles and collect Motor Vehicle Sales Tax in periodic payments, you must complete **Form AP-169**.

Motor Vehicle Gross Rental Tax - If you rent motor vehicles in Texas, you must complete **Form AP-143**.

Petroleum Products Delivery Fee - If you are required to be licensed under Texas Water Code, sec. 26.3574, you must complete **Form AP-154**.

Sales and Use Tax - If you engage in business in Texas; AND you sell or lease tangible personal property or provide taxable services in Texas to customers in Texas; and/or you acquire tangible personal property or taxable services form out-of-state suppliers that do not hold a Texas Sales or Use Tax permit, you must complete **Form AP-201**.

Sulphur Production Tax - If you own, control, manage, lease, or operate a sulphur mine, well, or shaft, or produce sulphur by an method, system, or manner, you must complete **Form AP-171**.

Texas Customs Broker License - If you had been licensed by the United States Customs Service AND want to issue export certificates, you must complete **Form AP-168**.

Telecommunications Infrastructure Fund - If you are a telecommunications utility company or a mobile service provider who collects and pays taxes on telecommunications receipts under Texas Tax Code, Chapter 151, you must complete **Form AP-201**.

TEXAS APPLICATION FOR SALES TAX PERMIT,
USE TAX PERMIT AND/OR
TELECOMMUNICATIONS INFRASTRUCTURE FUND ASSESSMENT SET-UP

- TYPE OR PRINT
- Do NOT write in shaded areas.   Page 1

ORGANIZATION TYPE

1. Business organization type

[X] Individual - Sole owner   [ ] Registered limited liability partnership   [ ] Texas limited liability company   [ ] Non-Texas limited liability company
[ ] Estate   [ ] Texas profit corporation   [ ] Non-Texas profit corporation   [ ] Professional corporation
[ ] General partnership   [ ] Texas nonprofit corporation   [ ] Non-Texas nonprofit corporation   [ ] Professional association
[ ] Limited partnership   [ ] Trust *(Please submit a copy of the trust agreement with this application)*
[ ] Association *(explain)* _____
[ ] Financial institution *(explain)* _____
[ ] Government *(explain)* _____

TAXPAYER IDENTIFICATION

2. Taxpayer number for reporting any Texas tax OR
   Texas identification number if you now have or have ever had one ....

3. Social security number (SSN) if you are an individual-sole owner .... 2 400 - 20 - 1000

4. Federal employer's identification number (FEIN) assigned by the Internal Revenue Service .... 1 86 - 75309

5. [ ] Check here if you do not have a SSN or FEIN.   3

6. Legal name of entity *(Sole owner, partnership, corporation, or other name)*

   Hank Dillon

   If you have registered a DBA (Doing Business As) with either the Texas Secretary of State or your local county clerk, enter below and attach documentation. If not, please leave blank.

   Chili Unlimited

BUSINESS TYPE

7. Principal type of business

[ ] Agriculture   [ ] Transportation   [ ] Retail Trade   [ ] Real Estate   [ ] Mining   [ ] Communications *(See Item 39)*
[ ] Finance   [ ] Services   [ ] Construction   [ ] Utilities   [ ] Insurance   [ ] Public Administration
[X] Manufacturing   [ ] Wholesale Trade   [ ] Other *(explain)* _____

8. Primary business activities and type of products or services to be sold   SIC _____

   Sales, manufacture and packaging of product; chili mix

TAXPAYER INFORMATION

9. Mailing address
   Street number, P.O. Box, or rural route and box number

   1818 Stockyard Plaza

City	State/province	ZIP code	County (or country, if outside the U.S.)
Abilene	Texas	73000	817-555-3492

10. Name and daytime phone number of person to contact regarding day to day business operations

    Hank Dillon   ___/___-___

If you are a sole owner, skip to Item 16.

11. If the business is a Texas profit corporation, nonprofit corporation, professional corporation, or limited liability company, enter the charter number and date. ....
    Charter number _____   Month ___ Day ___ Year ___

12. If the business is a non-Texas profit corporation, nonprofit corporation, professional corporation, or limited liability company, enter the state or country of incorporation, charter number and date, Texas Certificate of Authority number and date.

State/country of inc.	Charter number	Month	Day	Year	Texas Certificate of Authority number	Month	Day	Year

13. If the business is a corporation, have you been involved in a merger within the last seven years? .. [ ] YES [ ] NO   *If "YES," attach a detailed explanation.*

14. If the business is a limited partnership or registered limited liability partnership, enter the home state and registered identification number. ....
    State _____   Number _____

15. General partners, principal members/officers, managing directors or managers *(Attach additional sheets, if necessary.)*

Name	Title	Phone (Area code and number)
		___/___-___

Address	City	State	ZIP code

SSN or FEIN _____   Percent of ownership _____ %   County (or country, if outside the U.S.) _____

Position held   [ ] Partner   [ ] Officer   [ ] Director   [ ] Corporate Stockholder   [ ] Record keeper

Name	Title	Phone (Area code and number)
		___/___-___

Address	City	State	ZIP code

SSN or FEIN _____   Percent of ownership _____ %   County (or country, if outside the U.S.) _____

Position held   [ ] Partner   [ ] Officer   [ ] Director   [ ] Corporate Stockholder   [ ] Record keeper

Comptroller of Public Accounts FORM AP-201-4 (2-98)

TEXAS APPLICATION FOR SALES TAX PERMIT,
USE TAX PERMIT AND/OR
TELECOMMUNICATIONS INFRASTRUCTURE FUND ASSESSMENT SET-UP

• TYPE OR PRINT
• Do NOT write in shaded areas.   Page 2

16. Legal name of entity *(Same as Item 6)*	SSN or FEIN
Hank Dillon	400-20-1000

17. Is your business located outside Texas? .... ☐ YES ☒ NO

    If "YES," **skip to Item 27.**

18. Is your business located inside the boundaries of an incorporated city? .... ☒ YES ☐ NO

    If "YES," indicate city *(You may need to contact your local city/county planning offices for assistance in determining the city taxing jurisdiction for your business location address entered in Item 19.)*   Abilene

19. Business location name and address

    Business location name

    Chili Unlimited

Street and number *(Do not use P.O. Box.)*	City	State	ZIP code	County
1818 Stockyard Plaza	Abilene	TX	73000	Taylor

Physical location *(If business location address is a rural route and box number, provide directions)*	Business location phone
downtown Abilene; in a strip mall/plaza	817 / 555 - 3492

20. Name of person we can contact about this location

    Hank Dillon

Answer the questions below about the above location by checking "YES" or "NO."   X ☐ O/L

21. Is your business located inside a metropolitan transit authority/city transit department (MTA/CTD)? .... ☒ YES ☐ NO

22. Is your business located inside a special purpose district (SPD)? .... ☒ YES ☐ NO

23. Will you deliver in your own vehicles, provide taxable services, or have sales/service representatives going from this location to customers located in:

    another city? .... ☒ YES ☐ NO

    another county? .... ☒ YES ☐ NO

    another MTA/CTD? .... ☒ YES ☐ NO

    another SPD? .... ☒ YES ☐ NO

24. Will you ship from this location to other customers via common carrier? .... ☒ YES ☐ NO

25. Are you a seller with no established place of business selling at a temporary location (trade show, event, or door to door)? .... ☐ YES ☒ NO

26. Will you have out-of-state suppliers shipping taxable items directly to customers' locations in Texas? .... ☒ YES ☐ NO

27. Check the box that best represents your anticipated quarterly state sales tax collections: ☐ less than $250   ☒ $250-$1,500   ☐ greater than $1,500

28. Enter the date of the first business operation in the above location that is subject to sales or use tax, or the date you plan to start such business operation. ....   month day year   09-20-2000

29. Is your business operated all year? .... ☒ YES ☐ NO

    If "NO," list the months you will operate. _____

30. Will you sell any type of alcoholic beverages? .... ☐ YES ☒ NO

    If "YES," indicate the type of permit you will hold: .... ☐ mixed beverage   ☐ beer and wine

31. Brief description of your business activities *for this location*, and the primary products or services to be sold.   SIC _____

    Mixture of chili product, packaging and distribution and sales

32. Will you be required to report interest earned on sales tax *(See "Specific Instructions" on page 2)*? .... ☐ YES ☒ NO

33. Are you located out of state with representation in Texas? .... ☐ YES ☒ NO

    If "YES," complete Item 34. If "NO," skip to Item 35.

34. List names and addresses of all representatives, agents, salespersons, canvassers, or solicitors in Texas.

    (Attach additional sheets, if necessary.)

    Name *(First, middle initial, last)*

Street	City	State	ZIP code
			-

35. Location of all distribution points, warehouses, or offices in Texas *(Attach additional sheets, if necessary.)*

Street	City	State	ZIP code
1818 Stockyard Plaza	Abilene	TX	73000 -
		TX	-

178

TEXAS APPLICATION FOR SALES TAX PERMIT,
USE TAX PERMIT AND/OR
TELECOMMUNICATIONS INFRASTRUCTURE FUND ASSESSMENT SET-UP

• *TYPE OR PRINT*
• *Do NOT write in shaded areas.*   Page 3

---

36. Legal name of entity *(Same as Item 6)*

Hank Dillon

SSN or FEIN
400-20-1000

SALES/USE TAX

37. Name and daytime phone number of the person primarily responsible for filing sales/use tax returns

Name: Hank Dillon

Phone: 817 / 555 - 3492

For Comptroller Use Only
Tax type/reason
☐ ■ 00991   ■ 2.0
Reference no.
■

38. Address where you want to receive sales/use tax correspondence *(if different from Item 9)*
Street and number, P.O. Box, or rural route and box number

City | State/province | ZIP code | County (or country, if outside the U.S.)

TIF ASSESSMENT

39. Do you receive compensation for providing telecommunication services? .... ☐ YES   ☒ NO

If "YES," you are responsible for the Telecommunications Infrastructure Fund (TIF) assessment and should complete Items 40-43.
If "NO," skip to Item 44.

40. Date of the first business operation that is subject to the Telecommunications Infrastructure Fund assessment in Texas or the date you plan to start such business operation. ....
month | day | year

41. Telecommunications provider type .... ☐ Telecommunications Utility   ☐ Commercial Mobile Service Provider

42. Name and daytime phone number of the person primarily responsible for filing Telecommunications Assessment reports.
Name *(First, middle initial, last)* | Phone *(Area code and number)*

43. Address where you want to receive Telecommunications Assessment reports *(if different from Item 9).*
Street and number, P.O. Box, or rural route number | City | State/province | ZIP code | County (or country, if outside U.S.)

PREVIOUS OWNER INFORMATION

If you purchased an existing business or business assets, complete Items 44-47.

44. Previous owner's trade name.

N/A

Previous owner's taxpayer number *(if available)*

45. Previous owner's legal name, address and phone number, if available.
Name | Phone *(Area code and number)*

Address *(Street and number)* | City | State | ZIP code

46. Check each of the following items you purchased.
☐ Inventory   ☐ Corporate stock   ☐ Equipment   ☐ Real estate   ☐ Other assets

47. Purchase price of this business or assets and the date of purchase.
Purchase price $ | Date of purchase
month | day | year

SIGNATURES

48. The sole owner, all general partners, corporation or organization president, vice-president, secretary or treasurer, managing director, or an authorized representative must sign. A representative must submit a written power of attorney. *(Attach additional sheets if necessary.)*

Date of signature(s)
month day year
0.9 2.0 20.0.0

I (We) declare that the information in this document and any attachments is true and correct to the best of my (our) knowledge and belief.

Type or print name and title of sole owner, partner, or officer: Hank Dillon
Drivers license number/state: 3456789 / TX
sign here ▶ *Hank Dillon*

Type or print name and title of partner or officer:
Drivers license number/state: /
sign here ▶

Type or print name and title of partner or officer:
Drivers license number/state: /
sign here ▶

YOUR PERMIT MUST BE PROMINENTLY DISPLAYED IN YOUR PLACE OF BUSINESS. THE INFORMATION ON YOUR PERMIT IS PUBLIC INFORMATION.

OPEN RECORDS NOTICE - Your name, address, and telephone number are public information under the Texas Open Records Act, Chapter 552, Government Code.

Field office or section number _____ Employee Name _____ USERID _____ Date _____

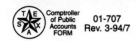

Do not write in the space above or the shaded areas

TEXAS SALES AND USE TAX BOND-SECURITY INFORMATION

1. Taxpayer Name *(Legal name of owner)*	2. Social Security No. or F.E.I. No.
Hank Dillon	400-20-1000

3. Business Trade Name	Business phone *(Area code and number)*
Chili Unlimited	817-555-3492

Location *(Street and number)*	City	State	ZIP Code
1818 Stockyard Plaza	Abilene	Texas	73000

ESTIMATED AMOUNT SUBJECT TO SALES AND USE TAX PER MONTH

4. 1st Qtr.	2nd Qtr.	3rd Qtr.	4th Qtr.	5. TOTAL ESTIMATED - 4 Qtrs.
6,250	6,250	6,250	6,250	25,000

5. Total Estimated - 4 Qtrs.	6. Divided by	7. Average monthly amount subject to tax (Item 5 ÷ Item 6
25,000	÷ 12	= 2,083

Comments

I CERTIFY THAT THE ABOVE STATEMENTS ARE CORRECT TO THE BEST OF MY KNOWLEDGE AND BELIEF.

sign here ▶ Taxpayer	Title	Date
Hank Dillon	owner	09/20/00

sign here ▶ E.O.	Field Office	Date

Instructions for Completing the Sales and Use Tax Bond-Security Information Worksheet

Purpose	This is a worksheet for use by the taxpayers and Comptroller personnel to determine whether or not bond/security will be required for a new tax payer. If bond is required, the tax payer will be notified.
	Taxpayers: send the completed worksheet along with the completed Sales and Use Tax Application, Form AP-100 or Form AP-157, to All Applications Section, Account Maintenance Division.
Items 1-3	Must exactly match the information on the Sales and Use Tax Application, Form AP-100 or Form AP-157.
Items 4-7	If purchasing a business, base estimates on prior owner's sales.
	For new businesses, base estimate on projected sales volume.
Signature	Taxpayer: The owner, partner, corporate president, corporate secretary or someone with power of attorney must sign the form. Preferably, the same person who signed the application signs the form.

TEXAS RESALE CERTIFICATE

Name of purchaser, film or agency	phone *(Area code and number)*
Hank Dillon	817-555-3492

Address *(Street & number, P.O. Box or Route number)*
1818 Stockyard Plaza

City, State, ZIP Code
Abilene, Texas 73000

Texas Sales or Use Tax Permit Number *(or out-of-state retailer's registration number or date applied for Texas Permit - must contain 11 digits if from a Texas permit)*

⌊12345678900⌋   *(Mexican retailer's must show their federal Taxpayers Registry (RFC) number on the certificate and give a copy of their Mexican registration form to the seller.)*

I, the purchaser named above, claim the right to make a non-taxable purchase for resale of the taxable items described below or on the attached order or invoice form:

Seller: **Abilene Restaurant Supply**

Street Address: **1729 Caine Drive**

City, State, ZIP code: **Abilene, Texas 73000**

Description of items to be purchased on the attached order or invoice:

aluminum foil, wrapping machines, paints, manila paper, etc.

Description of the type of business activity generally engaged in or type of items normally sold by the purchaser:

food production - packaging, distribution and sales of chili powder.

The taxable items described above, or on the attached order or invoice, will be resold, rented, or leased by me within the geographical limits of the United States of America, its territories and possessions, or within the geographical limits of the United Mexican States, in their present form or attached to other taxable items to be sold.

I understand that if I make any use of the items other than retention, demonstration or display while holding them for sale, lease or rental, I must pay sales tax on the items at the time of use based upon either the purchase price or the fair market rental value for the period of time used.

I understand that it is a criminal offense to give a resale certificate to the seller for taxable items that I know, at the time of purchase, are purchased for use rather than for the purpose of resale, lease, or rental and, depending on the amount of tax evaded, the offense may range from a Class C misdemeanor to a felony of the second degree.

sign here ▶ Purchaser *Hank Dillon*	Title owner	Date 09/20/00

This certificate should be furnished to the supplier. Do not send the completed certificate to the Comptroller of Public Accounts.

TEXAS SALES AND USE TAX EXEMPTION CERTIFICATION

Name of purchaser, film or agency	
St. John's Episcopal Church	
Address (Street & number, P.O. Box or Route number)	Phone (Area code and number)
1342 Holy Boulevard	817-555-3492
City, State, ZIP Code	
Abilene, Texas 73000	

I, the purchaser named above, claim an exemption from payment of sales and use tax for the purchase of the taxable items described below or on the attached order or invoice form:

Seller: __Chili Unlimited__

Street Address: __1818 Stockyard Plaza__ City, State, ZIP code: __Abilene, Texas 73000__

Description of items to be purchased on the attached order or invoice:

promotional "Firebreather Chili" bowls and napkins

Purchaser claims this exemption for the following reason:

religious exemption

I understand that I will be liable for payment of sales or use taxes which may become due for failure to comply with the provisions of the Tax Code: Limited Sales, Excise, and Use Tax Act; Municipal Sales and Use Tax Act; Sales and Use Taxes for Special Purpose Taxing Authorities; County Sales and Use Tax Act; County Health Services Sales and Use Tax; The Texas Health and Safety Code; Special Provisions Relating to Hospital Districts, Emergency Services Districts, and Emergency Services Districts in counties with a population of 125,000 or less.

I understand that it is a criminal offense to give a resale certificate to the seller for taxable items that I know, at the time of purchase, are purchased for use rather than for the purpose of resale, lease, or rental and, depending on the amount of tax evaded, the offense may range from a Class C misdemeanor to a felony of the second degree.

sign here ▶	Purchaser *Father Tyler Jones*	Title owner	Date 09/20/00

NOTE: This certificate cannot be issued for the purchaser, lease, or rental of a motor vehicle.
THIS CERTIFICATE DOES NOT REQUIRE A NUMBER TO BE VALID.
Sales and Use Tax "exemption Numbers" or "Tax Exempt" Numbers do not exist.

This certificate should be furnished to the supplier. Do not send the completed certificate to the Comptroller of Public Accounts.

Comptroller of Public Accounts FORM 01-114 (Rev. 9-96/22)

DDDD

b. ■

TEXAS SALES AND USE TAX RETURN

a. ■ 26100

c. Taxpayer number

Page 1 of

● Do not staple or paper clip.   ● Do not write in shaded areas.

d. Filing period

e.

f. Due date
12/21/00

■

Taxpayer name and mailing address

g.
Hank Dillon d/b/a Chili Unlimited
1818 Stockyard Plaza
Abilene, TX 73000

● Blacken this box if your mailing address has changed. Show changes by the preprinted information.———— 1. ■ ☐
● Blacken this box if you are no longer in business. Write in the date you went out of business.—————— 2. ■ ☐
● Blacken this box if one of your locations is out of business or has changed its address.———————— 3. ■ ☐

h. ■   i. ■

SALES TAX QUESTION?
CALL US!
1-800-252-5555

PLEASE PRINT YOUR NUMERALS LIKE THIS
0 1 2 3 4 5 6 7 8 9

k. NO SALES - *If you had zero to report in Items 1, 2 and 3 for all locations for this filing period, blacken this box, sign and date this return and mail it to the Comptroller's office.* ▶ 1 ■ ☐

6. Physical location (outlet) name and address
(Do not use a P.O. box address.)

Outlet no. ■ | 1

1. TOTAL SALES *(Whole dollars only)*____ ■	25,000.00
2. TAXABLE SALES *(Whole dollars only)*___ ■	25,000.00
3. TAXABLE PURCHASES *(Whole dollars only)*___ ■	2,000.00
4. Amount subject to state tax *(Item 2 plus Item 3)*____ ■	27,000.00
5. Amount subject to local tax *(Amount for city, transit, county and SPD must be equal.)*	15,000.00

7. AMOUNT OF TAX DUE FOR THIS OUTLET *(Dollars and cents)*
(Multiply "Amount subject to tax" by "TAX RATE" for state and local tax due)

TAX RATES

X ■ .07 = **7a. State tax** *(include in Item 8a)* 1,890.00

X ■ .07 = **7b. Local tax** *(include in Item 8b)* 150.00

■ 26180	■ 02 ■ STATE TAX - Column a	■ 04 ■ LOCAL TAX - Column b
8. Total tax due *(from all outlets or list supplements)* ————	1,890.00	150.00

01-114 (Rev. 9-96/22)

DDDD

	State	Local
9. Prepayment credit ———————————— −	<750.00>	<120.00>
10. Adjusted tax due *(Item 8 minus Item 9)* =	1,140.00	30.00
11. TIMELY FILING DISCOUNT——————— −	4.00	4.00
12. Prior payments ————————————— −	0	0
13. Net tax due *(Item 10 minus Items 11 & 12)* =	1,136.00	26.00
14. Penalty and interest ———————— +	0	0
	15a. Total state amount due	15b. Total local amount due
15. TOTAL STATE AND LOCAL AMOUNT DUE *(Item 13 plus Item 14)* ■ 02 = ■	1,136.00	■ 04 ■ 26.00

Mail to: COMPTROLLER OF PUBLIC ACCOUNTS
111 E. 17th Street
Austin, TX 78774-0100

■ T Code   ■ Taxpayer number   ■ Period

26020

16. TOTAL AMOUNT PAID *(Total of Items 15a and 15b)* 1,162.00

n. ■

Taxpayer name
Hank Dillon

I declare that the information in this document and any attachments is true and correct to the best of my knowledge.

sign here ▶ Taxpayer or duly authorized agent
Hank Dillon

Date 12/31/00

Daytime phone *(Area code & number)* 817-555-3492

Make check payable to:
STATE COMPTROLLER.

183

INSTRUCTIONS FOR COMPLETING TEXAS SALES AND USE TAX RETURN

GENERAL INSTRUCTIONS

WHO MUST FILE THE LONG FORM? If you meet any one of the following criteria, you must file the long form:
- you have more than one outlet;
- you report tax to more than one city, transit authority (MTA/CTD), county or special purpose district (SPD);
- you prepay your state and local taxes;
- you ship outside a transit authority (MTA/CTD); or
- you report use tax from out of state locations.

Returns must be filed for every period even if there is no amount subject to tax or any tax due. Complete and detailed records must be kept of all sales as well as any deductions claimed so that returns can be verified by a state auditor. Failure to file the return and pay applicable tax may result in collection action as prescribed by Title 2 of the tax code.

WHEN TO FILE - Returns must be filed or postmarked on or before the 20th of the month following the end of each reporting period. If the due date falls on a Saturday, Sunday or legal holiday, the next business day is the due date.

BUSINESS CHANGES - The boxes to the right of the taxpayer name and mailing address should be blackened if your mailing address has changed, if you are no longer in business, if you added a new location, or if one of you r locations is out of business or has changed addresses. If you prefer, you make make these changes via voice mail by calling 1-800-224-1844.

INSTRUCTIONS FOR FILING AMENDED TEXAS SALES AND USE TAX RETURNS To request forms to file an amended return, call 1-800-252-5555 toll free nationwide. The Austin number is 512-463-4600. Forms may be picked up at the Comptroller Field Office nearest you; *OR* you may photocopy the original, write "AMENDED RETURN" at the top, strike through **Item a**, strike through those figures that have changed, and write the new figures on the return. Sign and date the amended return.

FOR ASSISTANCE - If you have any questions regarding sales tax, you may contact the Texas State Comptroller's field office in your area or cal 1-800-252-5555, toll free, nationwide. The Austin number is 512/463-4600. If you are calling from a Telecommunications Device for the Deaf (TDD), our toll free number is 1-800-248-4099, or in Austin, 512/463-4621.

If typing, numbers may be typed consecutively as shown in the example.

```
0123456789
```

If any amounts entered are negative, bracket them as follows: <XXX,XXX.XX>.

SPECIFIC INSTRUCTIONS

Item c. If the return is not preprinted, enter the taxpayer number as shown on your sales tax permit. If you have not received your sales tax permit and you are a sole owner, enter your Social Security number. For other types of organizations, enter the Federal Employer's Identification Number (FEIN) assigned to your organization.

Item d. If the return is not preprinted, enter the filing period of this report (month, quarter or year) and the last day of the period in the space provided. Examples: "Quarter Ending 09-30-96" "Month Ending 10-31-96" "Year Ending 12-31-96."

Item k. If you had zero to report in items 1, 2, and 3 for all outlets during this filing period, blacken this box, sign and date this return and mail it to the Comptroller's office.

Item 1. Enter the total amount (not including tax) of all services and sales, leases and rentals of tangible personal property made during this reporting period for each outlet. Report whole dollars only. Enter "0" if no sales during the current reporting period.

Item 2. Enter the total amount of taxable services and taxable sales, leases and retails of tangible personal property made during the reporting period for each outlet. This amount is the total sales made LESS any deductions. Report whole dollars only. Enter "0" if you have no taxable sale to report.

Item 3. Enter the total amount of taxable purchases that were bought for your own use. This includes purchases from Texas or out-of-state sellers, items taken out of inventory for use, items given away, and items purchases for an exempt use but actually used in a taxable manner. Taxable purchases do not include inventory items being held exclusively for resale. Report whole dollars only. Enter "0" if you have no taxable purchased to report.

Item 4. Add Taxable Sales (Item 2) to Taxable Purchases (Item 3), and enter the result in Item 4. **Do not** include Total Sales (Item 1) in this total. Report whole dollars only.

Item 5. To report local tax by outlet, the amount subject to local tax must be the same for all local taxing authorities (city, transit, county, SPD) for that outlet. If any of these local amounts are different for the outlet, you MUST report your local tax on the List Supplement (Form 01-116-A). report whole dollars only. If "NOT APPLICABLE" is preprinted in Item 5, do not enter an amount.

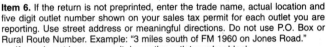

Item 6. If the return is not preprinted, enter the trade name, actual location and five digit outlet number shown on your sales tax permit for each outlet you are reporting. Use street address or meaningful directions. Do not use P.O. Box or Rural Route Number. Example: "3 miles south of FM 1960 on Jones Road."
- If you do not have a permit, leave the outlet number blank.
- If you are reporting use tax from out of state locations, use outlet number "00000."
- If the physical location (outlet) is no longer in business, write "out of business" and date of closing next to any outlet that is no longer in business.
- If the physical location address is different than the preprinted physical location address, make correction next to incorrect information.
- If a new outlet has been opened, write the outlet trade name, actual location and opening date in a blank space on the return along with a brief description of the business.

Item 7 (a,b). Multiply Item 4 by the state tax rate and enter in Item 7a. Multiply Item 5 by the local tax rate and enter in Item 7b. If your return is not preprinted, refer to the booklet, Texas Sales and Use Tax Rates (Pub. 96-132) for a list of the current city, transit, county and SPD rates. If "USE LIST" is preprinted in Item 7b, report the tax on the Texas List Supplement (Form 01-116-A).

Item 8. Combine the state tax due from all outlets (Item 7a) and enter the total tax in Column a. Combine local sales tax due from Item 7b from all pages and enter the total tax in Column b.

Item 9. The amount preprinted in Item 9 includes the amount of your prepayment plus the allowable prepayment discount.
- If you prepaid timely and the amount is not printed in Item 9, calculate the credit by dividing the amount you prepaid by .9825 and enter the result in Item 9.
- If the total tax due in either column of Item 8 is greater than the prepayment, enter the difference in Item 10, Multiply the difference by .005 and enter the result in Item 11.
- If the total tax due in either 8a or 8b is less than the prepayment credit in Item 9a or 9b enter the difference in Item 10a or 10b. Multiply the difference by .9825 and enter the result in Item 13 to determine the amount of refund. Bracket the amount as follows: <XXX.XX>.
- If you are filing your return and/or paying the tax late, mark out the preprinted amount in Item 9 and enter the actual amount paid with your prepayment report.

NOTE: *Discount applies only if all prepayment requirements are met AND your regular sales and use tax return AND any additional payments are postmarked by the due date.*

Item 10. Subtract the prepayment credit in Item 9 from the total tax due in Item 8, and enter the result in Adjusted tax due (Item 10).

Item 11. If you are filing your return and paying the tax due on or before the due date, multiply the Total Tax Due in Item 8 by 1/2% (.005) and enter the result in (PREPAYERS: See instructions for Item 9.) *NOTE: DO NOT TAKE THE DISCOUNT IF THE RETURN AND/OR PAYMENT IS NOT TIMELY.*

Item 12. If you requested that a prior payment and/or an overpayment be designated to this specific period, the amount is preprinted in Item 12 as of the date this return was printed.

Item 14. Penalty and interest
- 1-30 days late: Enter penalty of 5% (.05) of Item 13.
- 31-60 days late: Enter penalty of 10% (.10) of Item 13.
- Over 60 days late: Enter penalty of 10% (.10) of Item 13 plus interest calculated at the rate of 12% (.12) per annum of item 13.

NOTE: *An additional $50 penalty may be assessed after more than two returns are received with a postmark date later than the due date.*

OUT-OF-STATE TAXES 18

STATE SALES TAXES

In 1992, the United States Supreme Court struck a blow for the rights of small businesses by ruling that state tax authorities cannot force them to collect sales taxes on interstate mail orders (*Quill Corporation v. North Dakota*).

Unfortunately, the court left open the possibility that Congress could allow interstate taxation of mail order sales, and since then several bills have been introduced which would do so. One, introduced by Arkansas senator Dale Bumpers, was given the Orwellian "newspeak" title, *The Consumer and Main Street Protection Act*.

At present, companies are only required to collect sales taxes for states in which they *do business*. Exactly what business is enough to trigger taxation is a legal question and some states try to define it as broadly as possible.

If you have an office in a state, clearly you are doing business there and any goods shipped to consumers in the state are subject to sales taxes. If you have a full time employee working in the state much of the year, many states will consider you doing business there. In some states, attending a two-day trade show is enough business to trigger taxation for every order shipped to the state for the entire year. One loophole that works often is to be represented at shows by persons who are not your employees.

Because the laws are different in each state, you will have to do some research on a state-by-state basis to find out how much business you can do in a state without being subject to their taxation. You can request a state's rules from its department of revenue, but keep in mind that what a department of revenue wants the law to be is not always what the courts will rule that it is.

BUSINESS TAXES

Even worse than being subject to a state's sales taxes is to be subject to their income or other business taxes. For example, California charges every company doing business in the state a minimum $800 a year fee and charges income tax on a portion of the company's worldwide income. Doing a small amount of business in the state is clearly not worth getting mired in California taxation.

For this reason, some trade shows have been moved from the state and this has resulted in a review of the tax policies and some "safe-harbor" guidelines to advise companies on what they can do without becoming subject to taxation.

Write to the department of revenue of any state with which you have business contacts to see what might trigger your taxation.

INTERNET TAXES

State revenue departments are drooling at the prospect of taxing commerce on the internet. Theories have already been proposed that web sites available to state residents mean a company is doing business in a state.

Fortunately, Congress has passed a moratorium on taxation of the internet. This will be extended, hopefully, and will give us a new tax-free world, but don't count on it. Never before has a government let a new source of revenue go untapped. It would take a tremendous outcry to keep the internet tax-free. Keep an eye out for any news stories on proposals to tax the internet and petition you representatives against them.

CANADIAN TAXES

Apparently oblivious to the logic of the U.S. Supreme Court, the Canadian government expects American companies, which sell goods by mail order to Canadians, to collect taxes for them and file returns with Revenue Canada, their tax department.

Those that receive an occasional unsolicited order are not expected to register, and Canadian customers, who order things from the U.S., pay the tax plus a $5 fee upon receipt of the goods. But companies that solicit Canadian orders are expected to be registered if their worldwide income is $30,000 or more per year. In some cases, a company may be required to post a bond and to pay for the cost of Canadian auditors visiting its premises and auditing its books! For these reasons you may notice that some companies decline to accept orders from Canada. So much for the benefits of NAFTA.

THE END...AND THE BEGINNING 19

If you have read through this whole book, then you know more about the rules and laws for operating a Texas business than most people in business today. However, after learning about all the governmental regulations, you may become discouraged. You are probably wondering how you can keep track of all the laws and how you will have any time left to make money after complying with the laws. It's not that bad. People are starting businesses every day and they are making money, lots of money. At least we don't have laws like some countries which have marginal tax rates as high as 105%!

The regulations that exist right now are enough to strangle some businesses. Consider the Armour meat-packing plant. The Federal Meat Inspection Service required that an opening be made in a conveyor to allow inspection or they would shut down the plant. OSHA told them that if they made that opening they would be shut down for safety reasons. Government regulations made it impossible for that plant to be in business!

But what you have to realize is that the same incompetent bureaucrats who are creating this morass of laws to slow down businesses are the ones who are charged with enforcing the laws. And just as most government programs cost more than expected and fail to achieve their goals, most government regulations cannot be enforced against millions of people who do not wish to be controlled.

If our government cannot stop drug dealers, crime, the S & L crisis, or anything else it is supposed to do, how will it be able to keep track of your compliance with a thousand little regulations. The bureaucratic regulators are mostly people who do not have the skills to prosper in private industry. They all have their own problems and concerns. They are involved in petty office politics, they have kids to raise, birthdays to remember, bosses to please, lovers on the side to please, and bills to pay.

The government operates on fear. Laws are said to be sacred whether they make sense or not. We are told we must all obey every law or there will be chaos, but laws are not sacred. They are the preferences of those who control the government.

While serving on jury duty, the author and other jurors were told by the judge that the jury must enforce the law whether it is considered to be a fair and sensible law or not. Actually, this instruction was erroneous. The jury has the full power to pardon a person in spite of what any law says. One of the benefits of the jury system is that it may refuse to enforce a law which it considers unfair.

In a pure democracy, fifty-one percent of the voters can decide that all left-handed people must wear green shirts and that everyone must go to church three days a week. It is the Bill of Rights in our constitution which protects us from the tyrannical whims of the majority.

In America today, there are no laws regarding left-handed people or going to church but there are laws controlling minute aspects of our personal and business lives. Does a majority have the right to decide what hours you can work, what you can sell, or where you can sell it? You must decide for yourself and act accordingly.

One way to avoid problems with the government is to keep a low profile and avoid open confrontation. For a lawyer, it can be fun going to appeals court over an unfair parking ticket or making a federal case out of a $25 fine. But for most people the expenses of a fight with the government are unbearable. If you start a mass protest against the IRS or OSHA, they will be forced to make an example of you so that no one else gets any ideas.

The important thing is that you know the laws and the penalties for violations before making your decision. Knowing the laws will also allow you to use the loopholes in the laws to avoid violations.

Congratulations on deciding to start a business in Texas! I hope you get rich in record time. If you have any unusual experiences along the way, drop me a line at the following address. The information may be useful for a future book.

Sphinx Publishing
P.O. Box 25
Clearwater, FL 33757-0025

FOR FURTHER REFERENCE

The following books will provide valuable information to new businesses:

For inspiration to give you the drive to succeed:

Karbo, Joe. *The Lazy Man's Way to Riches*

Schwartz, David J. *The Magic of Thinking Big*

Hill, Napoleon. *Think and Grow Rich*

For hints on how to be successful:

Ringer, Robert J. *Looking Out for #1, Million Dollar Habits* and *Winning Through Intimidation*

For advice on bookkeeping and organization:

Kamoroff, Bernard. *Small Time Operator*

For good investment advice:

Tobias, Andrew. *The Only Other Investment Guide You'll Ever Need*

For an exposé on how bad our government bureaucracy is getting:

Simon, William E. *A Time For Truth*

For advice on how to avoid governmental problems:

Browne, Harry. *How I Found Freedom in an Unfree World*

The following is a list of self-help law books which may be helpful to your business. They are available from your local bookstore or from Sourcebooks, Inc.

Warda, Mark. *How to Negotiate Real Estate Contracts*, *How to Negotiate Real Estate Leases*, *How to Register Your Own Copyright*, and *How to Register Your Own Trademark*

Brown, William and Warda, Mark. *How to Win in Small Claims Court in Texas*

Eckert, W. Kelsea, Sartorius, Arthur & Mark Warda. *How to Form Your Own Corporation*

Herskowitz, Suzan. *Legal Research Made Easy*

Ray, James C. *The Most Valuable Business Forms You'll Ever Need* and *The Most Valuable Corporate Forms You'll Ever Need*

Ray, James C. Bonamer, Charles S. *Successful Real Estate Brokerage Management*

Also from Sourcebooks:

Gutmann, Jean E. *Accounting Made Easy on Computer*

Covello, Joseph and Hazelgren, Brian. *The Complete Book of Business Plans*

The Staff of Business Consumer Guide. *The Essential Business Buyer's Guide*

Bronson, Howard and Lange, Peter. *Great Idea! Now What?*

Mancuso, Joseph R. *Mancuso's Small Business Basics*

Frasier, Lynne Ann. *The Small Business Legal Guide*

Fleury, Robert. *The Small Business Survival Guide*

Koenig, Steve and Root, Hal. *The Small Business Start-Up Guide*

Wendover, Robert W. *Smart Hiring*

Covello, Joseph and Hazelgren, Brian. *Your First Business Plan*

The following web sites provide information which may be useful to you in starting your business:

The Internal Revenue Service: http://www.ssa.gov

The Social Security Administration: http://www.irs.ustreas.gov

The U.S. Business Advisor: http://www.business.gov

Appendix: Tax Timetable Business Startup Checklist& Ready-to-use Forms

The following forms may be photocopied or removed from this book and used immediately. Some of the tax forms explained in this book are not included here because you should use original returns provided by the IRS (940, 941) or the Texas Department of Revenue (quarterly unemployment compensation form).

These forms are included on the following pages:

TAX TIMETABLE

| | Texas | | | | | Federal | | | |
	Sales	Unem-ployment	Tangible	Intang-ible	Corp. Income	Est. Payment	Annual Return	Form 941*	Misc.
JAN.	20th	31st				15th		31st	31st 940 W-2 508 1099
FEB.	20th			28th 4% disc.					28th W-3
MAR.	20th		31st	31st 3% disc.			15th Corp. & Partnership		
APR.	20th	30th	1st	30th 2% disc.	1st	15th	15th Personal	30th	30th 508
MAY	20th			31st 1% disc.					
JUN.	20th			30th tax due		15th			
JUL.	20th	31st						31st	31st 508
AUG.	20th								
SEP.	20th					15th			
OCT.	20th	31st						31st	31st 508
NOV.	20th								
DEC.	20th								

* In addition to form 941, deposits must be made regularly if withholding exceeds $500 in any month

ASSUMED NAME RECORDS
CERTIFICATE OF OWNERSHIP FOR UNINCORPORATED BUSINESS OR PROFESSION

NOTICE: "CERTIFICATES OF OWNERSHIP" ARE VALID ONLY FOR A PERIOD NOT TO EXCEED 10 YEARS FROM THE DATE FILED IN THE COUNTY CLERK'S OFFICE (Chapter 36, Section 1, title 4 - Business and Commerce Code)

NAME IN WHICH BUSINESS IS OR WILL BE CONDUCTED

_____

BUSINESS ADDRESS:
CITY: STATE: ZIP CODE:
PERIOD (Not to Exceed 10 years) DURING WHICH ASSUMED NAME WILL BE USED:

BUSINESS IS TO BE CONDUCTED AS (Check one):
_____ Proprietorship   _____ Sole Practioner   _____ Joint Venture
_____ General Partnership   _____ Limited Partnership
_____ Joint Stock Company   _____ Real Estate Investment Trust
_____ Other: _____

_____

CERTIFICATE OF OWNERSHIP

I/We, the undersigned am/are the owner(s) of the above business and my/our name(s) and address(es) given is/are true and correct, and there is/are no ownership(s) in said business other than those listed herein below.

NAME OF OWNERS

NAME: _____ SIGNATURE: _____
    ADDRESS: _____
NAME: _____ SIGNATURE: _____
    ADDRESS: _____
NAME: _____ SIGNATURE: _____
    ADDRESS: _____
NAME: _____ SIGNATURE: _____
    ADDRESS: _____
NAME: _____ SIGNATURE: _____
    ADDRESS: _____

_____

STATE OF TEXAS   §
COUNTY OF _____   §

BEFORE ME, THE UNDERSIGNED AUTHORITY, on this day personally appeared

_____

_____

known to me to be the person__ whose name__ is/are subscribed to the foregoing instrument and acknowledged to me that __he__ is/are the owner__ of the above-named business and that __he__ signed the same for the purpose and consideration therein expressed.
GIVEN UNDER MY HAND AND SEAL OF OFFICE on _____, _____.

_____
Notary Public in and for the State of Texas

My Commission Expires:

_____

Corporations Section

ASSUMED NAME CERTIFICATE

1.   The name of the corporation, limited liability company, limited partnership, or registered limited liability partnership as stated in its articles of incorporation, articles of organization, certificate of limited partnership, application for certificate of authority or comparable document is_____

        _____

2.   The assumed name under which the business or professional service is or is to be conducted or rendered is_____

        _____

3.   The state, country, or other jurisdiction under the laws of which it was incorporated, organized or associated is _____, and the address of its registered or similar office in that jurisdiction is_____

        _____

4.   The period, not to exceed 10 years, during which the assumed name will be used is ___

        _____

5.   The entity is a (circle one):

                    Business Corporation
                    Non-Profit Corporation
                    Professional Corporation
                    Professional Association
                    Limited Liability Company
                    Limited Partnership
                    Registered Limited Liability Partnership

    If the entity is some other type of incorporated business, professional or other association, please specify below:

        _____

6.   If the entity is required to maintain a registered office in Texas, the address of the registered office is_____

        _____ and the name of its registered agent at such address is_____

        The address of the principal office (if not the same as the registered office) is_____

        _____

7.   If the entity is not required to or does not maintain a registered office in Texas, the office address in Texas is _____
and if the entity is not incorporated, organized or associated under the laws of Texas, the address of its place of business in Texas is _____
and the office address elsewhere is _____

_____

8.   The county or counties where business or professional services are being or are to be conducted or rendered under such assumed name are (if applicable, use the designation "ALL" or "ALL EXCEPT"):

_____

_____
Signature of officer, general partner, manager, representative or attorney-in-fact of the entity

State of Texas   §
                                      §
County of _____§

This instrument was acknowledged before me on _____by
                                                              (date)
_____
(name of person acknowledging)

(Notary Seal)

_____
Signature of Notary
Notary Public, State of Texas

Form No. 503
Revised 8/98

The Office of the Secretary of State does not discriminate on the basis of race, color, national origin, sex, religion, age or disability in employment or the provision of services.

**Office of the
Secretary of State**

Corporations Section
P.O. Box 13697
Austin, Texas 78711-3697

APPLICATION FOR
RESERVATION OF ENTITY NAME

The undersigned applicant hereby applies for reservation of the following entity name for a period of one hundred twenty (120) days:

_____

The name is being reserved for the following type of entity pursuant to the applicable statutory provision. The appropriate fee is enclosed with this application for the type of entity specified below:

___ *Corporation* (including business, non-profit, professional and foreign corporations and professional associations) pursuant to Article 2.06 of the Texas Business Corporation Act <u>OR</u> Article 2.04A of the Texas Non-Profit Corporation Act (*$40.00*).

___ *Limited Liability Company* (including foreign limited liability companies) pursuant to Article 2.04 of the Texas Limited Liability Company Act (*$25.00*).

___ *Limited Partnership* (including foreign limited partnerships) pursuant to Section 1.04 of the Texas Revised Limited Partnership Act (*$50.00*).

<u>Name reservations filed under one statute cannot be used for, or transferred to, filings made under any other statute.</u> In addition, once the application is filed, the name reservation will be recorded exclusively in the name of the applicant. Transfer of the reservation to another person may be made by filing a notice of such transfer executed by the applicant for whom the name was reserved and paying the appropriate fee.

Name and address of Applicant:

_____

_____

_____

Dated:_____

Signature:

_____

201

APPLICATION FOR REGISTRATION
OF TRADEMARK OR SERVICE MARK

The undersigned applicant has adopted and used, and is now using, a certain trademark or service mark in Texas and hereby makes application for registration of such mark, in accordance with Chapter 16 of the Texas Business & Commerce Code.

1.   Applicant: _____

2.   Address:_____

       City: _____State:_____Zip:_____

3.   Applicant is incorporated or organized as a _____
       and is incorporated or organized under the laws of _____

4.   Describe the mark (words and/or design) SHOWN ON THE ATTACHED DRAWING

       SHEET:

       _____

       _____

5.   Description of goods or services in connection with which the mark is being used: (BE

       SPECIFIC)

       _____

       _____

6.   The manner in which the mark is being used (labels, tags on the goods, etc; OR brochures,

       newspapers advertising the services, etc.): (A SAMPLE IS ATTACHED)

       _____

       _____

7.   Number and title of the class of goods or services:_____

8.   Date mark first used by applicant (BOTH SPACES MUST BE COMPLETED):

       (a) Anywhere:_____(b) In Texas:_____

9.   Applicant hereby appoints the secretary of state of Texas as its agent for service of process only in suits relating to the registration which may be issued if the applicant is or becomes a nonresident individual, partnership or association or foreign corporation, limited partnership, or limited liability company without a certificate of authority to do business in this state or cannot be found in this state.

10.   Applicant is the owner of the mark and, to the best of the applicant's knowledge, no other person is entitled to use the mark in this state in the identical form used by applicant, or in a form that is likely, when used in connection with the goods or services, to cause confusion or mistake, or to deceive, because of its resemblance to the mark used by the applicant.

Executed on this _____ day of _____ , 19____ .

_____

(Name of Applicant)

_____

(Signature of Applicant) (if applicable, title of officer, partner, or other authorized person)

INSTRUCTIONS

Submit an ORIGINAL and one copy of the application. <u>Prior to signing, please review carefully the statements set forth in the application. A person commits an offense under Section 16.31, Business & Commerce Code, if the person signs a document that is forged or that the person knows is false in any material respect with the intent that the document be delivered to the secretary of state for filing. The offense is a Class A misdemeanor. In addition, an application or registration procured by fraud is subject to cancellation pursuant to Sections 16.16 and 16.28, Business & Commerce Code.</u>

The application must be <u>typewritten</u> or <u>clearly printed in black ink</u>. Enclose two (2) copies of a <u>drawing</u> of the mark and two (2) <u>specimens</u> of use (examples of use listed in item 6).

The application processing fee of $50.00 also must be enclosed. Checks should be made payable to the secretary of state. <u>The processing fee is not refundable regardless of whether the application is subsequently registered, denied or abandoned.</u>

Documents should be mailed to the address shown in the heading of this form. The delivery address is James Earl Rudder Office Building, 1019 Brazos, Austin, Texas 78701. We will place one document on record and return a file stamped copy. The telephone number is (512) 463-5576, TDD: (800) 735-2989, FAX: (512) 463-5709.

TRADEMARK DRAWING SHEET

Applicant:

Address:

Goods/Services:

U.S. Department of Justice
Immigration and Naturalization Service

OMB No. 1115-0136

Employment Eligibility Verification

Please read instructions carefully before completing this form. The instructions must be available during completion of this form. **ANTI-DISCRIMINATION NOTICE.** It is illegal to discriminate against work eligible individuals. Employers CANNOT specify which document(s) they will accept from an employee. The refusal to hire an individual because of a future expiration date may also constitute illegal discrimination.

Section 1. Employee Information and Verification. To be completed and signed by employee at the time employment begins

Print Name: Last	First	Middle Initial	Maiden Name

Address (Street Name and Number)		Apt. #	Date of Birth (month/day/year)

City	State	Zip Code	Social Security #

I am aware that federal law provides for imprisonment and/or fines for false statements or *use of false documents in connection with the* completion of this form.

I attest, under penalty of perjury, that I am (check one of the following):
- ☐ A citizen or national of the United States
- ☐ A Lawful Permanent Resident (Alien # A_____)
- ☐ An alien authorized to work until ____/____/____
   (Alien # or Admission # _____)

Employee's Signature	Date (month/day/year)

Preparer and/or Translator Certification. *(To be completed and signed if Section 1 is prepared by a person other than the employee.) I attest, under penalty of perjury, that I have assisted in the completion of this form and that to the best of my knowledge the information is true and correct.*

Preparer's/Translator's Signature	Print Name

Address (Street Name and Number, City, State, Zip Code)	Date (month/day/year)

Section 2. Employer Review and Verification. To be completed and signed by employer. **Examine one document from List A OR examine one document from List B and one from List C** as listed on the reverse of this form and record the title, number and expiration date, if any, of the document(s)

List A	OR	List B	AND	List C
Document title: _____		_____		_____
Issuing authority: _____		_____		_____
Document #: _____		_____		_____
Expiration Date (if any): ___/___/___		___/___/___		___/___/___
Document #: _____				
Expiration Date (if any): ___/___/___				

CERTIFICATION - I attest, under penalty of perjury, that I have examined the document(s) presented by the above-named employee, that the above-listed document(s) appear to be genuine and to relate to the employee named, that the employee began employment on *(month/day/year)* ____/____/____ **and that to the best of my knowledge the employee is eligible to work in the United States. (State employment agencies may omit the date the employee began employment).**

Signature of Employer or Authorized Representative	Print Name	Title

Business or Organization Name	Address (Street Name and Number, City, State, Zip Code)	Date (month/day/year)

Section 3. Updating and Reverification. To be completed and signed by employer

A. New Name (if applicable)	B. Date of rehire (month/day/year) (if applicable)

C. If employee's previous grant of work authorization has expired, provide the information below for the document that establishes current employment eligibility.

Document Title:_____ Document #:_____ Expiration Date (if any):___/___/___

I attest, under penalty of perjury, that to the best of my knowledge, this employee is eligible to work in the United States, and if the employee presented document(s), the document(s) I have examined appear to be genuine and to relate to the individual.

Signature of Employer or Authorized Representative	Date (month/day/year)

INSTRUCTIONS
PLEASE READ ALL INSTRUCTIONS CAREFULLY BEFORE COMPLETING THIS FORM.

Anti-Discrimination Notice. It is illegal to discriminate against any individual (other than an alien not authorized to work in the U.S.) in hiring, discharging, or recruiting or referring for a fee because of that individual's national origin or citizenship status. It is illegal to discriminate against work eligible individuals. Employers **CANNOT** specify which document(s) they will accept from an employee. The refusal to hire an individual because of a future expiration date may also constitute illegal discrimination.

Section 1 - Employee. All employees, citizens and noncitizens, hired after November 6, 1986, must complete Section 1 of this form at the time of hire, which is the actual beginning of employment. **The employer is responsible for ensuring that Section 1 is timely and properly completed.**

Preparer/Translator Certification. The Preparer/Translator Certification must be completed if Section 1 is prepared by a person other than the employee. A preparer/translator may be used only when the employee is unable to complete Section 1 on his/her own. However, the employee must still sign Section 1 personally.

Section 2 - Employer. For the purpose of completing this form, the term "employer" includes those recruiters and referrers for a fee who are agricultural associations, agricultural employers, or farm labor contractors.

Employers must complete Section 2 by examining evidence of identity and employment eligibility within three (3) business days of the date employment begins. If employees are authorized to work, but are unable to present the required document(s) within three business days, they must present a receipt for the application of the document(s) within three business days and the actual document(s) within ninety (90) days. However, if employers hire individuals for a duration of less than three business days, Section 2 must be completed at the time employment begins. **Employers must record: 1)** document title; **2)** issuing authority; **3)** document number, **4)** expiration date, if any; and **5)** the date employment begins. Employers must sign and date the certification. Employees must present original documents. Employers may, but are not required to, photocopy the document(s) presented. These photocopies may only be used for the verification process and must be retained with the I-9. **However, employers are still responsible for completing the I-9.**

Section 3 - Updating and Reverification. Employers must complete Section 3 when updating and/or reverifying the I-9. Employers must reverify employment eligibility of their employees on or before the expiration date recorded in Section 1. Employers **CANNOT** specify which document(s) they will accept from an employee.

- If an employee's name has changed at the time this form is being updated/ reverified, complete Block A.

- If an employee is rehired within three (3) years of the date this form was originally completed and the employee is still eligible to be employed on the same basis as previously indicated on this form (updating), complete Block B and the signature block.

- If an employee is rehired within three (3) years of the date this form was originally completed and the employee's work authorization has expired **or** if a current employee's work authorization is about to expire (reverification), complete Block B and:
  - examine any document that reflects that the employee is authorized to work in the U.S. (see List A **or** C),
  - record the document title, document number and expiration date (if any) in Block C, and
  - complete the signature block.

Photocopying and Retaining Form I-9. A blank I-9 may be reproduced provided both sides are copied. The Instructions must be available to all employees completing this form. Employers must retain completed I-9s for three (3) years after the date of hire **or** one (1) year after the date employment ends, whichever is later.

For more detailed information, you may refer to the INS Handbook for Employers, (Form M-274). You may obtain the handbook at your local INS office.

Privacy Act Notice. The authority for collecting this information is the Immigration Reform and Control Act of 1986, Pub. L. 99-603 (8 U.S.C. 1324a).

This information is for employers to verify the eligibility of individuals for employment to preclude the unlawful hiring, or recruiting or referring for a fee, of aliens who are not authorized to work in the United States.

This information will be used by employers as a record of their basis for determining eligibility of an employee to work in the United States. The form will be kept by the employer and made available for inspection by officials of the U.S. Immigration and Naturalization Service, the Department of Labor, and the Office of Special Counsel for Immigration Related Unfair Employment Practices.

Submission of the information required in this form is voluntary. However, an individual may not begin employment unless this form is completed since employers are subject to civil or criminal penalties if they do not comply with the Immigration Reform and Control Act of 1986.

Reporting Burden. We try to create forms and instructions that are accurate, can be easily understood, and which impose the least possible burden on you to provide us with information. Often this is difficult because some immigration laws are very complex. Accordingly, the reporting burden for this collection of information is computed as follows: **1)** learning about this form, 5 minutes; **2)** completing the form, 5 minutes; and **3)** assembling and filing (recordkeeping) the form, 5 minutes, for an average of 15 minutes per response. If you have comments regarding the accuracy of this burden estimate, or suggestions for making this form simpler, you can write to both the Immigration and Naturalization Service, 425 I Street, N.W., Room 5304, Washington, D. C. 20536; and the Office of Management and Budget, Paperwork Reduction Project, OMB No. 1115-0136, Washington, D.C. 20503.

EMPLOYERS MUST RETAIN COMPLETED I-9
PLEASE DO NOT MAIL COMPLETED I-9 TO INS

Form SS-4
(Rev. February 1998)
Department of the Treasury
Internal Revenue Service

Application for Employer Identification Number
(For use by employers, corporations, partnerships, trusts, estates, churches,
government agencies, certain individuals, and others. See instructions.)

▶ Keep a copy for your records.

EIN

OMB No. 1545-0003

Please type or print clearly.

| 1 | Name of applicant (legal name) (see instructions) |

| 2 Trade name of business (if different from name on line 1) | 3 Executor, trustee, "care of" name |

| 4a Mailing address (street address) (room, apt., or suite no.) | 5a Business address (if different from address on lines 4a and 4b) |

| 4b City, state, and ZIP code | 5b City, state, and ZIP code |

6 County and state where principal business is located

7 Name of principal officer, general partner, grantor, owner, or trustor—SSN or ITIN may be required (see instructions) ▶ _____

8a Type of entity (Check only one box.) (see instructions)

Caution: *If applicant is a limited liability company, see the instructions for line 8a.*

- ☐ Sole proprietor (SSN) _____ | _____
- ☐ Partnership   ☐ Personal service corp.
- ☐ REMIC   ☐ National Guard
- ☐ State/local government   ☐ Farmers' cooperative
- ☐ Church or church-controlled organization
- ☐ Other nonprofit organization (specify) ▶ _____
- ☐ Other (specify) ▶ _____

- ☐ Estate (SSN of decedent) _____ | _____
- ☐ Plan administrator (SSN) _____ | _____
- ☐ Other corporation (specify) ▶ _____
- ☐ Trust
- ☐ Federal government/military
- (enter GEN if applicable) _____

8b If a corporation, name the state or foreign country (if applicable) where incorporated

| State | Foreign country |

9 Reason for applying (Check only one box.) (see instructions)
- ☐ Started new business (specify type) ▶ _____
- ☐ Hired employees (Check the box and see line 12.)
- ☐ Created a pension plan (specify type) ▶
- ☐ Banking purpose (specify purpose) ▶ _____
- ☐ Changed type of organization (specify new type) ▶ _____
- ☐ Purchased going business
- ☐ Created a trust (specify type) ▶ _____
- ☐ Other (specify) ▶

10 Date business started or acquired (month, day, year) (see instructions)

11 Closing month of accounting year (see instructions)

12 First date wages or annuities were paid or will be paid (month, day, year). **Note:** *If applicant is a withholding agent, enter date income will first be paid to nonresident alien. (month, day, year)* . . . . ▶

13 Highest number of employees expected in the next 12 months. **Note:** *If the applicant does not expect to have any employees during the period, enter -0-. (see instructions)* . . . . ▶

Nonagricultural	Agricultural	Household

14 Principal activity (see instructions) ▶

15 Is the principal business activity manufacturing? . . . . ☐ Yes ☐ No
If "Yes," principal product and raw material used ▶

16 To whom are most of the products or services sold? Please check one box.
- ☐ Public (retail)   ☐ Other (specify) ▶
- ☐ Business (wholesale)
- ☐ N/A

17a Has the applicant ever applied for an employer identification number for this or any other business? . . . . ☐ Yes ☐ No
Note: *If "Yes," please complete lines 17b and 17c.*

17b If you checked "Yes" on line 17a, give applicant's legal name and trade name shown on prior application, if different from line 1 or 2 above.
Legal name ▶   Trade name ▶

17c Approximate date when and city and state where the application was filed. Enter previous employer identification number if known.

Approximate date when filed (mo., day, year)	City and state where filed	Previous EIN

Under penalties of perjury, I declare that I have examined this application, and to the best of my knowledge and belief, it is true, correct, and complete.

| | Business telephone number (include area code) |
| Name and title (Please type or print clearly.) ▶ | Fax telephone number (include area code) |

Signature ▶   Date ▶

Note: *Do not write below this line. For official use only.*

Please leave blank ▶	Geo.	Ind.	Class	Size	Reason for applying

For Paperwork Reduction Act Notice, see page 4.   Cat. No. 16055N   Form **SS-4** (Rev. 2-98)

Form **SS-8**	**Determination of Employee Work Status**	
(Rev. June 1997)	**for Purposes of Federal Employment Taxes**	OMB No. 1545-0004
Department of the Treasury Internal Revenue Service	**and Income Tax Withholding**	

Paperwork Reduction Act Notice

We ask for the information on this form to carry out the Internal Revenue laws of the United States. You are required to give us the information. We need it to ensure that you are complying with these laws and to allow us to figure and collect the right amount of tax.

You are not required to provide the information requested on a form that is subject to the Paperwork Reduction Act unless the form displays a valid OMB control number. Books or records relating to a form or its instructions must be retained as long as their contents may become material in the administration of any Internal Revenue law. Generally, tax returns and return information are confidential, as required by Code section 6103.

The time needed to complete and file this form will vary depending on individual circumstances. The estimated average time is: **Recordkeeping, 34 hr., 55 min.; Learning about the law or the form,** 12 min.; and **Preparing and sending the form to the IRS,** 46 min. If you have comments concerning the accuracy of these time estimates or suggestions for making this form simpler, we would be happy to hear from you. You can write to the Tax Forms Committee, Western Area Distribution Center, Rancho Cordova, CA 95743-0001. **DO NOT** send the tax form to this address. Instead, see **General Information** for where to file.

Purpose

Employers and workers file Form SS-8 to get a determination as to whether a worker is an employee for purposes of Federal employment taxes and income tax withholding.

General Information

Complete this form carefully. If the firm is completing the form, complete it for **ONE** individual who is representative of the class of workers whose status is in question. If you want a written determination for more than one class of workers, complete a separate Form SS-8 for one worker

from each class whose status is typical of that class. A written determination for any worker will apply to other workers of the same class if the facts are not materially different from those of the worker whose status was ruled upon.

Caution: *Form SS-8 is not a claim for refund of social security and Medicare taxes or Federal income tax withholding. Also, a determination that an individual is an employee does not necessarily reduce any current or prior tax liability. A worker must file his or her income tax return even if a determination has not been made by the due date of the return.*

Where to file.—In the list below, find the state where your legal residence, principal place of business, office, or agency is located. Send Form SS-8 to the address listed for your location.

Location:	Send to:
Alaska, Arizona, Arkansas, California, Colorado, Hawaii, Idaho, Illinois, Iowa, Kansas, Minnesota, Missouri, Montana, Nebraska, Nevada, New Mexico, North Dakota, Oklahoma, Oregon, South Dakota, Texas, Utah, Washington, Wisconsin, Wyoming	Internal Revenue Service SS-8 Determinations P.O. Box 1231, Stop 4106 AUSC Austin, TX 78767
Alabama, Connecticut, Delaware, District of Columbia, Florida, Georgia, Indiana, Kentucky, Louisiana, Maine, Maryland, Massachusetts, Michigan, Mississippi, New Hampshire, New Jersey, New York, North Carolina, Ohio, Pennsylvania, Rhode Island, South Carolina, Tennessee, Vermont, Virginia, West Virginia, All other locations not listed	Internal Revenue Service SS-8 Determinations Two Lakemont Road Newport, VT 05855-1555
American Samoa, Guam, Puerto Rico, U.S. Virgin Islands	Internal Revenue Service Mercantile Plaza 2 Avenue Ponce de Leon San Juan, Puerto Rico 00918

Name of firm (or person) for whom the worker performed services	Name of worker	
Address of firm (include street address, apt. or suite no., city, state, and ZIP code)	Address of worker (include street address, apt. or suite no., city, state, and ZIP code)	
Trade name	Telephone number (include area code) ( )	Worker's social security number
Telephone number (include area code) ( )	Firm's employer identification number	

Check type of firm for which the work relationship is in question:

☐ **Individual** ☐ **Partnership** ☐ **Corporation** ☐ **Other** (specify) ▶ ....

Important Information Needed To Process Your Request

This form is being completed by: ☐ Firm ☐ Worker

If this form is being completed by the worker, the IRS **must** have your permission to disclose your name to the firm.

Do you object to disclosing your name and the information on this form to the firm? . . . . ☐ Yes ☐ No

If you answer "Yes," the IRS cannot act on your request. **Do not complete the rest of this form unless the IRS asks for it.**

Under section 6110 of the Internal Revenue Code, the information on this form and related file documents will be open to the public if any ruling or determination is made. However, names, addresses, and taxpayer identification numbers will be removed before the information is made public.

Is there any other information you want removed? . . . . ☐ Yes ☐ No

If you check "Yes," we cannot process your request unless you submit a copy of this form and copies of all supporting documents showing, in brackets, the information you want removed. Attach a separate statement showing which specific exemption of section 6110(c) applies to each bracketed part.

Cat. No. 16106T

Form **SS-8** (Rev. 6-97)

*This form is designed to cover many work activities, so some of the questions may not apply to you. **You must answer ALL items or mark them "Unknown" or "Does not apply."** If you need more space, attach another sheet.*

Total number of workers in this class. (Attach names and addresses. If more than 10 workers, list only 10.) ▶ _____

This information is about services performed by the worker from _____ to _____
                                                              (month, day, year)   (month, day, year)

Is the worker still performing services for the firm? . . . . ☐ **Yes** ☐ **No**

- If "No," what was the date of termination? ▶_____
                                              (month, day, year)

1a Describe the firm's business ....

  b Describe the work done by the worker ....

....

2a If the work is done under a written agreement between the firm and the worker, attach a copy.

  b If the agreement is not in writing, describe the terms and conditions of the work arrangement ....

....

  c If the actual working arrangement differs in any way from the agreement, explain the differences and why they occur ....

....

3a Is the worker given training by the firm? . . . . ☐ **Yes** ☐ **No**
- If "Yes," what kind? ....
- How often? ....

  b Is the worker given instructions in the way the work is to be done (exclusive of actual training in 3a)? . ☐ **Yes** ☐ **No**
- If "Yes," give specific examples ....

  c Attach samples of any written instructions or procedures.

  d Does the firm have the right to change the methods used by the worker or direct that person on how to
do the work? . . . . ☐ **Yes** ☐ **No**
- Explain your answer ....

....

  e Does the operation of the firm's business require that the worker be supervised or controlled in the
performance of the service? . . . . ☐ **Yes** ☐ **No**
- Explain your answer ....

....

4a The firm engages the worker:
  ☐ To perform and complete a particular job only
  ☐ To work at a job for an indefinite period of time
  ☐ Other (explain) ....

  b Is the worker required to follow a routine or a schedule established by the firm? . . . . ☐ **Yes** ☐ **No**
- If "Yes," what is the routine or schedule? ....

....

  c Does the worker report to the firm or its representative?. . . . . ☐ **Yes** ☐ **No**
- If "Yes," how often? ....
- For what purpose? ....
- In what manner (in person, in writing, by telephone, etc.)? ....
- Attach copies of any report forms used in reporting to the firm.

  d Does the worker furnish a time record to the firm? . . . . ☐ **Yes** ☐ **No**
- If "Yes," attach copies of time records.

5a State the kind and value of tools, equipment, supplies, and materials furnished by:
- The firm ....

....

- The worker ....

....

  b What expenses are incurred by the worker in the performance of services for the firm? ....

....

  c Does the firm reimburse the worker for any expenses? . . . . ☐ **Yes** ☐ **No**
- If "Yes," specify the reimbursed expenses ....

212

6a Will the worker perform the services personally? . . . . ☐ Yes ☐ No

b Does the worker have helpers? . . . . ☐ Yes ☐ No
  - If "Yes," who hires the helpers? ☐ Firm ☐ Worker
  - If the helpers are hired by the worker, is the firm's approval necessary? . . . . ☐ Yes ☐ No
  - Who pays the helpers? ☐ Firm ☐ Worker
  - If the worker pays the helpers, does the firm repay the worker? . . . . ☐ Yes ☐ No
  - Are social security and Medicare taxes and Federal income tax withheld from the helpers' pay? . . ☐ Yes ☐ No
  - If "Yes," who reports and pays these taxes? ☐ Firm ☐ Worker
  - Who reports the helpers' earnings to the Internal Revenue Service? ☐ Firm ☐ Worker
  - What services do the helpers perform? ....

7 At what location are the services performed? ☐ Firm's ☐ Worker's ☐ Other (specify) ....

8a Type of pay worker receives:
  ☐ Salary ☐ Commission ☐ Hourly wage ☐ Piecework ☐ Lump sum ☐ Other (specify) ....
b Does the firm guarantee a minimum amount of pay to the worker? . . . . ☐ Yes ☐ No
c Does the firm allow the worker a drawing account or advances against pay? . . . . ☐ Yes ☐ No
  - If "Yes," is the worker paid such advances on a regular basis? . . . . ☐ Yes ☐ No
d How does the worker repay such advances? ....

9a Is the worker eligible for a pension, bonus, paid vacations, sick pay, etc.? . . . . ☐ Yes ☐ No
  - If "Yes," specify ....
b Does the firm carry worker's compensation insurance on the worker? . . . . ☐ Yes ☐ No
c Does the firm withhold social security and Medicare taxes from amounts paid the worker? . . . . . ☐ Yes ☐ No
d Does the firm withhold Federal income tax from amounts paid the worker? . . . . ☐ Yes ☐ No
e How does the firm report the worker's earnings to the Internal Revenue Service?
  ☐ Form W-2 ☐ Form 1099-MISC ☐ Does not report ☐ Other (specify) ....
  - Attach a copy.
f Does the firm bond the worker? . . . . ☐ Yes ☐ No

10a Approximately how many hours a day does the worker perform services for the firm? ....
b Does the firm set hours of work for the worker? . . . . ☐ Yes ☐ No
  - If "Yes," what are the worker's set hours? _____ a.m./p.m. to _____ a.m./p.m. (Circle whether a.m. or p.m.)
c Does the worker perform similar services for others? . . . . ☐ Yes ☐ No ☐ Unknown
  - If "Yes," are these services performed on a daily basis for other firms? . . . . . ☐ Yes ☐ No ☐ Unknown
  - Percentage of time spent in performing these services for:
    This firm .... % Other firms .... % ☐ Unknown
  - Does the firm have priority on the worker's time? . . . . ☐ Yes ☐ No
  - If "No," explain ....
d Is the worker prohibited from competing with the firm either while performing services or during any later
  period? . . . . ☐ Yes ☐ No

11a Can the firm discharge the worker at any time without incurring a liability? . . . . ☐ Yes ☐ No
  - If "No," explain ....
b Can the worker terminate the services at any time without incurring a liability? . . . . ☐ Yes ☐ No
  - If "No," explain ....

12a Does the worker perform services for the firm under:
  ☐ The firm's business name ☐ The worker's own business name ☐ Other (specify) ....
b Does the worker advertise or maintain a business listing in the telephone directory, a trade
  journal, etc.? . . . . ☐ Yes ☐ No ☐ Unknown
  - If "Yes," specify ....
c Does the worker represent himself or herself to the public as being in business to perform
  the same or similar services? . . . . ☐ Yes ☐ No ☐ Unknown
  - If "Yes," how? ....
d Does the worker have his or her own shop or office? . . . . ☐ Yes ☐ No ☐ Unknown
  - If "Yes," where? ....
e Does the firm represent the worker as an employee of the firm to its customers? . . . . ☐ Yes ☐ No
  - If "No," how is the worker represented? ....
f How did the firm learn of the worker's services? ....

13 Is a license necessary for the work? . . . . ☐ Yes ☐ No ☐ Unknown
  - If "Yes," what kind of license is required? ....
  - Who issues the license? ....
  - Who pays the license fee?

14 Does the worker have a financial investment in a business related to the services performed?. . . . . ☐ **Yes** ☐ **No** ☐ **Unknown**
- If "Yes," specify and give amount of the investment ....

15 Can the worker incur a loss in the performance of the service for the firm? . . . . ☐ **Yes** ☐ **No**
- If "Yes," how? ....

16a Has any other government agency ruled on the status of the firm's workers? . . . . ☐ **Yes** ☐ **No**
- If "Yes," attach a copy of the ruling.

b Is the same issue being considered by any IRS office in connection with the audit of the worker's tax return or the firm's tax return, or has it been considered recently? . . . . ☐ **Yes** ☐ **No**
- If "Yes," for which year(s)? ....

17 Does the worker assemble or process a product at home or away from the firm's place of business? ☐ **Yes** ☐ **No**
- If "Yes," who furnishes materials or goods used by the worker? ☐ Firm   ☐ Worker   ☐ Other
- Is the worker furnished a pattern or given instructions to follow in making the product? . . . . . ☐ **Yes** ☐ **No**
- Is the worker required to return the finished product to the firm or to someone designated by the firm? ☐ **Yes** ☐ **No**

18 Attach a detailed explanation of any other reason why you believe the worker is an employee or an independent contractor.

Answer items 19a through o only if the worker is a salesperson or provides a service directly to customers.

19a Are leads to prospective customers furnished by the firm?. . . . . ☐ **Yes** ☐ **No** ☐ **Does not apply**
b Is the worker required to pursue or report on leads? . . . . ☐ **Yes** ☐ **No** ☐ **Does not apply**
c Is the worker required to adhere to prices, terms, and conditions of sale established by the firm? . . ☐ **Yes** ☐ **No**
d Are orders submitted to and subject to approval by the firm? . . . . ☐ **Yes** ☐ **No**
e Is the worker expected to attend sales meetings?. ☐ **Yes** ☐ **No**
- If "Yes," is the worker subject to any kind of penalty for failing to attend?. . . . . ☐ **Yes** ☐ **No**
f Does the firm assign a specific territory to the worker? . . . . ☐ **Yes** ☐ **No**
g Whom does the customer pay?   ☐ Firm   ☐ Worker
- If worker, does the worker remit the total amount to the firm? . . . . ☐ **Yes** ☐ **No**
h Does the worker sell a consumer product in a home or establishment other than a permanent retail establishment? . . . . ☐ **Yes** ☐ **No**
i List the products and/or services distributed by the worker, such as meat, vegetables, fruit, bakery products, beverages (other than milk), or laundry or dry cleaning services. If more than one type of product and/or service is distributed, specify the principal one ....
j Did the firm or another person assign the route or territory and a list of customers to the worker? . . ☐ **Yes** ☐ **No**
- If "Yes," enter the name and job title of the person who made the assignment ....
k Did the worker pay the firm or person for the privilege of serving customers on the route or in the territory? ☐ **Yes** ☐ **No**
- If "Yes," how much did the worker pay (not including any amount paid for a truck or racks, etc.)? $ ....
- What factors were considered in determining the value of the route or territory?.........................
l How are new customers obtained by the worker? Explain fully, showing whether the new customers called the firm for service, were solicited by the worker, or both ....
m Does the worker sell life insurance? . . . . ☐ **Yes** ☐ **No**
- If "Yes," is the selling of life insurance or annuity contracts for the firm the worker's entire business activity? . . . . ☐ **Yes** ☐ **No**
- If "No," list the other business activities and the amount of time spent on them ....
n Does the worker sell other types of insurance for the firm? . . . . ☐ **Yes** ☐ **No**
- If "Yes," state the percentage of the worker's total working time spent in selling other types of insurance.............. %
- At the time the contract was entered into between the firm and the worker, was it their intention that the worker sell life insurance for the firm: ☐ on a full-time basis   ☐ on a part-time basis
- State the manner in which the intention was expressed ....
o Is the worker a traveling or city salesperson? . . . . ☐ **Yes** ☐ **No**
- If "Yes," from whom does the worker principally solicit orders for the firm?...............................
- If the worker solicits orders from wholesalers, retailers, contractors, or operators of hotels, restaurants, or other similar establishments, specify the percentage of the worker's time spent in the solicitation .... %
- Is the merchandise purchased by the customers for resale or for use in their business operations? If used by the customers in their business operations, describe the merchandise and state whether it is equipment installed on their premises or a consumable supply

Under penalties of perjury, I declare that I have examined this request, including accompanying documents, and to the best of my knowledge and belief, the facts presented are true, correct, and complete.

Signature ▶   Title ▶   Date ▶

If the firm is completing this form, an officer or member of the firm must sign it. If the worker is completing this form, the worker must sign it. If the worker wants a written determination about services performed for two or more firms, a separate form must be completed and signed for each firm. Additional copies of this form may be obtained by calling 1-800-TAX-FORM (1-800-829-3676).

Form W-4 (1998)

Purpose. Complete Form W-4 so your employer can withhold the correct Federal income tax from your pay. Because your tax situation may change, you may want to refigure your withholding each year.

Exemption from withholding. If you are exempt, complete only lines 1, 2, 3, 4, and 7, and sign the form to validate it. Your exemption for 1998 expires February 16, 1999.

Note: You cannot claim exemption from withholding if (1) your income exceeds $700 and includes unearned income (e.g., interest and dividends) and (2) another person can claim you as a dependent on their tax return.

Basic instructions. If you are not exempt, complete the Personal Allowances Worksheet. The worksheets on page 2 adjust your withholding allowances based on itemized deductions, adjustments to income, or two-earner/two-job situations. Complete all worksheets that apply. They will help you figure the number of withholding allowances you are entitled to claim. However, you may claim fewer allowances.

New—Child tax and higher education credits. For details on adjusting withholding for these and other credits, see **Pub. 919**, Is My Withholding Correct for 1998?

Head of household. Generally, you may claim head of household filing status on your tax return only if you are unmarried and pay more than 50% of the costs of keeping up a home for yourself and your dependent(s) or other qualifying individuals.

Nonwage income. If you have a large amount of nonwage income, such as interest or dividends, you should consider making estimated tax payments using Form 1040-ES. Otherwise, you may owe additional tax.

Two earners/two jobs. If you have a working spouse or more than one job, figure the total number of allowances you are entitled to claim on all jobs using worksheets from only one W-4. Your withholding will usually be most accurate when all allowances are claimed on the W-4 filed for the highest paying job and zero allowances are claimed for the others.

Check your withholding. After your W-4 takes effect, use Pub. 919 to see how the dollar amount you are having withheld compares to your estimated total annual tax. Get Pub. 919 especially if you used the Two-Earner/Two-Job Worksheet and your earnings exceed $150,000 (Single) or $200,000 (Married). To order Pub. 919, call 1-800-829-3676. Check your telephone directory for the IRS assistance number for further help.

Sign this form. Form W-4 is not valid unless you sign it.

Personal Allowances Worksheet

A Enter "1" for **yourself** if no one else can claim you as a dependent . . . . **A** ____

B Enter "1" if:
- You are single and have only one job; or
- You are married, have only one job, and your spouse does not work; or
- Your wages from a second job or your spouse's wages (or the total of both) are $1,000 or less. **B** ____

C Enter "1" for your **spouse**. But, you may choose to enter -0- if you are married and have either a working spouse or more than one job. (This may help you avoid having too little tax withheld.). . . . . . . **C** ____

D Enter number of **dependents** (other than your spouse or yourself) you will claim on your tax return . . . . . . **D** ____

E Enter "1" if you will file as **head of household** on your tax return (see conditions under **Head of household** above) . **E** ____

F Enter "1" if you have at least $1,500 of **child or dependent care expenses** for which you plan to claim a credit . . **F** ____

G **New—Child Tax Credit:** • If your total income will be between $16,500 and $47,000 ($21,000 and $60,000 if married), enter "1" for each eligible child. • If your total income will be between $47,000 and $80,000 ($60,000 and $115,000 if married), enter "1" if you have two or three eligible children, or enter "2" if you have four or more . . . . **G** ____

H Add lines A through G and enter total here. Note: This amount may be different from the number of exemptions you claim on your return. ▶ **H** ____

For accuracy, complete all worksheets that apply.
- If you plan to **itemize or claim adjustments to income** and want to reduce your withholding, see the Deductions and Adjustments Worksheet on page 2.
- If you are **single**, have **more than one job**, and your combined earnings from all jobs exceed $32,000 OR if you are **married** and have a **working spouse or more than one job**, and the combined earnings from all jobs exceed $55,000, see the Two-Earner/Two-Job Worksheet on page 2 to avoid having too little tax withheld.
- If **neither** of the above situations applies, **stop here** and enter the number from line H on line 5 of Form W-4 below.

-------------------- Cut here and give the certificate to your employer. Keep the top part for your records. --------------------

---

Form W-4
Department of the Treasury
Internal Revenue Service

Employee's Withholding Allowance Certificate

▶ For Privacy Act and Paperwork Reduction Act Notice, see page 2.

OMB No. 1545-0010

1998

1 Type or print your first name and middle initial	Last name	2 Your social security number

Home address (number and street or rural route)

3 ☐ Single ☐ Married ☐ Married, but withhold at higher Single rate.
Note: If married, but legally separated, or spouse is a nonresident alien, check the Single box.

City or town, state, and ZIP code

4 If your last name differs from that on your social security card, check here and call 1-800-772-1213 for a new card . . . . . ▶ ☐

5 Total number of allowances you are claiming (from line H above or from the worksheets on page 2 if they apply) . **5** ____

6 Additional amount, if any, you want withheld from each paycheck . . . . **6** $ ____

7 I claim exemption from withholding for 1998, and I certify that I meet **BOTH** of the following conditions for exemption:
- Last year I had a right to a refund of **ALL** Federal income tax withheld because I had **NO** tax liability **AND**
- This year I expect a refund of **ALL** Federal income tax withheld because I expect to have **NO** tax liability.

If you meet both conditions, enter "EXEMPT" here . . . . ▶ **7** ____

Under penalties of perjury, I certify that I am entitled to the number of withholding allowances claimed on this certificate or entitled to claim exempt status.

Employee's signature ▶   **Date ▶** _____ , 19 ____

8 Employer's name and address (Employer: Complete 8 and 10 only if sending to the IRS)	9 Office code (optional)	10 Employer identification number

215

Deductions and Adjustments Worksheet

Note: Use this worksheet only if you plan to itemize deductions or claim adjustments to income on your 1998 tax return.

1	Enter an estimate of your 1998 itemized deductions. These include qualifying home mortgage interest, charitable contributions, state and local taxes (but not sales taxes), medical expenses in excess of 7.5% of your income, and miscellaneous deductions. (For 1998, you may have to reduce your itemized deductions if your income is over $124,500 ($62,250 if married filing separately). Get Pub. 919 for details.)	1 $
2	Enter: $7,100 if married filing jointly or qualifying widow(er) / $6,250 if head of household / $4,250 if single / $3,550 if married filing separately	2 $
3	**Subtract** line 2 from line 1. If line 2 is greater than line 1, enter -0-	3 $
4	Enter an estimate of your 1998 adjustments to income, including alimony, deductible IRA contributions, and education loan interest.	4 $
5	**Add** lines 3 and 4 and enter the total	5 $
6	Enter an estimate of your 1998 nonwage income (such as dividends or interest)	6 $
7	**Subtract** line 6 from line 5. Enter the result, but not less than -0-	7 $
8	**Divide** the amount on line 7 by $2,500 and enter the result here. Drop any fraction	8
9	Enter the number from Personal Allowances Worksheet, line H, on page 1	9
10	**Add** lines 8 and 9 and enter the total here. If you plan to use the Two-Earner/Two-Job Worksheet, also enter this total on line 1 below. Otherwise, **stop here** and enter this total on Form W-4, line 5, on page 1	10

Two-Earner/Two-Job Worksheet

Note: Use this worksheet only if the instructions for line H on page 1 direct you here.

1	Enter the number from line H on page 1 (or from line 10 above if you used the Deductions and Adjustments Worksheet)	1
2	Find the number in **Table 1** below that applies to the **LOWEST** paying job and enter it here	2
3	If line 1 is **GREATER THAN OR EQUAL TO** line 2, subtract line 2 from line 1. Enter the result here (if zero, enter -0-) and on Form W-4, line 5, on page 1. **DO NOT** use the rest of this worksheet	3

Note: If line 1 is **LESS THAN** line 2, enter -0- on Form W-4, line 5, on page 1. Complete lines 4–9 to calculate the additional withholding amount necessary to avoid a year end tax bill.

4	Enter the number from line 2 of this worksheet	4
5	Enter the number from line 1 of this worksheet	5
6	**Subtract** line 5 from line 4	6
7	Find the amount in **Table 2** below that applies to the **HIGHEST** paying job and enter it here	7 $
8	**Multiply** line 7 by line 6 and enter the result here. This is the additional annual withholding amount needed	8 $
9	Divide line 8 by the number of pay periods remaining in 1998. (For example, divide by 26 if you are paid every other week and you complete this form in December 1997.) Enter the result here and on Form W-4, line 6, page 1. This is the additional amount to be withheld from each paycheck	9 $

Table 1: Two-Earner/Two-Job Worksheet

Married Filing Jointly				All Others			
If wages from **LOWEST** paying job are—	Enter on line 2 above	If wages from **LOWEST** paying job are—	Enter on line 2 above	If wages from **LOWEST** paying job are—	Enter on line 2 above	If wages from **LOWEST** paying job are—	Enter on line 2 above
0 - $4,000	0	38,001 - 43,000	8	0 - $5,000	0	70,001 - 85,000	8
4,001 - 7,000	1	43,001 - 54,000	9	5,001 - 11,000	1	85,001 - 100,000	9
7,001 - 12,000	2	54,001 - 62,000	10	11,001 - 16,000	2	100,001 and over	10
12,001 - 18,000	3	62,001 - 70,000	11	16,001 - 21,000	3		
18,001 - 24,000	4	70,001 - 85,000	12	21,001 - 25,000	4		
24,001 - 28,000	5	85,001 - 100,000	13	25,001 - 42,000	5		
28,001 - 33,000	6	100,001 - 110,000	14	42,001 - 55,000	6		
33,001 - 38,000	7	110,001 and over	15	55,001 - 70,000	7		

Table 2: Two-Earner/Two-Job Worksheet

Married Filing Jointly		All Others	
If wages from **HIGHEST** paying job are—	Enter on line 7 above	If wages from **HIGHEST** paying job are—	Enter on line 7 above
0 - $50,000	$400	0 - $30,000	$400
50,001 - 100,000	760	30,001 - 60,000	760
100,001 - 130,000	840	60,001 - 120,000	840
130,001 - 240,000	970	120,001 - 250,000	970
240,001 and over	1,070	250,001 and over	1,070

Privacy Act and Paperwork Reduction Act Notice. We ask for the information on this form to carry out the Internal Revenue laws of the United States. The Internal Revenue Code requires this information under sections 3402(f)(2)(A) and 6109 and their regulations. Failure to provide a completed form will result in your being treated as a single person who claims no withholding allowances. Routine uses of this information include giving it to the Department of Justice for civil and criminal litigation and to cities, states, and the District of Columbia for use in administering their tax laws.

You are not required to provide the information requested on a form that is subject to the Paperwork Reduction Act unless the form displays a valid OMB control number. Books or records relating to a form or its instructions must be retained as long as their contents may become material in the administration of any Internal Revenue law. Generally, tax returns and return information are confidential, as required by Code section 6103.

The time needed to complete this form will vary depending on individual circumstances. The estimated average time is: **Recordkeeping** 46 min., **Learning about the law or the form** 10 min., **Preparing the form** 1 hr., 10 min. If you have comments concerning the accuracy of these time estimates or suggestions for making this form simpler, we would be happy to hear from you. You can write to the Tax Forms Committee, Western Area Distribution Center, Rancho Cordova, CA 95743-0001. **DO NOT** send the tax form to this address. Instead, give it to your employer.

Comptroller of Public Accounts FORM AP-201-3 (2-98)

TEXAS APPLICATION FOR SALES TAX PERMIT, USE TAX PERMIT AND/OR TELECOMMUNICATIONS INFRASTRUCTURE FUND ASSESSMENT SET-UP

- TYPE OR PRINT
- Do NOT write in shaded areas.

Page 1

ORGANIZATION TYPE

1. Business organization type
   - [ ] Individual - Sole owner
   - [ ] Estate
   - [ ] General partnership
   - [ ] Limited partnership
   - [ ] Registered limited liability partnership
   - [ ] Texas profit corporation
   - [ ] Texas nonprofit corporation
   - [ ] Trust *(Please submit a copy of the trust agreement with this application)*
   - [ ] Texas limited liability company
   - [ ] Non-Texas profit corporation
   - [ ] Non-Texas nonprofit corporation
   - [ ] Non-Texas limited liability company
   - [ ] Professional corporation
   - [ ] Professional association
   - [ ] Association *(explain)* _____
   - [ ] Financial institution *(explain)* _____
   - [ ] Government *(explain)* _____

TAXPAYER IDENTIFICATION

2. Taxpayer number for reporting any Texas tax OR
   Texas identification number if you now have or have ever had one ....

3. Social security number (SSN) if you are an individual-sole owner .... 2 ___ - ___ - ___

4. Federal employer's identification number (FEIN) assigned by the Internal Revenue Service .... 1 ___ - ___

5. [ ] Check here if you do not have a SSN or FEIN. 3 _____

6. Legal name of entity *(Sole owner, partnership, corporation, or other name)*

   If you have registered a DBA (Doing Business As) with either the Texas Secretary of State or your local county clerk, enter below and attach documentation. If not, please leave blank.

BUSINESS TYPE

7. Principal type of business
   - [ ] Agriculture
   - [ ] Finance
   - [ ] Manufacturing
   - [ ] Transportation
   - [ ] Services
   - [ ] Wholesale Trade
   - [ ] Retail Trade
   - [ ] Construction
   - [ ] Other *(explain)* _____
   - [ ] Real Estate
   - [ ] Utilities
   - [ ] Mining
   - [ ] Insurance
   - [ ] Communications *(See Item 39)*
   - [ ] Public Administration

8. Primary business activities and type of products or services to be sold   SIC _____

TAXPAYER INFORMATION

9. Mailing address
   Street number, P.O. Box, or rural route and box number

City	State/province	ZIP code	County *(or country, if outside the U.S.)*

10. Name and daytime phone number of person to contact regarding day to day business operations
    ___ / ___ - ___

If you are a sole owner, skip to Item 16.

11. If the business is a Texas profit corporation, nonprofit corporation, professional corporation, or limited liability company, enter the charter number and date. ....

    Charter number | Month Day Year

12. If the business is a non-Texas profit corporation, nonprofit corporation, professional corporation, or limited liability company, enter the state or country of incorporation, charter number and date, Texas Certificate of Authority number and date.

    State/country of inc. | Charter number | Month Day Year | Texas Certificate of Authority number | Month Day Year

13. If the business is a corporation, have you been involved in a merger within the last seven years? .. [ ] YES [ ] NO   *If "YES," attach a detailed explanation.*

14. If the business is a limited partnership or registered limited liability partnership, enter the home state and registered identification number. ....   State Number

15. General partners, principal members/officers, managing directors or managers *(Attach additional sheets, if necessary.)*

    Name | Title | Phone *(Area code and number)* ___ / ___ - ___

    Address | City | State | ZIP code

    SSN or FEIN | Percent of ownership ___ % | County *(or country, if outside the U.S.)*

    Position held [ ] Partner [ ] Officer [ ] Director [ ] Corporate Stockholder [ ] Record keeper

    Name | Title | Phone *(Area code and number)* ___ / ___ - ___

    Address | City | State | ZIP code

    SSN or FEIN | Percent of ownership ___ % | County *(or country, if outside the U.S.)*

    Position held [ ] Partner [ ] Officer [ ] Director [ ] Corporate Stockholder [ ] Record keeper

217

Comptroller
of Public
Accounts
FORM
AP-201-4
(2-98)

TEXAS APPLICATION FOR SALES TAX PERMIT, USE TAX PERMIT AND/OR
TELECOMMUNICATIONS INFRASTRUCTURE FUND ASSESSMENT SET-UP

• TYPE OR PRINT
• Do NOT write in shaded areas.   Page 2

16. Legal name of entity *(Same as Item 6)*	SSN or FEIN

BUSINESS LOCATION

17. Is your business located outside Texas? .... ☐ YES   ☐ NO
   If "YES," **skip to Item 27.**

18. Is your business located inside the boundaries of an incorporated city? .... ☐ YES   ☐ NO
   If "YES," indicate city *(You may need to contact your local city/county planning offices for assistance in determining the city taxing jurisdiction for your business location address entered in Item 19.)* _____

19. Business location name and address
   Business location name
   _____

   Street and number *(Do not use P.O. Box.)*   City   State   ZIP code   County

   Physical location *(If business location address is a rural route and box number, provide directions)*   Business location phone

20. Name of person we can contact about this location
   _____

Answer the questions below about the above location by checking "YES" or "NO."   ☐ O/L

21. Is your business located inside a metropolitan transit authority/city transit department (MTA/CTD)? .... ☐ YES   ☐ NO

22. Is your business located inside a special purpose district (SPD)? .... ☐ YES   ☐ NO

23. Will you deliver in your own vehicles, provide taxable services, or have sales/service representatives going from this location to customers located in:
   another city? .... ☐ YES   ☐ NO
   another county? .... ☐ YES   ☐ NO
   another MTA/CTD? .... ☐ YES   ☐ NO
   another SPD? .... ☐ YES   ☐ NO

24. Will you ship from this location to other customers via common carrier? .... ☐ YES   ☐ NO

25. Are you a seller with no established place of business selling at a temporary location (trade show, event, or door to door)? .... ☐ YES   ☐ NO

26. Will you have out-of-state suppliers shipping taxable items directly to customers' locations in Texas? .... ☐ YES   ☐ NO

SALES AND USE TAX

27. Check the box that best represents your anticipated quarterly state sales tax collections: ☐ less than $250 ☐ $250-$1,500 ☐ greater than $1,500

28. Enter the date of the first business operation in the above location that is subject to sales or use tax, or the date you plan to start such business operation. ....   month   day   year

29. Is your business operated all year? .... ☐ YES   ☐ NO
   If "NO," list the months you will operate. _____

30. Will you sell any type of alcoholic beverages? .... ☐ YES   ☐ NO
   If "YES," indicate the type of permit you will hold: .... ☐ mixed beverage   ☐ beer and wine

31. Brief description of your business activities **for this location**, and the primary products or services to be sold.   SIC __ __ __

32. Will you be required to report interest earned on sales tax *(See "Specific Instructions" on page 2)*? .... ☐ YES   ☐ NO

33. Are you located out of state with representation in Texas? .... ☐ YES   ☐ NO
   If "YES," complete Item 34. If "NO," skip to Item 35.

34. List names and addresses of all representatives, agents, salespersons, canvassers, or solicitors in Texas.
   (Attach additional sheets, if necessary.)
   Name *(First, middle initial, last)*
   _____

   Street   City   State   ZIP code

35. Location of all distribution points, warehouses, or offices in Texas *(Attach additional sheets, if necessary.)*
   Street   City   State TX   ZIP code

   Street   City   State TX   ZIP code

218

Comptroller of Public Accounts FORM AP-201-5 (2-98)

TEXAS APPLICATION FOR SALES TAX PERMIT, USE TAX PERMIT AND/OR TELECOMMUNICATIONS INFRASTRUCTURE FUND ASSESSMENT SET-UP

• TYPE OR PRINT
• Do NOT write in shaded areas.

Page 3

36. Legal name of entity *(Same as Item 6)*

SSN or FEIN

SALES/USE TAX

37. Name and daytime phone number of the person primarily responsible for filing sales/use tax returns

Name

Phone

For Comptroller Use Only
Tax type/reason
☐ ∎ 00991 ∎ 2 0
Reference no.
∎

38. Address where you want to receive sales/use tax correspondence *(if different from Item 9)*

Street and number, P.O. Box, or rural route and box number

City

State/province

ZIP code

County (or country, if outside the U.S.)

TIF ASSESSMENT

39. Do you receive compensation for providing telecommunication services? .... ☐ YES   ☐ NO

If "YES," you are responsible for the Telecommunications Infrastructure Fund (TIF) assessment and should complete Items 40-43.

If "NO," skip to Item 44.

40. Date of the first business operation that is subject to the Telecommunications Infrastructure Fund assessment in Texas or the date you plan to start such business operation. ....

month   day   year

41. Telecommunications provider type .... ☐ Telecommuncations Utility   ☐ Commercial Mobile Service Provider

42. Name and daytime phone number of the person primarily responsible for filing Telecommunications Assessment reports.

Name *(First, middle initial, last)*

Phone *(Area code and number)*

43. Address where you want to receive Telecommunications Assessment reports *(if different from Item 9)*.

Street and number, P.O. Box, or rural route number

City

State/province

ZIP code

County (or country, if outside U.S.)

PREVIOUS OWNER INFORMATION

If you purchased an existing business or business assets, complete Items 44-47.

Previous owner's taxpayer number *(if available)*

44. Previous owner's trade name.

45. Previous owner's legal name, address and phone number, if available.

Name

Phone *(Area code and number)*

Address *(Street and number)*

City

State

ZIP code

46. Check each of the following items you purchased.

☐ Inventory   ☐ Corporate stock   ☐ Equipment   ☐ Real estate   ☐ Other assets

47. Purchase price of this business or assets and the date of purchase.

Purchase price $

month   day   year

Date of purchase

SIGNATURES

48. The sole owner, all general partners, corporation or organization president, vice-president, secretary or treasurer, managing director, or an authorized representative must sign. A representative must submit a written power of attorney. *(Attach additional sheets if necessary.)*

Date of signature(s)
month   day   year

I (We) declare that the information in this document and any attachments is true and correct to the best of my (our) knowledge and belief.

Type or print name and title of sole owner, partner, or officer

Drivers license number/state

sign here▶ Sole owner, partner, or officer

Type or print name and title of partner or officer

Drivers license number/state

sign here▶ Partner or officer

Type or print name and title of partner or officer

Drivers license number/state

sign here▶ Partner or officer

YOUR PERMIT MUST BE PROMINENTLY DISPLAYED IN YOUR PLACE OF BUSINESS. THE INFORMATION ON YOUR PERMIT IS PUBLIC INFORMATION.

OPEN RECORDS NOTICE - Your name, address, and telephone number are public information under the Texas Open Records Act, Chapter 552, Government Code.

Field office or section number _____   Employee Name _____   USERID _____   Date _____

219

TEXAS RESALE CERTIFICATE

Name of purchaser, film or agency	phone *(Area code and number)*

Address *(Street & number, P.O. Box or Route number)*

City, State, ZIP Code

Texas Sales or Use Tax Permit Number *(or out-of-state retailer's registration number or date applied for Texas Permit - must contain 11 digits if from a Texas permit)*
(Mexican retailer's must show their federal Taxpayers Registry (RFC) number on the certificate and give a copy of their Mexican registration form to the seller.)

I, the purchaser named above, claim the right to make a non-taxable purchase for resale of the taxable items described below or on the attached order or invoice form:

Seller: _____

Street Address: _____

City, State, ZIP code: _____

Description of items to be purchased on the attached order or invoice:

Description of the type of business activity generally engaged in or type of items normally sold by the purchaser:

The taxable items described above, or on the attached order or invoice, will be resold, rented, or leased by me within the geographical limits of the United States of America, its territories and possessions, or within the geographical limits of the United Mexican States, in their present form or attached to other taxable items to be sold.

I understand that if I make any use of the items other than retention, demonstration or display while holding them for sale, lease or rental, I must pay sales tax on the items at the time of use based upon either the purchase price or the fair market rental value for the period of time used.

I understand that it is a criminal offense to give a resale certificate to the seller for taxable items that I know, at the time of purchase, are purchased for use rather than for the purpose of resale, lease, or rental and, depending on the amount of tax evaded, the offense may range from a Class C misdemeanor to a felony of the second degree.

sign here ▸ Purchaser	Title	Date

This certificate should be furnished to the supplier. Do not send the completed certificate to the Comptroller of Public Accounts.

TEXAS SALES AND USE TAX EXEMPTION CERTIFICATION

Name of purchaser, film or agency	
Address *(Street & number, P.O. Box or Route number)*	Phone *(Area code and number)*
City, State, ZIP Code	

I, the purchaser named above, claim an exemption from payment of sales and use tax for the purchase   of the taxable items described below or on the attached order or invoice form:

Seller: _____

Street Address: _____ City, State, ZIP code: _____

Description of items to be purchased on the attached order or invoice:

Purchaser claims this exemption for the following reason:

I understand that I will be liable for payment of sales or use taxes which may become due for failure to comply with the provisions of the Tax Code: Limited Sales, Excise, and Use Tax Act; Municipal Sales and Use Tax Act; Sales and Use Taxes for Special Purpose Taxing Authorities; County Sales and Use Tax Act; County Health Services Sales and Use Tax; The Texas Health and Safety Code; Special Provisions Relating to Hospital Districts, Emergency Services Districts, and Emergency Services Districts in counties with a population of 125,000 or less.

I understand that it is a criminal offense to give a resale certificate to the seller for taxable items that I know, at the time of purchase, are purchased for use rather than for the purpose of resale, lease, or rental and, depending on the amount of tax evaded, the offense may range from a Class C misdemeanor to a felony of the second degree.

sign ▶ here	Purchaser	Title	Date

NOTE: This certificate cannot be issued for the purchaser, lease, or rental of a motor vehicle.
THIS CERTIFICATE DOES NOT REQUIRE A NUMBER TO BE VALID.
Sales and Use Tax "exemption Numbers" or "Tax Exempt" Numbers do not exist.

This certificate should be furnished to the supplier. Do not send the completed certificate to the Comptroller of Public Accounts.

Comptroller
of Public
Accounts
FORM

01-707
Rev. 3-94/7

Do not write in the space above or the shaded areas

TEXAS SALES AND USE TAX BOND-SECURITY INFORMATION

1. Taxpayer Name *(Legal name of owner)*	2. Social Security No. or F.E.I. No.
3. Business Trade Name	Business phone *(Area code and number)*

Location *(Street and number)*	City	State	ZIP Code

ESTIMATED AMOUNT SUBJECT TO SALES AND USE TAX PER MONTH

4. 1st Qtr.	2nd Qtr.	3rd Qtr.	4th Qtr.	5. TOTAL ESTIMATED - 4 Qtrs.

5. Total Estimated - 4 Qtrs.	6. Divided by	7. Average monthly amount subject to tax (Item 5 ÷ Item 6
÷	**12** =	

Comments

I CERTIFY THAT THE ABOVE STATEMENTS ARE CORRECT TO THE BEST OF MY KNOWLEDGE AND BELIEF.

sign here ▶ Taxpayer	Title	Date
sign here ▶ E.O.	Field Office	Date

Instructions for Completing the Sales and Use Tax Bond-Security Information Worksheet

Purpose

This is a worksheet for use by the taxpayers and Comptroller personnel to determine whether or not bond/security will be required for a new tax payer. If bond is required, the tax payer will be notified.

Taxpayers: send the completed worksheet along with the completed Sales and Use Tax Application, Form AP-100 or Form AP-157, to All Applications Section, Account Maintenance Division.

Items 1-3

Must exactly match the information on the Sales and Use Tax Application, Form AP-100 or Form AP-157.

Items 4-7

If purchasing a business, base estimates on prior owner's sales.

For new businesses, base estimate on projected sales volume.

Signature

Taxpayer: The owner, partner, corporate president, corporate secretary or someone with power of attorney must sign the form. Preferably, the same person who signed the application signs the form.

DDDD

b. ■

TEXAS SALES AND USE TAX RETURN

a. ■ 26100

c. Taxpayer number

• *Do not staple or paper clip.*

• *Do not write in shaded areas.*

Page 1 of

d. Filing period

e.

f. Due date

Taxpayer name and mailing address

g.

• *Blacken this box if your mailing address has changed. Show changes by the preprinted information.* — 1. ■ ☐
• *Blacken this box if you are no longer in business. Write in the date you went out of business.* — 2. ■ ☐
• *Blacken this box if one of your locations is out of business or has changed its address.* — 3. ■ ☐

h. ■

i. ■

SALES TAX QUESTION?
CALL US!
1-800-252-5555

PLEASE PRINT YOUR NUMERALS LIKE THIS
0 1 2 3 4 5 6 7 8 9

k. NO SALES - *If you had zero to report in Items 1, 2 and 3 for all locations for this filing period, blacken this box, sign and date this return and mail it to the Comptroller's office.* ▶ 1 ■ ☐

6. Physical location (outlet) name and address *(Do not use a P.O. box address.)*

Outlet no. ■

1. TOTAL SALES *(Whole dollars only)* ■

2. TAXABLE SALES *(Whole dollars only)* ■

3. TAXABLE PURCHASES *(Whole dollars only)* ■

4. Amount subject to state tax *(Item 2 plus Item 3)* ■

5. Amount subject to local tax *(Amount for city, transit, county and SPD must be equal.)* ■

7. AMOUNT OF TAX DUE FOR THIS OUTLET *(Dollars and cents)*
(Multiply "Amount subject to tax" by "TAX RATE" for state and local tax due)

TAX RATES

X ■ . = **7a. State tax** *(include in Item 8a)*

X ■ . = **7b. Local tax** *(include in Item 8b)*

■ 26180

	■ 02 ■ STATE TAX - Column a	■ 04 ■ LOCAL TAX - Column b
8. Total tax due *(from all outlets or list supplements)*		

01-114 (Rev. 9-96/22)   DDDD

9. Prepayment credit —		
10. Adjusted tax due *(Item 8 minus Item 9)* =		
11. TIMELY FILING DISCOUNT —		
12. Prior payments —		
13. Net tax due *(Item 10 minus Items 11 & 12)* =		
14. Penalty and interest +		
	15a. Total state amount due	15b. Total local amount due
15. TOTAL STATE AND LOCAL AMOUNT DUE *(Item 13 plus Item 14)* =	■ 02	■ 04

Mail to: COMPTROLLER OF PUBLIC ACCOUNTS
111 E. 17th Street
Austin, TX 78774-0100

■ T Code   ■ Taxpayer number   ■ Period

16. TOTAL AMOUNT PAID *(Total of Items 15a and 15b)*

26020

Taxpayer name

n. ■

I declare that the information in this document and any attachments is true and correct to the best of my knowledge.

sign here ▶

Taxpayer or duly authorized agent | Date | Daytime phone *(Area code & number)*

Make check payable to:
STATE COMPTROLLER.

INDEX

Your #1 Source for Real World Legal Information...

SPHINX® PUBLISHING
A Division of Sourcebooks, Inc.®

- Written by lawyers
- Simple English explanation of the law
- Forms and instructions included

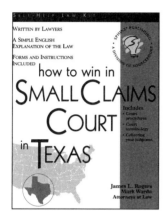

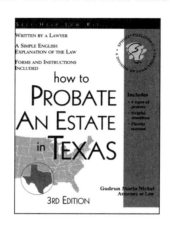

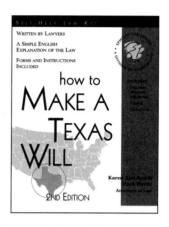

HOW TO WIN IN SMALL CLAIMS COURT IN TEXAS

File and defend your own case with critical information about filing your case, settling your case and collecting your judgment.

124 pages; $14.95;
ISBN 1-57248-012-2

HOW TO PROBATE AN ESTATE IN TEXAS, 2ND ED.

An easy-to-use handbook to the process of probate in Texas. Saves, time, money and frustration.

128 pages; $19.95;
ISBN 1-57071-418-5

HOW TO MAKE A TEXAS WILL, 2ND ED.

This book explains how you can make your own simple will. It covers joint ownership of property, guardianship of your children and their property, different ways to distribute your property, living wills, and anatomical gifts.

112 pages; $12.95;
ISBN 1-57071-417-7

See the following order form for books written specifically for California, Florida, Georgia, Illinois, Massachusetts, Michigan, Minnesota, New York, North Carolina, Pennsylvania, and Texas! *Coming soon—Ohio and New Jersey!*

What our customers say about our books:

"It couldn't be more clear for the lay person." —R.D.

"I want you to know I really appreciate your book. It has saved me a lot of time and money." —L.T.

"Your real estate contracts book has saved me nearly $12,000.00 in closing costs over the past year." —A.B.

"...many of the legal questions that I have had over the years were answered clearly and concisely through your plain English interpretation of the law." —C.E.H.

"If there weren't people out there like you I'd be lost. You have the best books of this type out there." —S.B.

"...your forms and directions are easy to follow." —C.V.M.

Sphinx Publishing's Legal Survival Guides
are directly available from the Sourcebooks, Inc., or from your local bookstores.
For credit card orders call 1–800–43–BRIGHT, write P.O. Box 372, Naperville, IL 60566,
or fax 630-961-2168

SPHINX® PUBLISHING'S NATIONAL TITLES
Valid in All 50 States

LEGAL SURVIVAL IN BUSINESS

How to Form a Limited Liability Company (April)	$19.95
How to Form Your Own Corporation (2E)	$19.95
How to Form Your Own Partnership	$19.95
How to Register Your Own Copyright (2E)	$19.95
How to Register Your Own Trademark (2E)	$19.95
Most Valuable Business Legal Forms You'll Ever Need (2E)	$19.95
Most Valuable Corporate Forms You'll Ever Need (2E)	$24.95
Software Law (with diskette)	$29.95

LEGAL SURVIVAL IN COURT

Crime Victim's Guide to Justice	$19.95
Debtors' Rights (3E)	$12.95
Defend Yourself against Criminal Charges	$19.95
Grandparents' Rights (2E)	$19.95
Help Your Lawyer Win Your Case	$12.95
Jurors' Rights (2E)	$9.95
Legal Malpractice and Other Claims against Your Lawyer (2E) (June)	$18.95
Legal Research Made Easy (2E)	$14.95
Simple Ways to Protect Yourself from Lawsuits	$24.95
Victims' Rights	$12.95
Winning Your Personal Injury Claim	$19.95

LEGAL SURVIVAL IN REAL ESTATE

How to Buy a Condominium or Townhome	$16.95
How to Negotiate Real Estate Contracts (3E)	$16.95
How to Negotiate Real Estate Leases (3E)	$16.95
Successful Real Estate Brokerage Management	$19.95

LEGAL SURVIVAL IN PERSONAL AFFAIRS

How to File Your Own Bankruptcy (4E)	$19.95
How to File Your Own Divorce (3E)	$19.95
How to Make Your Own Will	$12.95
How to Write Your Own Living Will	$9.95
How to Write Your Own Premarital Agreement (2E)	$19.95
How to Win Your Unemployment Compensation Claim	$19.95
Living Trusts and Simple Ways to Avoid Probate (2E)	$19.95
Neighbors' Rights	$12.95
The Power of Attorney Handbook (3E)	$19.95
Simple Ways to Protect Yourself from Lawsuits	$24.95
Social Security Benefits Handbook (2E)	$14.95
Unmarried Parents' Rights	$19.95
U.S.A. Immigration Guide (3E)	$19.95
Guia de Inmigracion a Estados Unidos (2E) (May)	$19.95

Legal Survival Guides are directly available from Sourcebooks, Inc., or from your local bookstores.

For credit card orders call 1–800–43–BRIGHT, write P.O. Box 372, Naperville, IL 60566, or fax 630-961-2168

SPHINX® PUBLISHING ORDER FORM

BILL TO:		SHIP TO:	
Phone #	Terms	F.O.B. Chicago, IL	Ship Date

Charge my: ☐ VISA ☐ MasterCard ☐ American Express

☐ **Money Order or Personal Check**

Credit Card Number

Expiration Date

Qty	ISBN	Title	Retail	Ext.
		SPHINX PUBLISHING NATIONAL TITLES		
	1-57071-166-6	Crime Victim's Guide to Justice	$19.95	
	1-57071-342-1	Debtors' Rights (3E)	$12.95	
	1-57071-162-3	Defend Yourself against Criminal Charges	$19.95	
	1-57248-082-3	Grandparents' Rights (2E)	$19.95	
	1-57248-087-4	Guia de Inmigracion a Estados Unidos (2E) (May)	$19.95	
	1-57248-021-1	Help Your Lawyer Win Your Case	$12.95	
	1-57071-164-X	How to Buy a Condominium or Townhome	$16.95	
	1-57071-223-9	How to File Your Own Bankruptcy (4E)	$19.95	
	1-57071-224-7	How to File Your Own Divorce (3E)	$19.95	
	1-57248-083-1	How to Form a Limited Liability Company (April)	$19.95	
	1-57071-227-1	How to Form Your Own Corporation (2E)	$19.95	
	1-57071-343-X	How to Form Your Own Partnership	$19.95	
	1-57071-228-X	How to Make Your Own Will	$12.95	
	1-57071-331-6	How to Negotiate Real Estate Contracts (3E)	$16.95	
	1-57071-332-4	How to Negotiate Real Estate Leases (3E)	$16.95	
	1-57071-225-5	How to Register Your Own Copyright (2E)	$19.95	
	1-57071-226-3	How to Register Your Own Trademark (2E)	$19.95	
	1-57071-349-9	How to Win Your Unemployment Compensation Claim	$19.95	
	1-57071-167-4	How to Write Your Own Living Will	$9.95	
	1-57071-344-8	How to Write Your Own Premarital Agreement (2E)	$19.95	
	1-57071-333-2	Jurors' Rights (2E)	$9.95	
	1-57248-090-4	Legal Malpractice and Other Claims against...(2E) (June)	$18.95	
	1-57071-400-2	Legal Research Made Easy (2E)	$14.95	
	1-57071-336-7	Living Trusts and Simple Ways to Avoid Probate (2E)	$19.95	
	1-57071-345-6	Most Valuable Bus. Legal Forms You'll Ever Need (2E)	$19.95	
	1-57071-346-4	Most Valuable Corporate Forms You'll Ever Need (2E)	$24.95	

Qty	ISBN	Title	Retail	Ext.
	1-57248-089-0	Neighbors' Rights	$12.95	
	1-57071-348-0	The Power of Attorney Handbook (3E)	$19.95	
	1-57248-020-3	Simple Ways to Protect Yourself from Lawsuits	$24.95	
	1-57071-337-5	Social Security Benefits Handbook (2E)	$14.95	
	1-57071-163-1	Software Law (w/diskette)	$29.95	
	0-913825-86-7	Successful Real Estate Brokerage Mgmt.	$19.95	
	1-57071-399-5	Unmarried Parents' Rights	$19.95	
	1-57071-354-5	U.S.A. Immigration Guide (3E)	$19.95	
	0-913825-82-4	Victims' Rights	$12.95	
	1-57071-165-8	Winning Your Personal Injury Claim	$19.95	
		CALIFORNIA TITLES		
	1-57071-360-X	CA Power of Attorney Handbook	$12.95	
	1-57071-355-3	How to File for Divorce in CA	$19.95	
	1-57071-356-1	How to Make a CA Will	$12.95	
	1-57071-408-8	How to Probate an Estate in CA (April)	$19.95	
	1-57071-357-X	How to Start a Business in CA	$16.95	
	1-57071-358-8	How to Win in Small Claims Court in CA	$14.95	
	1-57071-359-6	Landlords' Rights and Duties in CA	$19.95	
		FLORIDA TITLES		
	1-57071-363-4	Florida Power of Attorney Handbook (2E)	$12.95	
	1-57248-093-9	How to File for Divorce in FL (6E) (July)	$21.95	
	1-57248-086-6	How to Form a Limited Liability Co. in FL (April)	$19.95	
	1-57071-401-0	How to Form a Partnership in FL	$19.95	
	1-57071-380-4	How to Form a Corporation in FL (4E)	$19.95	
	1-57071-361-8	How to Make a FL Will (5E)	$12.95	
	1-57248-088-2	How to Modify Your FL Divorce Judgement (4E) (May)	$22.95	
	Form Continued on Following Page		**SUBTOTAL**	

To order, call Sourcebooks at 1-800-43-BRIGHT or FAX (630)961-2168 (Bookstores, libraries, wholesalers—please call for discount)

SPHINX® PUBLISHING ORDER FORM

Qty	ISBN	Title	Retail	Ext.
		FLORIDA TITLES (CONT'D)		
_____	1-57071-364-2	How to Probate an Estate in FL (3E)	$24.95	_____
_____	1-57248-081-5	How to Start a Business in FL (5E) (March)	$16.95	_____
_____	1-57071-362-6	How to Win in Small Claims Court in FL (6E)	$14.95	_____
_____	1-57071-335-9	Landlords' Rights and Duties in FL (7E)	$19.95	_____
_____	1-57071-334-0	Land Trusts in FL (5E)	$24.95	_____
_____	0-913825-73-5	Women's Legal Rights in FL	$19.95	_____
		GEORGIA TITLES		
_____	1-57071-376-6	How to File for Divorce in GA (3E)	$19.95	_____
_____	1-57248-075-0	How to Make a GA Will (3E)	$12.95	_____
_____	1-57248-076-9	How to Start a Business in Georgia (3E)	$16.95	_____
		ILLINOIS TITLES		
_____	1-57071-405-3	How to File for Divorce in IL (2E)	$19.95	_____
_____	1-57071-415-0	How to Make an IL Will (2E)	$12.95	_____
_____	1-57071-416-9	How to Start a Business in IL (2E)	$16.95	_____
_____	1-57248-078-5	Landlords' Rights & Duties in IL (February)	$19.95	_____
		MASSACHUSETTS TITLES		
_____	1-57071-329-4	How to File for Divorce in MA (2E)	$19.95	_____
_____	1-57248-050-5	How to Make a MA Will	$9.95	_____
_____	1-57248-053-X	How to Probate an Estate in MA	$19.95	_____
_____	1-57248-054-8	How to Start a Business in MA	$16.95	_____
_____	1-57248-055-6	Landlords' Rights and Duties in MA	$19.95	_____
		MICHIGAN TITLES		
_____	1-57071-409-6	How to File for Divorce in MI (2E)	$19.95	_____
_____	1-57248-077-7	How to Make a MI Will (2E)	$12.95	_____
_____	1-57071-407-X	How to Start a Business in MI (2E)	$16.95	_____
		MINNESOTA TITLES		
_____	1-57248-039-4	How to File for Divorce in MN	$19.95	_____
_____	1-57248-040-8	How to Form a Simple Corporation in MN	$19.95	_____
_____	1-57248-037-8	How to Make a MN Will	$9.95	_____
_____	1-57248-038-6	How to Start a Business in MN	$16.95	_____
		NEW YORK TITLES		

Qty	ISBN	Title	Retail	Ext.
_____	1-57071-184-4	How to File for Divorce in NY (March)	$19.95	_____
_____	1-57248-095-5	How to Make a NY Will (2E)	$12.95	_____
_____	1-57071-185-2	How to Start a Business in NY	$16.95	_____
_____	1-57071-187-9	How to Win in Small Claims Court in NY	$14.95	_____
_____	1-57071-186-0	Landlords' Rights and Duties in NY (March)	$19.95	_____
_____	1-57071-188-7	New York Power of Attorney Handbook	$19.95	_____
		NORTH CAROLINA TITLES		
_____	1-57071-326-X	How to File for Divorce in NC (2E)	$19.95	_____
_____	1-57071-327-8	How to Make a NC Will (2E)	$12.95	_____
_____	1-57248-096-3	How to Start a Business in NC (2E)	$16.95	_____
_____	1-57248-091-2	Landlords' Rights & Duties in NC (June)	$19.95	_____
		PENNSYLVANIA TITLES		
_____	1-57071-177-1	How to File for Divorce in PA	$19.95	_____
_____	1-57248-094-7	How to Make a PA Will (2E)	$12.95	_____
_____	1-57071-178-X	How to Start a Business in PA	$16.95	_____
_____	1-57071-179-8	Landlords' Rights and Duties in PA (June)	$19.95	_____
		TEXAS TITLES		
_____	1-57071-330-8	How to File for Divorce in TX (2E)	$19.95	_____
_____	1-57248-009-2	How to Form a Simple Corporation in TX	$19.95	_____
_____	1-57071-417-7	How to Make a TX Will (2E)	$12.95	_____
_____	1-57071-418-5	How to Probate an Estate in TX (2E)	$19.95	_____
_____	1-57071-365-0	How to Start a Business in TX (2E)	$16.95	_____
_____	1-57248-012-2	How to Win in Small Claims Court in TX	$14.95	_____
_____	1-57248-011-4	Landlords' Rights and Duties in TX	$19.95	_____

SUBTOTAL THIS PAGE _____

SUBTOTAL PREVIOUS PAGE _____

Illinois residents add 6.75% sales tax _____

Florida residents add 6% state sales tax plus applicable discretionary surtax _____

Shipping— $4.00 for 1st book, $1.00 each additional _____

TOTAL _____

Please send me information on legal requirements for new hire reporting.

Thank you.

Name _____
Company _____
Address _____
City _____ State _____ Zip _____

Please send me information on workers' compensation requirements for a new Texas business.

Thank you.

Name _____
Company _____
Address _____
City _____ State _____ Zip _____

Please send me information on tax requirements for a new business.

Thank you.

Name _____
Company _____
Address _____
City _____ State _____ Zip _____

Please send me information on unemployment tax requirements for a new business

Thank you.

Name _____
Company _____
Address _____
City _____ State _____ Zip _____

PLACE
POSTCARD
STAMP
HERE

Texas New Hire Reporting Program
PO Box 149224
Austin, TX 78714-9224

Workers' Compensation Commission
Public Information Office
4000 South I H 35
Austin, TX 78704-7491

PLACE
POSTCARD
STAMP
HERE

PLACE
POSTCARD
STAMP
HERE

Texas Comptroller of Public Accounts
P. O. Box 13528
Austin, TX 78711-3528

Texas Workforce Commission
Austin, TX 78714-9037

PLACE
POSTCARD
STAMP
HERE

Please send me a copy of your wage and hour and child labor posters and any other information available to a new business.

Thank you.

Name _____

Company _____

Address _____

City _____ State ____ Zip ____

Please send me a copy of the required OSHA poster and any other information available to a new business.

Thank you.

Name _____

Company _____

Address _____

City _____ State ____ Zip ____

Please send me a copy of your discrimination poster and any other information available to a new business.

Thank you.

Name _____

Company _____

Address _____

City _____ State ____ Zip ____

Please send me a copy of your *Handbook for Employers* and *Instructions for Completing Form I-9* and any other information available to a new business.

Thank you.

Name _____

Company _____

Address _____

City _____ State ____ Zip ____

PLACE
POSTCARD
STAMP
HERE

U.S. Department of Labor
200 Constitution Ave., NW, Room N-3101
Washington, DC 20210

U.S. Department of Justice
Immigration & Naturalization Service
425 I Street NW
Washington, DC 20536

PLACE
POSTCARD
STAMP
HERE

PLACE
POSTCARD
STAMP
HERE

U.S. Department of Labor
200 Constitution Ave., NW, Room S-3325
Washington, DC 20210

E. E. O. C.
2401 E Street NW
Washington, DC 20506

PLACE
POSTCARD
STAMP
HERE